Pioneer Irish in New England

Michael J. O'Brien. LL.D.

HERITAGE BOOKS
2012

HERITAGE BOOKS
AN IMPRINT OF HERITAGE BOOKS, INC.

Books, CDs, and more—Worldwide

For our listing of thousands of titles see our website
at
www.HeritageBooks.com

A Facsimile Reprint
Published 2012 by
HERITAGE BOOKS, INC.
Publishing Division
100 Railroad Ave. #104
Westminster, Maryland 21157

— Publisher's Notice —
In reprints such as this, it is often not possible to remove blemishes from the original. We feel the contents of this book warrant its reissue despite these blemishes and hope you will agree and read it with pleasure.

International Standard Book Numbers
Paperbound: 978-1-55613-106-6
Clothbound: 978-0-7884-9468-0

TO A GREATLY ESTEEMED FRIEND

MOST REV. FRANCIS W. HOWARD, D.D.

THIS BOOK IS DEDICATED BY

THE AUTHOR

PREFACE

by

REV. P. J. TEMPLE, S.T.D.

Pioneer Irish in New England is in some respects the most important work that has come from the pen of its distinguished author. It deals with a subject of deep historical interest, which is little known and about which there has been scant scientific investigation. In a previous work, *A Hidden Phase of American History,* Dr. O'Brien demonstrated conclusively that the Irish were in America in large numbers at the time of the Revolution. So numerous were they and so eager to take part in the fight for independence, that they constituted thirty-eight per cent of the Revolutionary Army. Our author's latest book goes even further. It establishes beyond cavil that the Irish were represented in the Colonies from the very beginning, even before the coming of the *Mayflower.*

As this work deals with the seventeenth century, it would be profitable to glance at the history of Ireland of that time to see at what periods we would expect Irish immigrants and what class these were likely to be.

In the first quarter of the century, after the Irish defeat at Kinsale (1602), and the flight of the Earls O'Neill and O'Donnell (1607), there was the Plantation of Ulster (1609-1625). The whole Catholic population of this province was unsettled as the English Protestants and the Scotch Presbyterians—about 8,000 families in all—moved in to occupy the confiscated lands.

In the second quarter, Charles I, instead of fulfilling promises made to the Irish gentry, Catholic and Protestant, interfered with their prosperous woolen trade. The outstanding event of this period was the Rebellion of 1641, in which many Protestants of Ulster were ousted from their lately acquired lands; but they were soon organized by Munroe and concentrated in Antrim and Down.

The year 1650 finds Cromwell crushing out the revolt in Ireland in savage bloodshed and destruction, leaving the country a veritable desert. The land was divided between Cromwell's army and English adventurers, and the Catholic proprietors were driven across the Shannon. About 34,000 Irish soldiers emigrated for the service of France, Spain, Austria and Venice. They were not accompanied by their wives and children, who were afterwards hunted down and sent to the worst form of tropic slavery. In fact the number of women and children transported to the West Indies and the Colonies has been estimated as over 20,000—some say as much as 100,000. What proportion reached the American mainland?[1] To which Colonies did they mostly go? What became of them? Did some of the Irish soldiers in Europe find ways of rejoining their transported relations? Such questions await a thorough investigation. For a short period after the Restoration (1660) some leniency was shown the Catholics, while on the other hand, through the enforcement of the Uniformity Act, Non-Conformists underwent a persecution that drove a number to the Puritan Colonies of New England.

The leniency received by Irish Catholics in the opening years of the last quarter of the 17th century was ended by the Titus Oates Plot in England (1678). However, they received preferential treatment under James II (1685-1689),

[1] In this book Dr. O'Brien mentions a few who reached the Colonies from Barbados. I heard the late Monsignor Segourney Fay of Philadelphia say that he traced his ancestry back to an Irish fugitive from Barbados.

especially from Richard Talbot, Earl of Tyrconnell. This change in policy resulted in driving a number of Protestants to emigrate to the Colonies "for fear of Popery." The coming of Thomas Dongan, an Irish Catholic, as Governor of New York (1683-1688), occasioned the bringing of some of his countrymen to this Colony. For we find Governor Dongan writing on Sept. 8, 1687, to the Lord President of the Council at London, requesting that a number of his countrymen be sent over to colonize New York, "as many as the King will find convenient to send." [2] Those who were dispatched arrived in the following year and settled in Long Island and in Dutchess County along the Hudson River.

During the three years' War of the Revolution in Ireland there were more confiscations and some political prisoners were sent to Virginia. It was brought to an end by the Treaty of Limerick, 1692, which allowed the Irish soldiers to go to France with the returning French army. The 11,000 who did so formed the nucleus of the famous Irish Brigade which for a century was recruited from the flower of Irish manhood.

The Treaty of Limerick was broken to shreds by the dreadful Penal Code of 1695-1710. These most inhuman of all laws ever enacted by a government were aimed at the extinction of the Catholic religion in Ireland, and a consequence was that most of the Catholic gentry who had kept their estates after the Acts of Settlement and Explanation or who had been reinstated by James II were dispossessed, while the few who were not were deprived of all political power. Besides, the restrictive laws against the Irish industries of wool, glass, cotton and silk affected Protestants even more than Catholics. When the first of these was passed in 1689, it is estimated that about 42,000 Protestant families and about 14,000 Catholic families were engaged in the woolen business.

[2] Edmund B. O'Callaghan, *Documentary History of the State of New York*, Vol. I, p. 157.

As a result, Protestant weavers emigrated to Germany, Holland and France, while those of the Catholic faith went to Spain. In 1699, England passed the first great act restricting all the foreign business of Ireland. Trade with the Colonies had been forbidden in 1663 and 1670, yet had been kept alive. Now the Navigation Laws, shutting off all direct trade with the Plantations, crippled Irish industries and destroyed all hope of prosperity. This started the tide of Irish emigration to the West Indies and the Colonies in 1699, and by 1725 it reached large steady proportions. As an example of the heavy American immigration from Ireland, I may mention that according to the shipping statistics of the Philadelphia Custom House for the eighteen years between 1733 and 1750, the number of Irish who arrived at that port was about 138,900, of whom 36% came in vessels from Ulster ports, and 64% from all other Irish ports.[3] At the opening of the American Revolution, it is estimated there were nearly half a million Irish in the Colonies.

As our interest here is centered in the Irish emigration to New England in the seventeenth century, it is worth quoting from a letter written by the crafty, double-dealing James Butler, Marquis of Ormond, at a crucial point in the century, namely in 1660, when the claims of the new settlers for land in Ireland—planters, adventurers and soldiers—as well as those of some of the old native Irish, were clamoring for a hearing.

"If the adventurers and soldiers," wrote Ormond, "must be satisfied to the extent of what they suppose intended to them by the declaration, and if all that accepted and constantly adhered to the peace of 1648 be restored, as the same declaration seems also to intend, there must be new discoveries made *of a new Ireland*, for the old will not serve to

[3] "Shipping Statistics of the Philadelphia Custom House," by M. J. O'Brien, *Journal of American Irish Historical Society*, 1923, Vol. XXII, p. 138.

satisfy these engagements. It remains then to determine which party must suffer in default of means to satisfy all." [4]

A "new Ireland" had to be discovered to satisfy the wants of even the newcomers, and a "new Ireland" was in process of formation across the Atlantic to serve as a home for numerous Irish, Catholic and Protestant. The population of Ireland, when Ormond wrote in that critical year of 1660, is estimated at about 1,100,000, of whom 800,000 were Catholic, 100,000 Episcopalians, 100,000 Presbyterians, and 100,000 English non-Conformists, like the Quakers, etc. This was after half a million Catholics had been disposed of through war, famine and transportation, and after the Cromwellian settlement, to which there was nothing similar in the history of Europe "except the conquests effected by the Northern barbarians in the dark ages." [5] The result was, to quote Ormond again, "as divided and unsettled a country as is or ever was in Christendom." Catholics had held two-thirds of the land, but now three-fourths [6] of it were in the hands of Protestants and five-sixths of the housing. In fact the three great confiscations that practically included the whole island and that sometimes overlapped, affected mostly the Catholics, who, therefore, frequently during that dreadful century were without lands or homes and would be most liable to go abroad if the means could be at all found. Ireland swarmed with disinherited Catholics, a result of which was the frequent formation of bands of outlaws to prey on the planters and spoilers. They were first called "Tories" and in the last half of the century, "Rapparees," whose desperate deeds have come down in song

[4] Carte, *Life of the Dukes of Ormond*, IV, p. 81.

[5] Prendergast, *Ireland from the Restoration to the Revolution*, 3.

[6] Sir William Petty, *Political Anatomy*, at first says two-thirds, but afterwards admits three-fourths. See *Studies in Irish History*, 1649-1775, being Lectures before the Irish Literary Society of London, edited by Barry O'Brien, 2d edition, p. 115.

and story. These intrepid spirits would be likely to seek adventure in the Western Hemisphere, and obviously the British Government would be glad to be rid of them. Some of the chiefs, such as the O'Moores and the O'Carrolls, dispossessed of their lands in Ireland, received grants of land in South Carolina and Maryland, respectively.

The great persecutions and confiscations brought about almost a complete destruction of the Old Gaelic order of things, the chiefs, bards, brehons, and so forth; so that vast numbers ousted from their holdings would be anxious to go almost anywhere. The statement made that all the Catholic emigrants went to the European continent needs to be reexamined, for except for the clergy and the soldiers and a few other professionals, we do not hear of the ordinary people going there in large numbers; indeed there were not unoccupied lands for them in Europe as there were in America.

We can now, with a fair degree of accuracy, answer the question: what kind would we expect the Irish emigrants to be who came to the Colonies in the seventeenth century?

1. The chiefs and the landed gentry dispossessed of their estates.

2. Those affected by the confiscations who would not move to a different part of the island, but instead became "Rapparees." These would prefer to join one of the European armies, but they would also be likely to seek adventure in the New World.

3. People of all religious beliefs who were discouraged by the frequent political disturbances, or who suffered religious persecution, or who lost their business in the ruin of the woolen trade.

4. The thousands of the poor and helpless transported by Cromwell in the middle of the century. These undoubtedly formed the bulk of the "indentured servants" spoken of in this book.

5. Protestants, especially during the periods 1665-1675 and 1685-1699.

The picture of the Catholic four-fifths, unsettled and crushed, which the seventeenth century history of Ireland presents, fits in with the facts described by Dr. Michael J. O'Brien in the present work. The data he furnishes refute the "authorities" who say that the American Colonies in the first century of their history had few Irish, and that all of these were "Scotch-Irish Presbyterians." This painstaking research challenges all such views and calls for a thorough unbiased investigation.

No one can deny that most of the names listed in this book, which the author found in the early New England records, represent Catholic Irish, at least in the seventeenth century. It was the Penal Laws of the early eighteenth century, it must be remembered, that encouraged defections among the old Irish families and caused apostasy of about 5,000 individuals. These infamous enactments provided that if a son turned Protestant he could disinherit his father. Also in the eighteenth and nineteenth centuries, many Irish in America lost their faith, mainly because of the lack of opportunity of practising it; and no longer do we find Irish names proof that the bearers are Catholic. But it was different in the beginning of Colonial history before such changes began; and we can, therefore, place reliance on the names Dr. O'Brien supplies. The differences in the spelling of these names are explained by the fact that the vast majority of the Catholic Irish of the seventeenth century spoke the Gaelic language, and they had no academic institution to guide them in the process of anglicising their names. The language question is also the reason why they left so few written records behind them in the Colonies.

Would it be too much to expect that as a result of the labors of this indefatigable historian others will be encouraged to follow his inspiring example? There is a fruitful field to be explored in epitaphs in old cemeteries, in old records of deeds and wills, court dockets, town and county records, notices of ships, passenger lists, and family memoranda both here and in Europe. The collection of such data would enable us to form a more accurate idea of the number of Irish who came to the American Colonies in the first century of their history.

CHAPTER I

A challenge accepted—the author lists six hundred examples of Irish names, from New England records of the seventeenth century—the "indentured servants"—Irish merchants, tradesmen and husbandmen in New England—a so-called "First Census of the American People" refuted.

THIS book owes its origin to a pseudo-critic, who has issued a citation commanding me to "come into Court with some real proof" of the authenticity of certain statements I made in a newspaper article about the Irish in America. Despite the evidence to the contrary afforded by the public records, he wants the world to know that the English were the only national element in New England in the seventeenth century, and in support of his thesis he compiled and circulated a pamphlet entitled "Our Anglo-Saxon Forebears." It abounds in historical inaccuracies, some of which will be noted from the paragraphs hereunder quoted:

". . . Some Irish writers make even still more extravagant claims. Recently, I read at the Boston Public Library an article on 'Ireland and the American Colonies,' by a Dr. Michael J. O'Brien. It contains an assertion, which, according to my understanding of our history, is purely imaginative, that 'large numbers of Irish were in New England in the seventeenth century.' But, of these 'large numbers' of alleged 'Irish,' the author mentioned only three of them by name, John Cogan, Richard Dexter and John Kelly, and it just so happens that all three were English men and came to the colonies from England.

"I was amused at a somewhat similar legendary tale before, and cannot believe that these writers expect themselves to be taken seriously. For although the Scots-Irish to some extent took part in our revolution, not more than one genuine Irishman is mentioned by name in New England history of the seventeenth century. That was Bryan Morfrey, an Irish bondman, who, Mr. Justin Winsor says, was married in Boston to Margaret Mahoone sometime in the sixteen hundreds.

"I would not want it to be understood from these remarks that I bear any animus toward the Irish. I admire their many fine qualities and freely acknowledge that they have contributed something to the upbuilding of the country. But, when it comes to a question of the first settlements in the colonies, it is pure fiction to say that the Irish have any history in this country. The assertion that 'large numbers of Irish were in New England in the seventeenth century' is manifestly absurd on its face, because there were then no Roman Catholics in New England, and it is very doubtful that any Irish came here until the forepart of the last century.

"It is a fact, so well established by historians as to be indisputable, that our original stock was wholly English, and I don't see how there can be any question about it. A glance at Clemens' 'First Census' at once shows that practically all the colonial families had English names and none were Catholics, and we have the assurance of Messrs. Lodge and Palfrey that Massachusetts in the seventeenth century was even more English than any English shire. An authority on Massachusetts history informs me 'there is not a particle of truth in what this man says,' that 'the purpose of such articles is well understood, being part of an organized plan by the Irish in this country to establish for themselves a factitious place in American history, from which to launch attacks on any movement in which the Mother Country and ourselves may be mutually interested.'

"I am at a loss to understand how Dr. O'Brien expects those who are familiar with the details of New England history to accept his reckless statement. To my mind, it is unproveable and I challenge him to produce an iota of evidence to substantiate it. It would certainly be interesting to New Englanders to know what possible authority he can have for what he says about these elusive Irishmen, but until he comes into Court with some real proof, his *ipse dixit* must be thrown out as valueless. People who venture into this field should deal with facts, not romance."

Anyone having the slightest knowledge of the contents of the public records will at once see that all this amounts to nothing more than the "threshing of old straw." No new theory or principle concerning our forebears, Anglo-Saxon or otherwise, is advanced; its author presents no new facts; he only repeats in substance what certain New England historians have been saying, times out of mind, about "the homogeny of the English and American peoples." But, like many other persons with only a superficial knowledge of the history of the period, it is clear that he is thoroughly convinced that what the historians have said constitutes the last word on the subject.

That the article objected to should excite the risible sensibilities of one so poorly equipped with information, does not create surprise, because there is widespread misunderstanding about the racial composition of the people of this country in the seventeenth century. A coterie of historians appear to have been of one mind as to the extent to which they should acknowledge the presence of the Irish among the Colonists, and much that they have said about the racial origin of the colonial population is antipodal to the facts of record. Generally speaking, all we hear about in New England are the Puritans, in the Middle Colonies the Dutch, and in Virginia the Cavaliers, leading the public to understand that the pioneer settlers were comprised wholly of the English and the Dutch, with the former in a vast majority. The French, the Germans and the Scandinavians get very little credit, and the Irish none at all; and since special emphasis is laid upon the English, not only in the standard histories of the country but by the teachers in the public schools and colleges, American youth have grown up with the erroneous idea that this race alone constituted the original stock, which impression remains with them all their lives.

Unfortunately, some Irish-American papers have published articles about the Irish in the Colonies, without any reference to their sources of information, even sometimes containing misstatements of fact, which have not enhanced the Irish reputation for truth. Several contributors to historical magazines wax eloquent on the subject; but since they failed to examine the real sources of information, they were unable to offer any concrete evidence or any particulars such as would serve to convince skeptical readers of the genuineness of their "researches." So it is possible, as has been the case with many other people, that some such articles have come under the "eagle eye" of the present critic and have influenced him against the Irish. Aside from that, however, his own contribution to "history" is a striking example of the misinformation that is sometimes disseminated among the reading public; yet, since the challenger has such urgent yearning for "some real proof" that the Irish came to New England in the seventeenth century, I willingly supply some of the missing "facts," and will leave the "romance" to those who habitually indulge in it. In stating the case, I shall not content myself with generalities, but will be specific in the mention of names, dates, places and facts obtained from the public records and other equally reliable sources.

Obviously, the answer to the question raised here must be based upon specific data. Mere assertions, not shown to be founded on authority, would be of no avail. To meet the challenge properly requires an intensive study of American records, and to some extent, knowledge of the formation of Irish names and of the changes wrought in such names in this country. The proof that there were "genuine Irishmen" in this country in "large numbers" in the formative period of its history, and that they are entitled to mention among its pioneers, abounds to such an extent in the public records, that I estimate it would require a volume of many hundred pages to relate the facts. That proof has not yet been obtained to its fullest extent, and cannot be until certain shipping lists of the seventeenth century, still preserved at Somerset House and at the Public Record Office in London, are consulted and the names of the passengers extracted therefrom. But, in the absence of this important data, information is available on this side of the Atlantic, from the files of the Courts, probate, administration and land office records, the baptismal, marriage and burial registers, the rolls of the troops who served in the colonial wars, the town books or their printed reproductions, authentic transcripts of public documents published by historical societies, and sundry other public records of the period wherein it was customary to mention people by name. Far from being "elusive," numerous Irishmen are mentioned in these records, and the fact that they comprised part of the population of the country in the seventeenth century is by no means "unproveable."

It is difficult, and sometimes impossible, to uproot opinions such as those set forth in the pamphlet before quoted, because they have become firmly embedded in the public mind for almost a century. In view of this, the admission on the part of one so "familiar with the details of New England history," that there was at least one "genuine Irishman" in Boston in the seventeenth century, shows that we are making some progress. And it is hoped that before this "doubting Thomas" reaches the end of the chapter, he will be ready to go a step further and acknowledge that the "romance" is mainly on the side of the "authorities" on whom he so implicitly relies.

I appreciate the position of those who are obliged to depend for their information on historical works such as those published by Lodge and Palfrey, and who consequently are skeptical of the truth of any statement tending to contradict the historians. When we consider their inadequate sources of information on the subject at issue, it seems an almost perfectly natural attitude for them to take. In the case of the Irish, I know of no better way to substantiate the fact of their presence in New England at any given period, than by assembling the Irish names which appear in the records of the time. And since such names may serve as a means of gratifying the critic's curiosity, if they will not actually open up a new line of thought and enlarge his horizon, I append a list showing examples of the names of some of the men and women who resided in New England at various times in the seventeenth century.

The six hundred persons listed in the appendix make a decidedly interesting group, and I doubt that any one will seriously question the racial origin of people so named. These six hundred are witnesses testifying by their presence in the Colony, that "large numbers" of Irish came to New England during the period in question, and the entries concerning whom in the public records effectively shatter the popular belief, long fostered by certain historians, that the pioneer settlers were exclusively English. It may be thought that six hundred were an inconsiderable part of the population, but it must not be assumed that this number represents all of the Irish who were in New England in the seventeenth century. In the first place, it should be borne in mind that many public records have been destroyed; secondly, that others are not available, and lastly, that in any event the number of people whose names get into the records at any time usually is small; so, therefore, the number here listed should be regarded merely as symptomatic of the total number of Irish who came to the Colony. Besides, this does not take into consideration at all the sons and daughters of these people, born in New England. As a rule, Irish families are large, and on a conservative estimate, it is probable that the offspring of the men here listed, living in New England in the seventeenth century, numbered not less than two thousand five hundred persons, a very respectable proportion of the population of that early day. Another consideration is the fact that large numbers of young Irishwomen were transported to the Colonies in the seventeenth century. That is clearly indicated by the records hereinafter quoted. At that period, the male population far exceeded the females, and since it is fair to assume that many of these women were married in this country to men of races other than their own, their names were not handed down. Hence, it follows there were more Irish in the Colonies than the records show.

The extent and diffusion of the inhabitants of the Colonies at this period, either in total numbers or by nationalities, must not be contrasted with the figures of later times; the number of inhabitants in some localities was then reckoned in no larger units than tens and twenties. Statistics indicate that about the opening of the seventeenth century there were in all America not more than 2,000 white men and women; in 1630, in Manhattan Island, there were only 300 persons; in 1660 Brooklyn had only 134 souls, and by 1790, when the first Census was taken, the entire population of the City of Boston could easily be accommodated in one-third the space of one of our present-day baseball parks!

The best information available indicates that the bulk of the Irish in the Colonies in the seventeenth century were brought here as "servants" or "redemptioners," and as such were indentured for a term of years to work out the cost of their passage overseas. For that reason, it may be that they were looked down upon or were regarded as of "no account" by the historians, notwithstanding the fact that the majority of the first settlers began life in this country in the capacity of "servants." The use of the term "servants" in those days, however, was not confined to persons employed in domestic service only, but was invariably applied to artisans, laborers, mechanics, mariners, husbandmen, tradesmen and all who earned their living by manual labor. Even manufacturers and schoolmasters were sometimes classed as "servants." There is one case on record where a Dr. McCarthy, surgeon to the forces under the command of Captain Daniel Henchman of Boston, in the war with the Narragansett Indians in 1675, known as "King Philip's War," was described as "Mr. Mackarty, servant to Captain Henchman!"

From the historical collections of the American Antiquarian Society we learn that "persons of the better and upper classes were not infrequently among the redemptioners," which "may be the reason why no possible stigma was attached to the condition"; and we are also told that "many members of the Virginia House of Burgesses had been servants before they ruled others as legislators." When their terms of service had expired and the redemptioners paid their debts, they either bought lands for themselves or received grants of land from the colonial or town government, and were then on an equality with those other emigrants who had enough money on their arrival to pay their passage. In many cases, the women among them married their masters or their masters' sons; and family histories show that in some instances these women were the wives or mothers of men who founded some of the leading American families of the present day. That this was also the case in New England, will become clear to anyone consulting the public records and the genealogies.

The other class of emigrants, those able to pay their own way, were, in some colonies, called "gentlemen emigrants of means." As a rule, the Irish so classified were substantial people, who, becoming discouraged at the terrible conditions at home, had sold their properties after deciding to try their fortunes in the new country. The redemptioners, however, constituted the major part of the Irish. Though some of these reached positions of comparative independence after they had redeemed themselves from service, yet for many years they had to occupy such lowly stations in life and were so seriously handicapped in the struggle for existence, that only a comparatively small number of them reached a standing which would justify their being mentioned individually in the public records. Some students of history seem to be of the opinion that all the early comers from Ireland to America were "bondmen," but that impression is entirely erroneous, as is clear from the entries in such records as those of the probate and the land offices.

It cannot be said that more than a few of them were in the professions or in politics, or were entrusted with public office. Yet, the extracts from the records of the time, herein quoted, prove conclusively that among the New England Irish there were many merchants, tradesmen, artisans and tillers of the soil, the class of men most needed in the Colonies; that they bought and sold real estate, as the deeds on record show; that they were in business, just like their English neighbors; that they bequeathed property to their children and their wills were recorded; and that in many instances their sons and daughters married into English families who were deemed worthy of mention by the historians. All this clearly demonstrates that Lodge and Palfrey and other writers mislead the public, by giving them to understand that England was the only European country which sent people to colonize New England in the seventeenth century. In effect, these men did a grave injustice to the Irish, for which I venture to predict true history will yet condemn them; because, despite all opinion to the contrary, the Irish colonists were as much entitled to consideration by historians as the people of any other race.

Not that the Irish demand preferential treatment in American history, or that it is claimed the historians should have mentioned by name every Irish person recorded in New England, which would be impracticable and wholly unnecessary. All that is asked for them is simple justice. For many years past Americans of Irish blood have labored under the illusion that the early records were not available to them, or if available, that they are of so nebulous a character that they lack information as to the history of the people of their race in this country in the seventeenth and eighteenth centuries. While they believed the early Irish settlers had a creditable record in America, they knew little of its details, and since until recent years no one consulted original records for data of this character, they were unable to submit the proofs or point to any authoritative sources of information. But, all that is now changing. In accordance as the Irish have been acquiring knowledge of the contents of the public records, the consciousness and the conviction have been growing up in them that their people were deliberately ignored in American history, and they now rightfully demand that the truth and the whole truth shall be told.

It is true that town historians make occasional references to Irishmen who settled in their localities. Also, the publications of historical societies contain unabridged copies of town, county and family records from which valuable information on the subject is obtainable. Indeed, the Irish in America are very much indebted to these historical societies for their impartiality in publishing verbatim copies of the entries in the public records, thus affording them an opportunity to obtain information which it would be impossible to secure without consulting the originals. Foremost in this regard may be mentioned the Massachusetts Historical Society, the Essex Institute of Salem, the New England Historic-Genealogical Society and the Historical Commission of the City of Boston. But, since the general public are not interested in local history, and the journals of the historical societies are consulted only by a comparatively few special students, the average person is unacquainted with the real facts, and the only information he has is that which is imparted to him in the larger works brought out by the State and National historians. What Americans of our race object to in particular is the work of these latter historians. Their complaint is based chiefly on the ground of the almost total omission of any reference to the fact that the Irish constituted part of the Colonial population, and that some at least among them occupied stations in life of as much importance as many of the English who receive due credit in history.

A good example of the so-called "information sources" upon which some readers of history depend, is a compilation by one William M. Clemens, which he misnamed "The First Census of the American People—1699." His "Census" consists of a list of several thousand residents of America before the opening of the eighteenth century, and he points to the names in this list in support of the theory that "from the very beginning the inhabitants of this country have been Anglo-Saxons," to the exclusion of all other races of men. While it is true that most of the names in the Clemens list have an English complexion, he overlooked an important point in that he gave no consideration to the probability that some of those who bore them were not English. In my criticism of this work,[1] I submitted facts exposing the falsity of its premises and conclusions; I gave the names, with the places where they resided, of two thousand Irish men and women who came to this country in the seventeenth century, all of whom were omitted by Clemens from his so-called "Census"; and I quoted the authority of the English Public Record Office proving that these two thousand persons represented only

[1] *An Alleged First Census of the American People*, New York, 1930.

part of the great number of Irish people who came to the American Colonies in the seventeenth century. Mr. Clemens was challenged to refute my statements, but he made no reply. And so it is with the standard histories of the United States, which purport to show that the Irish were non-existent in this country in the seventeenth century. Since it must be assumed that the authors of these histories, when searching for the basic material for their work, found in the public records many references to Irish residents of the Colonies, the conclusion is inescapable that they deliberately omitted them.

CHAPTER II

Irish "Redemptioners" shipped to Massachusetts, 1627-1643—Evidence from the English State Papers—11,000 people transported from Ireland to the West Indies, Virginia and New England between 1649 and 1653—550 Irish arrived at Marblehead, Mass., in the Goodfellow *from Cork, Waterford and Wexford in 1654—"stollen from theyre bedds" in Ireland.*

WE are told that "the passengers on the *Mayflower* (1620) were of English, Dutch, French and Irish ancestry, and thus typical of our national stock." [1] While it has been said that John Alden and Christopher Martin were Irish,[2] no definite proof of it has been established, though there can hardly be much question about the nationality of William Mullins, father of the famous Priscilla, wife of John Alden. Historians differ as to the racial origin of William Mullins, although by inference they agree that he could not have been Irish, because he had lived in England and was of the "established religion." Some claim he was "a French Huguenot" and others that he was "of English descent"; but none has offered any evidence supporting either theory; yet all who have discussed the matter of his nationality have evaded the question of his Irish name. The name, Mullins, is distinctively Irish and comes from O'Maolain. It is one of the commonest surnames in Ireland and is found in almost every part of the country, but in a great variety of anglicised forms, such as

[1] *Brave Little Holland and What She Taught Us,* by Rev. William Elliot Griffis, p. 218, Albany, N. Y., 1894.

[2] Statements by Thomas Hamilton Murray and Rev. Madison C. Peters, in *Journal of the American Irish Historical Society,* Vol. 8, p. 223, and Vol. 10, p. 144.

O'Mullane, Mullane, Mullen, MacMullen, Mallin, Mollan and Mullins. It does not occur among the English. William Mullins, son of William of the *Mayflower*, was one of the first settlers at Duxbury, Mass. There is a record showing that in 1662 he purchased lands on the Namasket River in the Plymouth Colony from Josiah Wampatuck,[3] and "after a long life of eminent usefulness, the last of the little band of Pilgrims who first stepped upon Plymouth Rock, he died on the 12th of September, 1687, aged 88."[4] William Mullins, supposed to have been his son, is listed among the "original proprietors at Middleboro, Mass., 1661."[5] Much has been said about the remarkable longevity of his descendants, one example of whom was his grandson, John Mullins, who died at Middleboro, in the year 1821, at the age of 102. He had 19 children, 62 grandchildren, 134 great-grandchildren and 7 great-great-grandchildren, 172 of whom were living at the time of his death! The death of William Mullins (2) was recorded at Braintree on December 12, 1672.

Governor William Bradford of the Plymouth Colony, in his manuscript history, mentioned under "1626-7" the arrival in Barnstable Bay, Mass., of "a ship with passengers and servants, many being Irish." Nothing is known of their names or their history; all we are assured of is, by this most competent of authorities, that "many" of these people were "Irish"; but we do know that within the next few years there were Irish families in New England. Between April and October, 1633, several vessels sailed from English ports destined for Virginia and Massachusetts, and among the passengers in these vessels, as shown by lists published by the New England Historic-Genealogical Society, were the following:

[3] *New England Historic-Genealogical Register*, Vol. 3, pp. 334-5.
[4] *Ibid.*, p. 338.
[5] *History of Middleboro*, by Thomas Weston, p. 585, Boston, 1906.

Clement Barry *
Bryan Bourke *
Nicholas Brogan *
Joseph Bryan *
William Buckley *
Daniell Burcke *
John Butler
Matthew Calland *
Henry Carroll
John Cassedy *
Walter Collins *
Patrick Conly *
Daniel Connelly *
Thomas Conner
John Conniers *
Patrick Connyer *
Margaret Conway *
John Couney *
Bryan Crowley *
John Dellahay *
Jude Donley *
Edmond Farrell
Simon Farrell
Peter Fleming *
Thomas Fludd *
John Fox *
John Fynn *
Owen Garret *
Thomas Garret *
Matthew Gibbons *
Thomas Gill *
William Goff *
Ann Griffin *
John Griffin
Thomas Griffin *
John Haies
James Haies
William Haies *
Bryan Hare
Suzan Hare
Matthew Hely *
John Heron *
Ann Holland
Darby Hurlie *
Bryan Kelley
John Kennedy
Humfrey Kerby
Tego Leare *
John Lyon
Peter Manning
Edward Mawfrey * (Murphy)
John Moore *
Thomas Moore *
Dennis Mortagh *
Dorothy Moyle
Elizabeth Murrin *
Dennis McBrian *
John McCoury *
Teague Nacton *
Desmond O'Bryan *
Thomas Pendergrass *
Walter Piggott
Edward Plunkett *
Rowland Plunkett *
Thomas Plunkett *
Teague Quillin
Thomas Riley *
Richard Sexton
Robert Sexton
Peter Starkie
Joseph Welsh *
Michael White *
Teague Williams *
Patrick Wood

Those who came in the vessels destined to Massachusetts are marked with an asterisk (*). Their nationality cannot be determined with any certainty, but, since such names are of common occurrence in Ireland, I believe it can be fairly stated that most of these people were Irish. There can be little doubt that all were indentured servants, but there is no information obtainable of their history, and only very few of them can be identified in New England records.

From the *Journal* of John Winthrop, the first Governor of the Colony of Massachusetts Bay, we learn that in July, 1634, word was received "from the north of Ireland," that "many good Christians in those parts resolved to come hither, if they might receive satisfaction concerning some questions." [6] Thus we find that by orders of the General Court lands were granted on the Merrimack River in Essex County for the proposed settlement. That some were Irish is indicated by the records of the Court under date of September 25, 1634, wherein there is an entry: "It is ordered that the Scottishe and Irishe gentlemen wch intends to come hither shall have liberty to sitt downe in any place upp Merimacke Ryver, not possessed by any." [7] In the winter of the same year, Governor Winthrop went to England. His vessel was driven by foul weather "upon the coast of Ireland, not known by any in the ship," but finally arrived at Galway. Thence he journeyed to Dublin and afterwards to Antrim, where he conferred with the authorities "about the voyage to New England," of a number of persons who intended to settle in the colony.[8] There is no positive evidence of the presence of these people in the Colony, as far as I can find, and their arrival is not mentioned in any record now available, except insofar as the records show that many Scotch and Irish lived in Essex County adjacent to the Merrimack River within the next few years.

The Plymouth Colony gave recognition to the fact that there were Irish in that territory in 1636, for at a session of the General Court in that year, "it was enacted by the Court that all Scotes and Irishmen as are in any Township of the $Gou^{r}ment$ shall beare Armes and traine as others, except such as are servants from month to month." An exactly similar law dealing with "the Scots and Irish" was passed by the

[6] Winthrop's *Journal*, p. 135.
[7] Records of the General Court, Vol. 1, p. 129.
[8] Winthrop's *Journal*, p. 172.

Court on July 2, 1655.[9] It will be noted from the references to these people as Scots *and* Irish, that the colonial officials differentiated between them. The term "Scotch-Irish" was never used in those days.

In 1636, a vessel named the *Eagle Wing* sailed from Carrickfergus, Ireland, with 140 passengers for the Massachusetts Bay settlements, but the vessel had to put back "owing to stress of weather," and the project was abandoned for several years. Three years later, a number of Irishmen, on their refusal to take the oath of allegiance to Charles I, on the demand of the then Deputy in Ireland, the Earl of Strafford, were transported to the Colonies. The record is silent as to their names, or where they were located, but since we find a Dermod O'Mahony and his son, Teague, at Salem, Mass., in 1639, it is probable they were landed at that place and were bound out as indentured servants.

In 1640, a number of emigrants from Ireland arrived at Boston, and under date of May 13th of that year this interesting entry appears in the records of the General Court: "It is ordered that the goods of the persons come from Ireland shal bee free from this rate" [10] (tax); and there is a marginal notation on the record to the effect that "Irish goods now land free from ye rate." From what part of Ireland these people came cannot be stated definitely, nor are their numbers or names on record. But in at least one instance in 1640, it is clear that emigrants came by way of Cork, Ireland, to Massachusetts, since on July 6, 1640, "John Downes of Bandon Bridge, in the County of Cork, merchant," gave bond in Boston for the payment of £80 to George Luxon and others, to permit the landing of passengers from "the ship *John and*

[9] Plymouth Colony Records, Vol. 11, pp. 65, 106 and 182.

[10] *The Records of the Colony of Massachusetts Bay in New England*, Vol. 1, p. 295, published by the State Legislature, 1853.

Francis of Youghal, in England or Ireland." [11] Bandon Bridge and Youghal being in the County of Cork, it is probable that the persons here referred to were from the south of Ireland. In the next decade of years there is a gradual increase in the number of Irish names in the records, although it is not practicable to determine how many Irish came at this period. Yet, since the influx to Virginia and Maryland increased regularly, because of the constant demand for labor, it is to be supposed, like conditions prevailing in New England, that the Irish redemptioners brought to that territory were not an inconsiderable number.

On January 31, 1643, the English Parliament resolved: "that the agents for the affairs of New England shall have liberty to collect free contributions . . . for the transportation of divers poor children driven out of Ireland." [12] Thus, in the same year a vessel arrived at Boston with "twenty children" whose passages had been paid by money collected in London. In January, 1652, a company of settlers arrived in Massachusetts in "the *John and Sarah* of London," which sailed "for Boston in New England on November 11, 1651," and at the Suffolk County Registry of Deeds [13] may be seen a list of the passengers, clearly indicating by their names that it was of mixed Irish and Scotch composition. There is no other reference to these people in Massachusetts records, nor is anything said about their nationality; but the fact that a large number of them bore the prenomen, Patrick, led one historical writer to assume that all were Irishmen. That assumption, however, is not always warranted; for while it is true that today the baptismal name, Patrick, occurs almost exclusively among the Irish, yet in the seventeenth and eight-

[11] Thomas Lechford, *Note Book*, pp. 151 and 288.

[12] *Proceedings and Debates of the British Parliament Respecting North America*, edited by Leo F. Stock, Washington, D. C., 1924.

[13] Lib. 1, fol. 5.

eenth centuries it was a popular name in certain Highland Scotch families. Entries such as these in the official records of the time prove beyond question that Ireland contributed some share to the settlement of the Colony of Massachusetts Bay. And that fact being established, the next step is to ascertain the places where these people settled, and if possible, what their fate or fortune was among the dominant element in New England.

Next to the persecutions of the priests and the schoolmasters in Ireland in the seventeenth century, the saddest chapter of Irish history was the wholesale confiscation by the English invaders of the lands and other property of Irish families, thus driving the unfortunate people into exile. Prendergast, in *The Cromwellian Settlement of Ireland*, a work of such indubitable authority that no historian has ever questioned it, deals at length with the deportations of the people to the West Indies and the American plantations, and says:

"While the Government were employed in clearing the ground for the Adventurers and Soldiers, the English capitalists of that day, by making the nobility and gentry yield up their ancient inheritances and withdraw to Connaught, they had agents actively employed through Ireland, seizing women, orphans and the destitute, to be transported to Barbadoes and the English Plantations in America. The thirteen years war, 1641 to 1654, followed by the departure of 40,000 Irish soldiers, with the chief nobility and gentry, to Spain, had left behind a vast mass of widows and deserted wives with destitute families. There were plenty of other persons too, who, as their ancient properties had been confiscated, had no visible means of livelihood. Just as the King of Spain sent over his agents to treat with the Government for the Irish swordmen, the merchants of Bristol had agents treating with it for men, women and girls to be sent to the sugar plantations in the West Indies. The Commissioners for Ireland gave them orders upon the governors of garrisons to deliver to them prisoners of war, upon the keepers of goals for offenders in custody, upon masters of work houses for the destitute in their care, and gave directions to all in authority to seize those who had no visible means of livelihood and deliver them to these agents of the Bristol sugar merchants, in execution of which latter direction Ireland must have exhibited scenes in every part like the slave hunts in Africa. How many girls of gentle birth must have been caught and hurried to the private prisons of these mancatchers none can tell. But at last the evil became too shocking and notorious, particularly when these dealers in Irish flesh began to seize the daughters of the English themselves, and to force them aboard their slave ships; then, indeed, the orders, at the end of four years, were revoked." [14]

In the Calendar of English State Papers there are many references to "Orders in Council" relating to the transportation of the Irish to Virginia, New England and the islands of the West Indies. On April 16, 1649, the Council of State informed a "Committee of Merchants in Mincing Lane" (London), that "there are 170 Irish taken at sea in a Holland ship who pretende to be going for Galway," and who "are now at Milford." It goes on to direct that "the common men be sent to the plantations in America," and the Committee was requested "to treat such as trade hither to transport them there where use may be made of their services for the advancement of those plantations." On April 20, 1650, there came before the Council of State the "petition of Col. William Herbert for carrying 100 Irish men and women to Virginia for the Committee of Plantations," [15] and on September 16, 1651, the Council authorized "the Committee for prisoners to dispose of the persons upon the propositions made for 1,000 to be sent to Bristol in order to sending them to New England." One of the most active of the many persons engaged in the transportation of the Irish to Massachusetts

[14] *The Cromwellian Settlement of Ireland*, by John P. Prendergast, pp. 245-6.
[15] *Interregnum Entry Book*, Vol. 92, p. 287.

was one David Sellecke, a Boston merchant. There is an entry in the Colony records of October 19, 1652, relating to "Mr. David Sellake craveing pardon for his offence in bringing some of the Irish men on shoare" at Boston, for which "offence" he "hath his fine remitted so as the first optunitie be taken to send them out of this jurisdiction." [16]

Again, according to the English State Papers, on October 4, 1652, Colonel Marcus Trevor was ordered by the Council "to remove 500 Irish out of Ulster to Carlingford for transportation," [17] and on February 4, 1653, "150 or 200 Irish or Scotch youths, unless English can be procured," were ordered "to be sent to New England and let out to persons there who will pay for their services there in commodities necessary for shipping." [18] On April 1, 1653, the Council of State granted to Sir John Clotworthie "a license to transport into America 500 natural Irishmen," [19] and on June 8, 1653, it was "Ordered that the governors of the several precincts be authorized to transport 8,000 Irish." [20] On September 24th of the same year, Richard Netherway of Bristol and Sir Richard Nethersole received licenses, each "to transport 100 Irish toryes to Virginia," [21] and in the following month the Council of State requested "Alderman Tichborne to present to Parliament a draft of an Act concerning the transporting of poor Irish children to New England and the Western Plantations."

The excerpts here quoted from the English State Papers, show that the total number of Irish ordered for transporta-

[16] *Records of the Colony of Massachusetts Bay in New England*, Vol. 3, p. 291, published by order of the Legislature, 1853.

[17] Orders in Council, English State Papers, A 82, fol. 363.

[18] *Interregnum Entry Book*, Vol. 67, pp. 2 and 5.

[19] *Ibid.*, Vol. 69, p. 45.

[20] Orders in Council, A-84, fols. 216-7.

[21] *Interregnum Entry Book*, Vol. 98, p. 405.

tion was upwards of 11,000, divided between the West Indies, Virginia and New England. Prendergast states that

> "... In the course of four years they had seized and shipped about 6,400 Irish, men and women, boys and maidens, when on the 4th of March, 1655, all orders were revoked. These men-catchers employed persons (so runs the order) 'to delude poor people by false pretences into by-places, and thence they forced them on board their ships. The persons employed had so much a piece for all they so deluded, and for the money sake they were found to have enticed and forced women from their children and husbands, children from their parents, who maintained them at school, and they had not only dealt so with the Irish, but also with the English,' which last was the true cause, probably, of the Commissioners for Ireland putting an end to these proceedings." [22]

It is not possible to state how many of these people were brought to New England, and we are also without information as to what proportion of the 11,000 mentioned in the State Papers came to that Colony. But it is evident that the number must have been very large, and one shipment alone from Kinsale, Ireland, to Massachusetts in 1653 consisted of 300 males and 250 females, all apparently from the Counties of Cork, Waterford and Wexford.

Under date of September 6, 1653, there is an entry in the records of the Council of State that "upon petition of David Sellecke of Boston, New England, Merchant, for a licence for the *Goodfellow* of Boston, George Dalle, Master, and the *Providence* of London, Thomas Swanley, Master, to pass to New England and Virginia where they intend to carry 400 Irish children, directing a warrant to be granted, provided security is given to sail to Ireland and within two months to

[22] From "Order Books of the Commissioners of the Parliament of the Commonwealth of England for the Affairs of Ireland," A-10, fol. 283; in Prendergast's *The Cromwellian Settlement of Ireland*, p. 245.

take in 400 Irish children and transport them to those plantations." [23] And Prendergast states:

"Captain John Vernon was employed by the Commissioners for Ireland into England, and contracted in their behalf with Mr. David Sellick and Mr. Leader, under his hand, bearing date the 14th September, 1653, to supply them with 250 women of the Irish nation above twelve years and under the age of forty-five, also 300 men above twelve years of age and under fifty, to be found in the country within twenty miles of Cork, Youghal and Kinsale, Waterford and Wexford, to transport them into New England. Messrs. Sellick and Leader appointed their shipping to repair to Kinsale, but Roger Boyle, Lord Broghill, whose name, like that of Sir Charles Coote, seems ever the prelude of woe to the Irish, suggested that the required number of men and women might be had from the wanderers and persons who had no means to get their livelihood, in the County of Cork alone. Accordingly, on the 23d of October, 1653, he was empowered to search for them and arrest them, and to deliver them to Messrs. Sellick and Leader, who were to be at all the charge of conducting them to the waterside, and maintaining them from the time they received them; and no person, being once apprehended was to be released but by special order in writing under the hand of Lord Broghill." [24]

There are entries in the records of the Suffolk County, Mass., Registry of Deeds,[25] covering George Dell's accounts with the owners of the *Goodfellow,* which indicate that on October 28, 1653, Dell was licensed to proceed on his voyage, and that the vessel sailed from Ireland to England before her departure for New England.[26] Under English law, no vessel

[23] *Interregnum Entry Book,* Vol. 98, p. 338.

[24] "Order Books of the Commissioners of the Parliament of the Commonwealth of England for the Affairs of Ireland," A-84, fol. 663, in Prendergast's *The Cromwellian Settlement of Ireland.*

[25] Lib. 1, fols. 196-7.

[26] *Calendar of State Papers, America and West Indies,* pp. 407-10.

could sail for its destination direct from Ireland, being required to call first at an English port where clearance papers would be issued for the voyage, and where a "head tax" had to be paid on every individual leaving for the colonies. The *Goodfellow* arrived in January, 1654, at Marblehead, Mass., where the master of the vessel disposed of part of his human cargo and then proceeded to Boston. Only in the cases of

Edmund Dear	William Danford	Dennis McCormack
John Downing	John Ring	Jael Sullivan
William Downing or Dalton	Edward Nealand	Owen Swiney
		Philip Welsh

is any information obtainable as to the names of the passengers, the places where they were located or what their history might have been, though it is evident that many of those hereinafter mentioned came in the *Goodfellow*, and that all were bound as indentured servants.

Some interesting information concerning those above listed is found in the public records and in the *Hammett Papers*. Edmund Dear first appears on record on March 3, 1660, when he married Elizabeth Griffin at Ipswich,[27] and they were the parents of Edward, Thomas, Elizabeth and Mary, all born at Ipswich between 1662 and 1666.[28] By deed dated April 3, 1665, or only two years after he had redeemed himself from service, Edmund Dear bought land at Ipswich from Samuel Varnum.[29] He is said to have been a carpenter by trade, and in 1669 the town gave him three acres of timberland. In 1678 he was made a "Commoner" of the town of Ipswich. In course of time he became a man of some local prominence, and like his English neighbors, he was regularly recorded as performing the usual public duties required of a citizen and

[27] Vital Records, Ipswich, Mass., Vol. 2, p. 130.

[28] *Ibid.*, Vol. 1, p. 114.

[29] Ipswich Deeds, Lib. 2, fol. 246.

a freeman. By his will dated August 12, 1696, he divided his real and personal property among his wife, children and grandchildren.

Savage, in his *Genealogical Dictionary of the First Settlers of New England*,[30] mentions "Edward Welch, an Irish youth," and "William Dalton, an Irish youth," who were "brought in the *Goodfellow*, sold by the shipmaster, George Dell, to Samuel Symonds, May 10, 1654, having been sent by the command of the English government after the triumphs of Cromwell in Ireland." "Philip Welsh, an Irishman, servant to Mr. Samuel Symonds," was brought before the Essex County Court, on March 27, 1660, at the instance of his master, who complained of his "stubborness and other offences," and the Court "respitted him until his master again has cause to complain." [31] It appears, however, that Edward and Philip were one and the same person, since a correction was made in his name. An entry in the records of the Court shows that Philip Welsh spoke both Irish and English, indicating that he received some education in Ireland. It is probable also that the passengers on the *Goodfellow* used the Irish language as their ordinary medium of intercourse, since this entry was in part as follows: ". . . in the said writing he is called Edward, and upon his arrivall at Ipswich such as doe well understand his language say he owneth his name to be Philip." [32]

On June 25, 1661, Samuel Symonds charged "his two servants, William Downing and Philip Welch," with desertion from his service, claiming there were two more years to run under their indentures, and, while it may seem an exaggeration to say so, the address to the jury [33] of these two Irish

[30] Vol. 4, pp. 23 and 454.

[31] Records and Files of the Essex County, Mass., Quarterly Court, Vol. 2, p. 197.

[32] *Ibid.*, p. 295.

[33] *Ibid.*, pp. 293-97, 310-11.

"servants" was one of the most intelligent statements found in the records of the Court of this period. Among the witnesses for the defence were three of their countrymen, John Ring, John Downing and Edmund Dear. Ring's testimony was thus recorded: "This deponent saith that he with divers others were stollen in Ireland by some of ye English soldiers in ye night out of theyre bedds and brought to Mr. Dill's ship, where the boate lay ready to receive them, and in the same way as they went some others they tooke with them against their consents and brought them aboard ye said ship where there were divers others of their countrymen weeping and crying because they were stollen from theyr friends, they all declaring the same, and amongst the rest were these two men, William Downing and Philip Welsh, and there they were kept until upon a Lord's morning ye master set saile."

In support of his case, Symonds produced "a Bill of Sale" [34] dated May 10, 1654, "from George Dell, master of the ship *Goodfellow*," under which he "sould unto Mr. Samuel Symonds two of the Irish youthes" he "brought over by order of the State of England," and since it appeared they were bound "to serve him for the space of nine years in consideration of 26 li. in merchantable corne or live cattle," the jury brought in a verdict for the complainant. Downing and Welsh announced their intention to appeal the case to the higher Court, and in the records of the "General Court of the Colony of Massachusetts Bay" there was incorporated the following "Declaration of Deputy Governor Samuel Symonds":

"TO THE HONORABLE COURT:

The plaintiff declareth as followeth, viz.: That in the yeare of our Lord 1654, he, wanting servants and being in Boston, at a Generall Court, endeavoured to purchase a supply out of ye ship that was newly come from Ireland. And, accordingly he made a Bargan

[34] Copy in Essex County Court Records, Vol. 2, p. 295.

with George Dell, m'r of ye ship called *Goodfellow* for a certayne sume, mentioned in ye writing betweene the said master and the plaintiff, which sume was also truly paid according to the condic'ons therein expressed. And because there had come over many Irish before that time (1654) the plaintiff p'ceived that some questions were stirring in ye Court whether it were not best to make some stop (in reference to people of that nation) which occasioned the plaintiff to make a p'viso for good assurance, as it is in the first part of said writing. . . . The m'r of ye ship (*Goodfellow*) said he brought them over by order of ye then State of Engl: he meant (it seemeth) such as then ruled in all the 3 nations, who, if he did oughte amisse against them that he brought over, they should have had their remedy at his hands pr'sently, or after have sought it at the hands of executors (not as ye purchasers as it is supposed) vnless the Bargans of soe many in the Country should be dissolved which as is thoughte the Lawe will not admitt; noe, not of any other Country that we heare of.

SAMUEL SYMONDS."

The "declaration" of the Deputy Governor verifies the extracts previously quoted from the English State Papers, that "many Irish" were brought to New England prior to 1654. Up to that time the transportation of the Irish to this country was so extensive that the colonial authorities became alarmed, and "some questions were stirring in ye Court" as to the best means to handle the situation and prevent the influx of "soe many (Irish) in the Country." While there is nothing in Massachusetts records to indicate that Irish immigration to the Colony was prohibited and no historian has thrown any light upon the point, the General Court passed an Act on October 29, 1654, levying a penalty of £50. on every Irish person entering the Colony, "on account of their hostility to the English nation." Notwithstanding this, it is probable that no action was taken, since there is ample evidence that the Irish continued to come to the Colony in the period which elapsed between 1654 and the end of the century.

The John Ring who came in the *Goodfellow* married Mary Bray at Ipswich on November 8, 1664, and had sons, David, Thomas and John. In the same year he owned "a share in Plum Island as tenant to Edward Bragg," [35] and his name is perpetuated in Ring's Island near Ipswich. He was a miller, and for at least four generations the Ring family operated mills at Ipswich and at Gloucester, Mass.,[36] and in 1705 John Ring (2) was the town schoolmaster at Gloucester. Later Philip Welsh settled in Topsfield, Mass. After his marriage to Hannah Haggett on February 20, 1666, they lived at Topsfield for twenty-two years and were the parents of six children, whose births were recorded there between 1668 and 1685. At the Salem Court in June, 1678, Philip Welsh and three of his countrymen petitioned for a subdivision of a sum of "£ 25. left for them in the hands of John Ring by Robert Darton, an Irishman, when leaving the country." It appeared that in his nuncupative will Robert Darton "ordered it so that if he came not here within the space of three years, then he willed the said summes with the use thereof to four of his countrymen, Edmund Dear, William Danford, Philip Walsh and John Ring." [37] One Richard Welsh, who also probably came in the *Goodfellow*, was bound "to serve Michaell Smith as an apprentice for six years, February 1, 1656, and to be taught navigation." [38] In a genealogy of the Welch family,[39] covering six generations of Philip Welsh's New England descendants, it is said that "Philip Welch was Scotch-Irish"

[35] The *Hammatt Papers.*

[36] *Trades and Tradesmen of Essex County*, by Henry W. Belknap, The Essex Institute, 1929.

[37] Probate Records of Essex County, Vol. 3, p. 230, and Essex County Court Files, Vol. 7, p. 37.

[38] Court Files, Vol. 2, p. 163.

[39] In *New England Historic-Genealogical Register*, Vol. 23, pp. 417-32.

and "came from the north part of Ireland." But that assumption on the part of the genealogist is effectively disproven by the entries before quoted from the "Order Books of the Commissioners of the Parliament," showing that the passengers in the *Goodfellow* were from "Cork, Youghal and Kinsale, Waterford and Wexford," or from "the County of Cork alone."

Many of the *Goodfellow's* passengers were brought to Ipswich, and a local historian, in commenting upon this fact, says: "Cromwell treated the Irish with great cruelty and many young Irishmen were taken by violence and sent overseas . . . the simple story of their sorrowful experiences reveals the tragedies that resulted in the coming of the Irish to New England." [40] Edward Nealand, one of the passengers in the *Goodfellow*, was described in the records of the Essex County Court as "Edward Nealand of Ipswich, Irishman." [41] By deed dated April 28, 1664, or only one year after the expiration of his indentures, "Edward Neland, Irishman," bought of John Baker, a "half acre with an orchard" [42] in the town of Ipswich, which he transferred to John Woodman on December 10th of the same year.[43] And by deed dated June 5, 1664, Joseph and Thomas Metcalfe, "in consideration of work to be performed," sold seven acres of land to "Edward Nealand of Ipswich, Irishman." [44] Pope also states that in 1665 "Joseph Metcalf, one of the proprietors of Ipswich and a member of the Massachusetts General Court, with his wife, Elizabeth, sold land in Ipswich to Edward Neland, a certain Irishman," [45] although no record of such a deed can be located. In the roll of Major Appleton's company, enlisted

[40] *Ipswich in the Massachusetts Bay Colony*, by Thomas F. Waters, Vol. 2, p. 221.

[41] Essex County Court Files, Vol. 3.

[42] Ipswich Deeds, Lib. 2, fol. 270.

[43] *Ibid.*, Lib. 4, fol. 76.

[44] Essex County Court Records, Vol. 3, p. 326.

[45] *Pioneers of Massachusetts*, by Rev. Charles Henry Pope.

for service in King Philip's War in 1675, appears "Edward Neland of Ipswich"; in the next year he served as a trooper in Captain William Whipple's company,[46] and as late as 1703 he was one of a committee chosen "to lay out the bounds between Ipswich and Topsfield."[47] He is mentioned frequently as a resident of Essex County; he left many descendants whose names appear in the town records of Ipswich and Topsfield all through the eighteenth century, in such forms as Nealand, Neland and Kneeland.

The records of the York County (Maine) Court[48] show that on July 5, 1654, one John Pickering of Piscataqua bought "the remaining five years service of an Irish servante man who had been brought over as a captive by George Dell." The "captive" was called in the Court records "Dennis, the Irishman," but in other County records his name was mentioned as Dennis McCormack. Apparently, he had some difficulties with his "master," for on July 2, 1657, the Court ordered "that he serve the full five years for which Pickering had bought him." On July 11, 1659, John Pickering was ordered by the Court "to pay him £3 sterling and dismiss him," and in the next year, on the expiration of the period of his indentures, a plot of land was assigned to Dennis McCormack at Portsmouth, N. H., where he was "admitted an inhabitant."[49] The case of Dennis McCormack well illustrates the struggles of recording clerks in their efforts to spell Irish names; it was written in York County records at different times in such forms as McCormack, Mackermecke, Cormick, Ackormack and Occormacke!

We again meet with one of the Irish "captives" on the

[46] *Soldiers of King Philip's War*, by Rev. George M. Bodge, pp. 155 and 283, Boston, 1906.

[47] Topsfield Town Records.

[48] Quoted by Rev. Charles Henry Pope, in his *Pioneers of Maine and New Hampshire*, Boston, 1908.

[49] *Ibid.*

Goodfellow, in the person of Jael Sullivan, the entry of whose marriage to William McIntosh thus appears in Braintree, Mass., town records: "William Tosh and Jael Swilivan were marrry^{ed} the 12th mo 7th 1660 by Major Autherton."[50] In the genealogy of the Mott family of Massachusetts it is stated that "Jael Sullivan was evidently one of the shipload of Irish captives sent to New England in 1654,"[51] and that "McIntosh was among the Scotch prisoners shipped to New England by Cromwell in 1651." When a company of residents of Braintree set out to colonize Block Island, off the Rhode Island coast, in 1661, McIntosh and his wife accompanied them and were among the first settlers on the island. He became a man of much prominence there and was made a freeman in 1664. Mary, daughter of William and Jael McIntosh, married John Mott, son of Nathaniel Mott of Scituate, on October 16, 1683, and Sarah Tosh married Nathaniel Mott (2) on January 23, 1691, both at New Shoreham, Block Island, at which place there were recorded, down to the year 1735, the births of twenty-two children bearing the name Tosh, all descendants of William and Jael (Sullivan) McIntosh.[52]

[50] Braintree, Mass., Town Records, p. 717.

[51] "Nathaniel Mott of Scituate and His Sons," in *New England Historic-Genealogical Register*, Vol. 67, p. 24.

[52] Vital Records of Rhode Island, Vol. 4, part 4, p. 36.

CHAPTER III

Irish in Virginia, 1609—Francis Maguire wrote an account of the Colony in the Gaelic language in 1610—English names no indication of nationality—changes in Irish names—Michael Donnell, pioneer of Topsfield, Mass.—Mulligan,. O'Cane, O'Deave, O'Kelly and Carney—the Irish origin of the Whitcombs.

BUT, even long before the period covered by the records before quoted, the Irish had been coming to the colonies. It is recorded that only two years after Captain John Smith's arrival in Virginia, an Irishman named Francis Maguire was in the colony. Alexander Brown, in *The Genesis of the United States,* quotes from documents at the Department of State of the Spanish government at Simancas, relating to an enterprise on the part of an English colonization company, which in 1609 was "negotiating with the Baron of Arundel that he shall engage to go with 500 Englishmen and with as many Irishmen to settle in Virginia." These documents indicate that Maguire took a leading part in the adventure, that he remained in Virginia for eight months, and on his return he delivered a report to the Spanish government, written in Gaelic, which was translated into Spanish by "Fr. Florencio Conroy, Archbishop of Tuam," then exiled in Spain. Brown's description of this enterprise is of extraordinary interest, especially as showing that one of the earliest accounts of the Colony of Virginia was written by an Irishman, and in his native language!

Daniel Gookin, an Anglo-Irishman born in Carrigoline, in the County of Cork, came to Virginia with "a multitude of people and cattle from England and Ireland," in a ship named the *Flying Harte* which sailed from the port of Cork and arrived at Newport News on November 22, 1621.[1] Among the authorities for this statement, we have that of Captain John Smith, who in his *Generall Historie of Virginia* wrote: "1621, The 22 of November arrived Master Gookin out of Ireland with fiftie men of his owne and thirtie Passengers, exceedingly well furnished with all sortes of Provisions and cattle, and planted himself at Nuport-Newes." That these people were a welcome addition to the population of the colony is evidenced by Governor Wyatt's letter in January, 1622, to "The London Company," reporting their arrival, wherein he expressed the "great hope if the Irish plantation prosper that from Ireland great multitudes of people will be like to come hither.[2] In the same year (1621) a book by an English Puritan Minister named John Brinsley was printed in London. Its author called it "a plea for learning and the schoolmaster," and announced that it was his "unfeigned desire to adopt the book for all functions and places, and more particularly to every ruder place, and especially to that poor Irish nation with our loving countrymen in Virginia."

In Hening's *Statutes at Large* may be seen references to Acts of the Virginia Legislature, showing that the presence of the Irish in that colony at this period was officially recognized. In March, 1654, an Act was passed by the "Grand Assembly" that "all Irish servants that from the 1st of September, 1653, have bin brought into this Collony without indenture . . . shall serve as followeth, vizzt. all above sixteen yeares old to serve six yeares and all under to serve till

[1] *Records of The Virginia Company*, Vol. 1. See also *Virginia Carolorum*, compiled from documents of the period by Rev. Edward D. Neill, p. 82, Albany, N. Y., 1886, and *Life and Letters of Daniel Gookin*, by Frederick W. Gookin, privately printed, Chicago, Ill., 1912.

[2] *Records of The Virginia Company*, Vol. 1.

they be 24 yeares old." [3] But, this Act proved a serious deterrent to the settlement of the colony, and the planters themselves, finding that it operated to their disadvantage, induced the Assembly to declare that "the Act requiring Irish servants coming in without identures should serve six yeares should be repealed," because they found that "the length of time they have to serve discouraged them from coming into the country and by this means the peopling of the country is retarded." [4] Accordingly, the Act was repealed in March, 1659. Enactments were also passed specifically mentioning "Irish Papists," and on the statute books of Virginia there are several Acts of the Legislature dealing with "the importation of Irish Papists," large numbers of whom entered Virginia and thence passed over into Maryland.

These Virginia statutes are here referred to, because they prove conclusively, not only that the Irish came to this country in large numbers in the middle of the seventeenth century, but as a matter of fact Irish immigration was encouraged in order that "the peopling of the country" would not be "retarded." And since they were described as "Papists," it is evident that they were of the old native stock. In Hotten's *Original Lists of Emigrants*, the records at the offices of the Land Commissioners for the States of Virginia and Maryland, the collections of the Virginia Historical Society and other equally authoritative sources of information may be seen the names of hundreds of Irish settlers in those Colonies prior to the year 1700. So, in view of all these facts, it is not surprising that we find similar names in New England records as early as the seventeenth century.

I do not doubt that our critic honestly believes that he is "familiar with the details of New England history." But it is quite clear that his knowledge is confined to what he has

[3] Hening's *Statutes at Large*, Vol. 1, p. 411.

[4] *Ibid.*, pp. 558-9.

obtained from the work of the historians before mentioned, and his reference to the "English names" and the religious beliefs of the early colonists shows that he has arrived at a rather hasty conclusion. "Jumping at conclusions" is a common failing among persons not equipped with first-hand information, and in the case of a name whose spelling or sound gives it the appearance of being English, people often mistakenly assume that the person bearing that name is, necessarily, of English origin. He evidently believes that the "English names" borne by "practically all the colonial families" in New England are a strong point in support of his contention. But, a man's surname is not always a test of his nationality or race, because certain family names occur in different countries. For that reason it is not always safe to say that a person is English because he bears a name that may be common in England, and for the same reason a person is not necessarily Irish because his name may be common in Ireland. That, however, does not apply to the old clan names, which invariably are of unquestioned Irish origin.

There are indications, because of the manner in which certain surnames were spelled by recording officers, that historical writers were led to believe that all who bore them were English, though, as a matter of fact, some of these people were Scotch or Irish. Among the Irish, there are many families of the old native stock whose names give no indication at all of their racial origin. This was the result of the operations of a law enacted by the English Parliament in the year 1465, under which families in Ireland living within the "Pale," by which the territory then within the military jurisdiction of England was called, were compelled to change or disguise their names, or adopt names after trades, occupations, colors or places. Outside the "Pale," this law was not effective. This Act was entitled:

"An Act that the Irishmen dwelling in the Counties of Dublin, Myeth, Uriell and Kildare, shall goe apparrelled like Englishmen and weare their beards after the English maner, sweare alleageance and take English surnames." The wording of the Act was, in part, as follows: "At the request of the Commons it is ordeyened and established by authority of said parliament that every Irishman that dwells betwixt or amongst Englishmen in the County of Dublin, Myeth, Uriell or Kildare . . . . . shall take unto him an English surname of one towne, as Sutton, Chester, Trym, Corke, Kinsale; or colour, as white, blacke, browne; or arte or science, as smith or carpenter; or office, as cooke, butler; and he and his issue shall use this name under payne of forfeyting of his goods yearely till the premises be done, to be levied two times by the yeare to the King's warres according to the discretion of the lieutenant of the king or his deputy."

Heads of Irish families resorted to different methods of complying with this law. Some dropped the "Mac" or "O," and in course of time their names were further disguised by dropping or inserting a letter or a syllable; others, putting a literal construction on the law, took names that were entirely foreign to or had no resemblance whatsoever to their Irish patronymics. But the more frequent method was to translate their names into their English equivalents. Thus we can understand how a native of Ireland bearing the name Smith or Johnson, for example, can be of as ancient Irish origin as if he bore the original family name, MacGowan or MacShane, whose literal meaning is "the son of the smith" or "the son of Shane or John," respectively. A great many instances of similarly "translated" names can be cited.

So also with Irish families bearing such names as Black, White and Gray, Cook, Carpenter, Taylor and Mason, Bacon and Lamb, Hill, Vale, Stone and Wood, and other names of like character that are borne by English-speaking people, such names in many instances being arbitrary adoptions enforced in obedience to the law before referred to. Numerous people bearing such names emigrated from Ireland to the colonies before 1699, but unless there is positive information as to the birth, antecedents or history of such people, it is not always practicable to differentiate as to their racial origin. In the case of the old Gaelic names that have remained practically unchanged, there is no element of doubt to be considered, and seldom or never is there any dispute as to the racial origin of people so named; they are invariably regarded as of the Irish Race.

From this we see that, to some extent, one needs to acquaint himself with the origin and meaning of family names before he can be considered competent to deal with the subject. And he may find it to his advantage and it will broaden his knowledge if, when in doubt, he consults such works as those of the learned Irish archaeologists, O'Donovan and O'Curry, the topographical appendix to O'Mahony's translation of Keating's *History of Ireland,* Rev. Patrick Woulfe's *Irish Names and Surnames,* Joyce's *Irish Names of Places* and O'Flanghhaile's contributions to the subject in *The Tongue of the Gael.* But, a genealogist or historical critic who classifies as "English" all persons bearing names such as those cited, without other evidence that these people were of the English Race, is apt to find himself in an indefensible position, since the names alone do not justify any such arbitrary classification.

One historian tells us that the American families of Laflin and Claflin are of English descent, notwithstanding the fact that their immigrant ancestor was one Robert McLaughlin, who settled at Wenham, Mass., some time before the year 1662. In those days it was not uncommon for New Englanders to spell names phonetically, and they were frequently so recorded, as many such instances of Irish names noted in this book bear witness. In the case of McLaughlin, some of the recording clerks seem to have assumed that its proper pronunciation was as its separate syllables would be articulated, *i.e.*, Mac-*laugh*-lin, and thus we find "Robert Mackclafflin" recorded as receiving a grant of land at Wenham in 1669. In time, "Mackclafflin" came to be the accepted mode of pronouncing and spelling the name in some localities. So we can readily understand the transition of the name into its present forms of Laflin and Claflin, once the prefix was dropped, as was the custom in those days in the case of nearly every name commencing with "Mac" and "O." There were many almost similar cases.

Whence Robert McLaughlin came, or what his nationality was, is not on record, but although a genealogist of the family thinks he was a Scotsman, there is considerable doubt about it, and competent authorities on family nomenclature are inclined to the belief that he was an Irishman. The name was formed from the words, *loch*, meaning a sea or lake, and *lon*, meaning powerful, and both words were adopted from the Danish as a tribute to the power of the Danes at sea. The family name originally was O'Lochloin, hence MacLochlainn, and eventually McLaughlin, McLoughlin, O'Loughlin and Loughlin. There was a William McLoughlin at Boston, who was recorded [5] under that form of the name, as well as "Macloughlin," in entries covering the births and baptisms of his children in the years 1689-1694. As "William Mackloflin" he was taxed at Boston in 1688, and as "Mackcloghan" his widow was taxed in the year 1700. Some of his descendants were written down "Mclaughflin," "McClothlin" and "McClofflin," and "Daniel Mack Clafelin of Framingham" was so listed in the roll of a Sudbury, Mass., military company which took part in an expedition to Canada in the year 1690. When in later generations they too dropped the "Mac," we see at once that the name was almost completely angli-

[5] In Boston Town Books, Vol. 9, pp. 185, 196, 215.

cised, and thus numerous persons are of the opinion that the Laflins and Claflins are of the Anglo-Saxon race! There are also American families named Loffren and Lochren, whose family name originally was Loughran.

The vagaries of the colonial recording clerks in spelling people's names are sometimes difficult to understand, and in American records one observes many peculiar changes from the names borne by the original immigrants, which in some cases totally disguised them. There are families in North Carolina named Dula, descended from an Irishman named William Dooley of Patrick County, Virginia, a soldier of the Revolution. We find Fitts and Fitch for Fitzpatrick, Gerould, Jarrell and Jerl for Fitzgerald, Opherl (with the short sound of "o") for O'Farrell, Maness for MacManus, Bryant and Obryant for O'Brien, and so on. There are American families named Dennis, descended from one Dennis O'Deave who came from Ireland to Maryland in the year 1665, and two years later he "proved his rights" to a grant of land in Talbot County. In the "Lists of Early Settlers, 1633 to 1680," [6] he was recorded "Dennis O'Deere," in the land patent books as "Deer O Dennis," but he signed his will "Dennis O'Deave." Another such instance is that of Roger O'Cane of Somerset County, Md. At the Land Commissioner's office in Annapolis there is a record of a land grant to him, under date of June 26, 1679. He called his "home plantation" Waterford, doubtless after his birthplace in Ireland. His name was written in the body of the document, "Roger O'Cane," but in the margin it was entered "Keene O Roger," and in the probate records he appears as "Keine O Roger." On the marriage of his son, Donogh Dennis O'Cane, to Elise Nehulian at Hungar's Parish Church, Northampton County, Va., on July 31, 1661, his name was recorded "Donock Dennis," thus making it appear that his surname was "Dennis."

[6] At the Land Commissioner's Office, Annapolis, Md.

In each of these two cases, after the death of the father, the family adopted the names "Dennis" and "Roger," respectively, in the belief that in order to have legal title to the estate, it was necessary that their names should conform to the manner in which the owners of the property were recorded. Similar instances are met with occasionally in the records of all the colonies, and few of the new names are recognizable as Irish.

There are many American families whose names for several generations have been spelled Dunnel, Dwinnell, Dwoinell and by other variations. They are erroneously believed to be "of Scotch or French origin," notwithstanding the proven fact that they are descended from an Irishman named Michael Donnell, who I am convinced was an O'Donnell. This Michael Donnell first appears at Ipswich, Mass., in 1655, as an indentured servant to Samuel Appleton, which makes it reasonably certain that he was one of the passengers in the *Goodfellow*, which sailed from Kinsale, Ireland, in 1653. Evidently, he refused or neglected to attend services at the local Protestant church, for on April 9, 1657, "Andrew Tarvarse and Michaell, the Irishman, servants to Lieutenant Appleton," were summoned before the County Court on a charge of "absenting themselves from meeting." They were ordered "to acknowledge their offence at the next lecture at Ipswich, or pay a fine." [7] There can be no doubt that "Michaell, the Irishman," was Michael Donnell.

In the seventeenth century, the language of the great majority of the Irish was Gaelic, and to many of them English was an unknown tongue. They were taught to spell and write their names in Gaelic; but, after coming to this country, how to anglicise the names so as to make them understood by others, was a task, which, for many of them, was extremely difficult. Naturally, the efforts of the English offi-

[7] Essex County Court Records, Vol. 2, p. 41.

cials to spell Gaelic names did not lessen the difficulty, and thus we find not only a great lack of uniformity in the way such names were recorded, but some of the most ludicrous attempts at spelling them. In the case of Michael Donnell, there is no way of ascertaining whether he spelled his name in its original form, O'Donnell or MacDonnell, or simply Donnell, but, at any rate, it is clear the Town Clerks wrote it down as the fancy seized them. As time went on, the different branches of the family accepted and used the forms of the name as entered in the records. The births of seven of his children were thus recorded in Topsfield:

Mary, daughter of Michael Dwenell, born January 21, 1668.
Michaell, son of Michaell Dwinell, born November 5, 1670.
Thomas, son of Michaell Doenel, born November 20, 1673.
John, son of Mikell Dwinill, born December 16, 1674.
Elizabeth, daughter of Michael Donell, born April 17, 1677.
Magdalen, daughter of Michael Donnell, born February 24, 1679.
Joseph, son of Michael Dunnell, born January 26, 1681.

As early as 1660 he was possessed of a farm at Topsfield. As "Mikall Dwoinell" he appears under "Town Rate made January 27, 1668," and "Mickall Donell" was listed under "County Rate made the 18 of November, 1668, for Topsfield."[8] As "Myhill Dwinell" he appears in the court records as witness for the defence in an action at law entitled "William Pateson *vs.* Anthony Carroll," tried on March 31, 1668; as "Micall Donnell" he was recorded in 1670, as "Mikal donil" in 1679, and as "Michael Donnill" in 1680.[9] By deed dated October 24, 1672, he purchased fifty acres of land in Topsfield from Francis Peabody, and in his will dated June 29, 1711, he bequeathed this property to his "son Dr. Michael." At "a lawfull towne meeting 7 March 75/76,"

[8] Town Records, in *Topsfield Historical Society Collections*, Vol. 2, p. 51.
[9] Court Records, Vol. 4, p. 250, and Vol. 7, pp. 161, 238, 362.

several residents of Topsfield were declared to be "Commenars," one of whom was "Micall Donnell"; [10] among residents of the town who "took the oath of alegiance and fidelity" on December 18, 1678, was "Michael Dunniell," [11] and "Mikall Donel" was assessed for his share of the minister's salary in 1681.

The crude orthography of the town records in itself is sufficient to show why the Town Clerks were unable to write Michael Donnell's name in its correct form. For example, at a town meeting on April 30, 1673, it was "voated" that "Mickall Dunell is Chosene by ye seclectmen to Looke to ye yoaking and ringing of hoges and ye sd Doniell is to have one halfe of ye forfite for his payenes as is expressed in ye order above Wrighteen and other halfe hee is to returne to ye selectmen." [12] Again, in 1694, when Salem declared its right to tax the Donnell farm as being within the limits of that town, and the Topsfield town board protested its action, the Town Clerk made a record of their "resolve" in the following words: "At a lawfull towne meeting on December 18, 1694. Whareas sum of Salem lays Claime to mikell Dwoinells land for which ye said Dwonnill is attached ye Towne did manifest that they would stand by ye said Dwonill in this case. Voted Lieut Thomas Baker is Chosen in ye behalfe of ye Towne to stand by Mikell Dwonill sen^r in ye defence of his lands as is Claimed as above said." Also, "at a lawfull meeting of ye Towne of Topsfield ye 8th day ganuery 1695 ye Towne have made choyce of Lieut Thomas Baker to manage Mikell Donill Senr his cause against Salem farmes and to asosiate to himselfe whom he will to strengthen ye Cause and to prosicut it from Court to Court till ye case be ended ye mening in this case

10 *Topsfield Historical Society Collections,* Vol. 2, p. 18.

11 *Ibid.*, p. 47.

12 *Ibid.*, p. 15.

now comminsed against ye said Dwonill and ye Towne will bare him out in all his lawfull proseedings tharein." [13]

There are many other references to Michael Donnell in Topsfield records. He was several times chosen a town officer and there are indications that he and his sons, Michael and Thomas, were very active in local affairs. The name, with its many curious variations, is entered more than two hundred times in Topsfield vital records of the seventeenth and eighteenth centuries. It also appears frequently in the records of several other Massachusetts towns, and in the muster rolls of the colonial and revolutionary wars. His son, Michael, was described in deeds in the year 1697 as "Mikell Donnell, Jr., physician and chirurgeon," but his name nearly always appeared as Dwinnell, and in a sketch of the career of "Dr. Michael Dwinell, the first recorded physician in Topsfield," [14] it is said that "he was one of nine children of Michael and Mary Dwinell. Michael, the father, may have come from Scotland or Ireland, though the family tradition says he came from France." Likewise, in a genealogy of the family brought out by Dr. Henry Gale Dunnel of New York, he stated that he was "uncertain" as to whether his immigrant ancestor was from "the Macdonnels of Scotia, the O'Donnells of the Green Isle or the Duinnels of France."

However, there was another of the family who apparently was better informed, and he handed down to his descendants a certain record which clarifies the point. Solomon Dwinell, of the third generation in descent from Michael Donnell, was a soldier of the Revolution, serving, as he said himself, "from the siege of Boston to the siege of Yorktown." During the war he kept a diary, in which he made many entries of a family nature and of his personal observations and experiences, and in this interesting chronicle Solomon Dwinell

[13] *Ibid.*, pp. 87-88.

[14] *In Topsfield Historical Society Collections*, Vol. 16.

wrote that he was a "great-grandson of Michael Donnell, who was born in Ireland and came to America, settling in Massachusetts." The diary is in the possession of Rev. Walter S. Elliot of Portland, Oregon, a descendant of Solomon Dwinell, and from the entry here quoted it is reasonable to suppose that Michael Donnell, the immigrant, sprang from the O'Donnells or the McDonnells of Ireland, and was one of those "genuine Irishmen" of whom our critic can find no trace in history. The genealogist of the family quoted at length from deeds and other documents, showing the successive variations of the name, and said there are more than a thousand families spread over the Eastern and Middle States, all descended from Michael Donnell. "The original deeds to lands owned by Michael Donnell in 1672 and later are still preserved," and "his original farm has never passed out of the family and is in possession of a Dwinel."[15]

It is strange what a weakness some Americans have for trying to make believe they are not of Irish descent! A Dr. Mulliken, who died in Baltimore a few years ago, ridiculed the suggestion that his ancestors were Irish, notwithstanding the fact that I traced his family back in a direct line without a break to Patrick Mulligan, who was transported from Ireland to Maryland in 1661,[16] and who in the next year received four grants for a total of 1350 acres of land on the Eastern Shore.[17] A Massachusetts physician named Kelley, although admitting that his family was "a branch of the Kelleys of Cape Cod," denied his Irish descent. There have been many families of the name on the Cape Cod Peninsula, and all were descended from the David O'Kelly hereinafter mentioned, who settled at Yarmouth before 1655, and who

15 *The True Genealogy of the Dunnel or Dwinell Family,* by Dr. Henry Gale Dunnel, New York, 1862.

16 *Index of Early Settlers,* Vol. 1, at Land Commissioner's office, Annapolis, Md.

17 Maryland Land Records, Lib. 5, fols. 56, 243-4, 463.

was referred to in local records of the year 1657 as "an Irishman."

A New England family named Carney has been written up by one of their descendants, Dr. Sydney Howard Carney of New York, who insisted they are of French origin. His basis for that conclusion is that his immigrant ancestor, Mark Carney, a soldier of the Revolution, located near some French families in Lincoln County, Maine, where he married a Frenchwoman named Goux, and that it is "probable" he too came from France and was of "the French family of Marconnet or Marconnay." In his efforts to prove the point, Dr. Carney went to the Department of Haut Sonne in France, whence the Goux family emigrated, but failed to secure verification. And later, his lovely theory was exploded by the discovery of a letter written by Daniel Carney, son of Mark, in which he said: "I have understood that my father, Mark Carney, with David Clancy, William O'Brian and Richard Whaling, came to this part of the country when very young by way of Newfoundland." That his father was an Irishman, is seen from Daniel Carney's further statement, that "there are many of our name in the County of Kilkenny, but whether my father was an orphan or had parents living when he left Ireland, I do not recollect to have heard him or my mother say." This Daniel Carney was a prominent citizen of Boston in the early part of the last century and was the father of twenty-two children, and descendants of Mark Carney are mentioned in records and local histories of New England towns.

Many instances can be cited showing how family names affect people's opinions as to their racial origin, one of the most striking being the name, Whitcomb, of frequent occurrence in New England. Some years ago a lady of that name in Massachusetts asked if it were possible for me to verify a family tradition, to the effect that "the first of the Whitcombs in New England was an emigrant from Ireland and a Catholic, who settled in Maine about the year 1720." Since she herself is a Congregationalist, and as far back as she knows all her people were of that faith, she could not understand how her immigrant ancestor could have been "an Irish Catholic," especially since he bore "a name so obviously English." I collected all the data concerning the Whitcombs available from American records and sent it to Dr. Joseph Bigger of Belfast, then editor of the *Ulster Journal of Archaeology*, with the result that he obtained information from Irish sources, showing that the Whitcombs in Ireland came from an old family whose original name was Kirwan! Dr. Bigger explained at length the methods by which Irish names were formed in ancient times. He determined that the derivatives of the name Kirwan were the two Gaelic words, *cior bhan* (pronounced as if spelled *keer waun*); that the Kirwans in County Meath, Ireland, when compelled by the Penal Laws to take an English name and adopt English manners and customs, translated their name into what *cior bhan* means in English, viz., a "white comb," and in due course they adopted the name, Whitcomb. It was a very interesting case; Miss Whitcomb became thoroughly satisfied as to the correctness of the family tradition and rejoiced at being informed by such a good authority as Dr. Bigger that she is of Irish descent.

CHAPTER IV

Many Irish mentioned in Boston Records—Cormac Annis from Enniskillen, Ireland, at Newbury, 1666—Emigrants from Dublin at Dedham, Mass., 1640—Edward Mortimer, a prominent Boston Irishman, 1676—strange case of "Daniel Missilloway," or Daniel O'Sullivan—one of the ancestors of Joseph H. Choate, American Ambassador to England.

IN many cases, as the records attest, a variety of phonetic interpretations of the surnames has been handed down by colonial recording officers, whose ears were unattuned to the correct pronunciation of old Irish names. In some of these cases the changes were so radical that it is now difficult to determine or even to form an opinion as to the nationality of those who bore these names. Many persons were also recorded whom it would be very unsafe to place in any particular racial category, because the same names occur in English as well as in Irish family nomenclature, and although some of these latter probably were Irish, all doubtful cases have been eliminated from consideration in this study. Take, for instance, the following surnames, where the average reader of history would be apt to assume that the persons who bore them were not Irish: Annis, Bacon, Beers, Bird, Brasier, Bieck, Grasier, Hay, King, Mickery, Morrell, Mortimore, Reylean, Smith, Ward and Missilloway. These people evidently named Ireland to the recording officers as the country of their nativity; they called themselves "Irish," not "Anglo-Irish" or "Scotch-Irish," and therefore they are here included in the former category.

"Cormac alias Charles Annis" of Newbury, Mass., was

married at that place to Sarah Chase on May 15, 1666.[1] He lived at Topsfield for fifty years, had eight children whose births were recorded there between 1667 and 1681 and he died there on December 19, 1717. From the fact that he was christened Cormac his nationality may be safely assumed, but in any event there is an entry in the marriage register to the effect that the bridegroom was "born in Ennis-Killen, Ulster County, Ireland, in 1638." Needless to say, the registrant intended to say Enniskillen, Fermanagh County, Province of Ulster, Ireland. Cormac is the Irish name corresponding to the English Charles, and, as shown by O'Hart,[2] the surname originally was McGinnis, anglicised Magennis, Guiness, Ennis, Innis and Annis. Cormac Annis left many descendants, who are mentioned generally in Massachusetts and New Hampshire records as substantial people and active in town affairs. Two of them, Daniel and John Annis, lived at Bradford, Mass., in 1740. About 1745 Daniel sold his property there and he and one Reuben Kimball removed to what is now Warner, N. H. They were the first two settlers to locate there, and the town historian in referring to this fact, says that "Charles (Cormac) Annis is believed to be the common ancestor of all the Annis's in New England." [3]

Michael Bacon came from Dublin, Ireland, with Samuel Cook and John Smyth, and according to Dedham, Mass., town records, all three were "proposed as proprietors (3) 1640 at Dedham." [4] In Dedham town records under date of "6th of the 12 month, 1642," there is a list of the "first grantees of land," among whom were Michael Bacon and Samuel Cook.[5]

1 Newbury, Mass., Vital Records, Vol. 2, p. 19. Also Annis Genealogy, in *Essex Antiquarian*, Vol. 3, pp. 184-7.

2 *Irish Pedigrees*, Vol. 1, p. 311.

3 *History of Warner, N. H.*, by Walter Harriman, Concord, N. H., 1879.

4 Dedham, Mass., Town Records. See also Pope's *Pioneers of Massachusetts*, pp. 26-27.

5 Town Records, fol. 1, p. 81.

William, brother of Michael Bacon, came to Salem in 1641 and was recorded as "a resident of Dublin, Ireland, in 1639." Ordinarily, the fact that people had lived in Ireland and emigrated from that country is no assurance that they were Irish, but in the case of Michael Bacon, he is referred to several times in Massachusetts records as "an Irishman." At the first recorded meeting of "Charlestown Village" (now Woburn) on April 13, 1644, Michael Bacon was appointed one of the "surveyors of highways," [6] and on June 29, 1674, he sold lands at Woburn to his countryman, Daniel McGinnis. Michael Bacon had three sons, Michael, John and Daniel. The former came with his father from Ireland, and served as a soldier in King Philip's War (1675) from Billerica, Mass., and eleven Bacons from Dedham, descended probably from the Dublin emigrant of 1640, served in the army of the Revolution.[7] Some entries in Dedham town records read thus: "Mr. John Smith from Dublin, Ireland, partner with Samuel Cooke, March 10, 1639. His wife Hannah received as an inhabitant at Dedham, lately arrived from Ireland, 23 (4) 1640, and admitted to ye Church at Boston 21 (10) 1640-1. The rate levied against John Smith was remitted 30 (11) 1642, upon consideration of the great losses that have of late befallen him in Ireland." [8] Mary Smith, supposed to be the widow of John, died at Boston on August 23, 1696, and in her will, dated May 13th of that year, she named as one of the legatees her "Granddaughter, Elizabeth Mulligan."

In the record of the marriage of Edmond Cousins and Margaret Bird at Boston in November, 1656, the bride was referred to as "Margaret Bird, an Irish maide"; and in Boston

[6] Woburn, Mass., Town Records.

[7] *An Historical Memoir of Billerica*, by John Farmer, p. 11, Amherst, N. H., 1816.

[8] Boston Town Books, Vol. 2, p. 71, and Pope's *Pioneers of Massachusetts*, p. 422.

town records [9] this entry appears under date of November 28, 1681: "Madeline Brasier, an Irishwoman, came lately from New London." One Robert Beers, described as "an Irishman," resided at Rehoboth, Mass. During King Philip's War a band of Indians laid the town in waste, and we are told "the town records give the name of only one person slain by the Indians at this time, Robert Beers, slain ye 28 March, 1676. He was an Irishman and a brickmaker by trade." [10] According to Boston town records, "Robert Breck, m'chant, was marryed to Sarah Hawkins 4:11:53, by Richd Bellingham, Dep^t^ Gover^r^"; and the will of "Edward Brecke of Dorchester" was filed in the Suffolk County Probate Court on November 10, 1662. Since both are referred to as "of Galway in Ireland," it is assumed they were natives of that place.

In Boston town records [11] under the year 1658 there is an entry: "James Webster, a Scotishman, and Mary Hay, an Irish maide, were marryed the 14th Febr." She is supposed to have been a daughter of Thomas and Bridget Hay who were at Boston about that time, and who some years later were referred to as "Thomas and Bridget Hayes." We are told that "Edward King, an Irishman, was one of the oldest settlers of this vicinity"—Windsor, Conn.[12] In 1656, "Edward King, an Irishman," was mentioned in the town records as a resident of and owner of "a house and woodland" at East Windsor, "near Podunk on the Connecticut River," and on September 16, 1662, "Edward King, Irishman," had "land set out to him by the town in addition to that previously sold to him by

9 Vol. 10, p. 59.

10 *History of Rehoboth, Mass.*, by Leonard Bliss, p. 96, Boston, 1836. Also *History of Rehoboth*, by Rev. George H. Tilton, p. 78, Boston, 1918.

11 Vol. 9, p. 67.

12 *First Puritan Settlers of Connecticut*, by Royal R. Hinman.

Thomas Ford on the south side of Podunk brook."[13] He was also mentioned as "Edward King, an Irishman," at a town meeting in Windsor in June 27, 1659,[14] and in all references to him in the town records he was so called.[15] In 1663 he joined other residents of Windsor in a petition relative to the establishment of a new settlement, at what is now Killingworth,[16] and in 1680 he signed a "petition of inhabitants on the east side of the Great River." It is probable that a countryman of Edward King also was in this vicinity in the late years of the seventeenth century, since the town records of Wethersfield say that "John King, an Irishman, was dr. in the Great River by Ry. H. about the 16th of May 1702, as he was going over the river,"[17] *i.e.*, he was drowned in the Connecticut River near Rocky Hill, Conn.

"Garrett Mickery, an Irishman, drowned August 10, 1660," appears in the vital records of Sudbury, Mass.[18] In 1652, one John Morrell was an indentured servant to John Hart of Boston, and Boston town records inform us that "John Morrell, an Irishman, was married to Lysbell Morrell, an Irishwoman, the 31st of August, 1659, by John Endicott, Govr.,"[19] and in the next year they removed to Ipswich. In 1660, Daniel Grasier contracted to build a house for Richard Dummer at Ipswich, but after a disagreement between the parties, Dummer sued Grasier in the County Court in March, 1661. In the same month the Ipswich Selectmen, under a law passed by the General Court in 1659, respecting the settlement of "poor strangers," gave "notice to Daniel

[13] Town Records, quoted in *History and Genealogies of Ancient Windsor*, by Dr. Henry R. Stiles, Vol. 1, p. 550, Hartford, 1892.

[14] *Ibid.*, p. 82.

[15] *Ibid.*, p. 425.

[16] *Towns and Lands*, Vol. 1, in Connecticut State Archives.

[17] Town Records, quoted in Dr. Henry R. Stiles' *Ancient Wethersfield*.

[18] P. 316.

[19] Boston Town Records. Also *New England Historic-Genealogical Register*, Vol. 19, p. 29.

Grasier and John Morill, Irishmen, that they were not willing to receive them as inhabitants, and they, not removing, complaint was made to the Court."[20] That they were permitted to remain, however, is shown by the records of the Court, wherein they were mentioned as residents of Ipswich in 1667,[21] and "John Morrell" was on the Topsfield tax list in the following year. An entry in Boston town records under 1661 says that "John Reylean, an Irishman, and Margaret Brene, an Irishwoman, were married ye 15th March by John Endicott, Govr."[22] From the same source we also learn that "James Risley came from Ireland to Boston" in 1681.[23]

In August, 1676, Edward Mortimore was enrolled in a Marlborough, Mass., company under Captain Samuel Wadsworth, for service in King Philip's War, and in the Boston Town Books of the year 1678 he was referred to as "Edward Mortimer, an Irishman." He signed his name "Edward Mortemor" to a deed in 1681.[24] He was a member of "the fire-engine company" in 1678, and in the *Journal of John Dunton*,[25] an Englishman who opened a book store in Boston in 1685, he mentioned several prominent persons in Boston, among them "Mr. Richard Wilkins, formerly a bookseller in Limerick, Ireland," and "Mr. Mortimer who came from Ireland, an accomplished merchant, a person of great modesty who could answer the most abstruse points in algebra, navigation and dialling." As Edward Mortimore, he was taxed at Boston in 1688,[26] and under the same form of the name he received a license for a "Publique House of Entertainment" on August 18, 1690. But as Edward Mortimer he was re-

20 Records of the Essex County Court, Vol. 2, p. 280.

21 *Ibid.*, Vol. 3, p. 430.

22 Boston Town Records, Vol. 9, p. 81.

23 *Ibid.*, Vol. 10, p. 59.

24 Suffolk Deeds, Lib. 12, fol. 94.

25 Published by the Massachusetts Historical Society, 2d Ser., Vol. 2.

26 Town Records, Vol. 10.

corded in 1695, and he is referred to by Samuel Gardiner Drake, in his *History and Antiquities of Boston*,[27] as "an Irishman." Notwithstanding all this, a New England historical writer disputes the nationality of Edward Mortimer, "because of his name," though willing to admit that "perhaps he may have been Anglo-Irish." But, if he had consulted the authorities upon Irish names and how they were derived, it would have been of considerable help to him before arriving at that hasty conclusion. As a baptismal name, Mortimer is "as old as the hills" in Ireland and is very popular in certain Irish families, though neither it nor Mortimore is often heard of as a surname. It comes from the Gaelic words, *morty mōr,* which mean literally a man of large stature bearing the baptismal name, Morty or Murty.

The marriage of "Robert Ward of Youghall, County Munster, Ireland," and Margaret Peachie was recorded at Charlestown on October 22, 1692. But, as in the case of Cormac Annis, "Youghal, County Cork, Province of Munster, Ireland," obviously was meant. There are English as well as Irish families named Ward. The name is quite common in Ireland, especially in Donegal, and comes from the original *Mac an Bhaird,* meaning "the son of the bard," anglicised Ward and MacWard. They have an Irish crest and coat of arms and O'Hart [28] numbers them among the "Bardic Families of Ireland" in the fifteenth century.

One of the strangest cases involving name changes was that of "Daniel Missilloway," who on June 14, 1672, married Anne Chase,[29] mother of the Anne Chase who married Cormac Annis at Newbury, Mass., on May 15, 1666. Savage [30] mentions "Daniel Mussilloway of Newbury, an Irishman, servant in 1665 to Joseph Plummer." At a session of the

[27] P. 463.

[28] *Irish Pedigrees,* Vol. 1.

[29] Newbury, Mass., Vital Records, Vol. 2, p. 330.

[30] *Genealogical Dictionary of the First Settlers of New England.*

Essex County Quarterly Court at Salem in September, 1669, "Daniel Musseleway" was arraigned on a charge of "abusing" some of his neighbors. One of the witnesses testified that "Daniel had threatened to knock John Ewers on the head," and "considering his being of the Irish blood, made me fearfull of some mischevious intent." [31] The town historian of Newbury refers to him as "Daniel Mussilaway, alias Roger Waldron, an Irishman." [32] All this seems fairly well to establish it as a fact that he was an Irishman. The vital records show that "An, wife of Daniell Mussuloway," died at Newbury on April 21, 1687; as "Daniel Sillaway" he was recorded as marrying Mary Griffin on September 7, 1687, and in one reference to him his name was spelled "Mussullowain." He left many descendants, but in no case did they use the forms of the name by which he himself was recorded. Two sons were born at Newbury to "Daniel and Mary Mussilloway," John on September 6, 1690, and Daniel on February 13, 1692, and their names are in the birth records as "Mussilloway." Yet, when John married Abigail Thurla on April 24, 1714, he was recorded "John O Shulaway," and on Daniel's marriage to Sarah Stevens on December 30, 1714, he was recorded "Daniel O'Siliway." [33] Again, when Daniel, son of Daniel and Sarah (Stevens) O'Siliway, married Mary Thorla on April 14, 1752, he was recorded "Daniel Sillaway," but when his sister, Mary, married Daniel Merrill on November 27, 1759, her name was written in the record "Mary O'Sillaway." [34]

Further, the birth of "Joanna O Sillaway," daughter of Daniel and Mary (Thorla) Sillaway, was so recorded at Newbury in 1753; the entry of the birth of her sister, Mary, in 1755 was written "Osiloway," and their brother, John, de-

[31] Essex County Court Records, Vol. 4, p. 179.

[32] *History of Newbury, Mass.*, by Joshua Coffin, p. 311.

[33] Newbury Vital Records, Vol. 2, p. 368.

[34] *Ibid.*

scribed as the "son of Daniel and Mary Sullivay," was baptised at the Fourth Church, Newburyport, on December 25, 1757. When the above mentioned "Joanna O'Sillaway" declared her "intentions" (to marry) John Choat at Newburyport, her name was entered in the parish register as "Osuleman"; but the entry of their marriage under date of October 2, 1771, appears as "John Choat and Joanna O'Sullivan," [35] undoubtedly a return to the name borne originally by her great-grandfather, Daniel Missilloway, or his predecessors. It is an interesting fact that John and Joanna (O'Sullivan) Choat were ancestors of the distinguished New York lawyer, Joseph H. Choate, who at one time was United States Ambassador to England.[36]

The name also appears at Sudbury, Mass., in the year 1750 as "O'Silloway," and in the Boston Census of 1790 two of Daniel's descendants were listed as John and Daniel "Osylavay." Thus, the various forms here mentioned can be followed through the eighteenth and nineteenth century records, one generation after another, with the name changing back and forth. Today, the living descendants of the man first recorded "Daniel Missilloway" bear the name "Siloway." The inference is that Daniel came to Newbury before 1665, was bound as a servant to Joseph Plummer, and that he remained in service for the usual period of five years. And his marriage to Anne Chase in 1672 indicates that he became a "respectable" member of the community, since the genealogy of the Chase family shows that she was the widow of Captain Aquila Chase, mentioned prominently as a sailing master at Newbury. There was recorded in Norfolk County a deed dated February 1, 1674, by which "Aquilla Chace of Newbery," son of Captain Aquila Chase, sold to "Daniell Musilowa of Newbery" sixty-six acres of land at Haverhill, Mass., for

[35] Newburyport Vital Records, Vol. 2, pp. 89 and 352.

[36] *John Choat and His Descendants,* by E. D. Jamison, Boston, 1896.

£33.[37] The births of three children of "Joseph and Bridgett O'Sillaway" appear in Haverhill vital records between 1750 and 1757,[38] and "Bridget Siloway, aged 84," died at Haverhill in 1810.

Despite the various authorities before quoted as to Daniel's nationality, some may question the statement that he was an Irishman. And while nothing can be found on record that would explain it more clearly than is here stated, it is the opinion of leading Gaelic scholars that the recorded forms of his name were only crude attempts to take down the phonetic pronunciation of *Ua Suileabbain* (O'Sullivan),[39] from the lips of an Irish speaker with a superficial knowledge of English, and who consequently could not explain the meaning of his name or its spelling in English. The pronunciation of the prefix *Ua* in Irish names cannot be produced correctly by any combination of letters in English. The English-speaking person can learn these sounds only from a native speaker by ear, and even then the tongue will generally trip up in the effort to pronounce them. The prefix "O" in English is a poor attempt at giving anything like a satisfactory rendering of the Gaelic *Ua*, which means a descendant or grandson. It is this difficulty that often confronted the early American recording officers, who produced for us a metamorphosis in so many Irish family names that now makes them almost unintelligible. The second part of the name, *Suil-dubh-ain*, means "the dark-eyed person"; the name is written Suileabhain and is pronounced *Sool-awhaain;* the termination, *āin*, a

37 Norfolk County Records, in *Essex Antiquarian*, Vol. 13, p. 106.

38 Haverhill, Mass., Vital Records, Vol. 2.

39 The name Sullivan also appears in the records of other colonies in such forms as Suiflan, Shoolavaw, Shulavan, Shulavay, Sillivan, Suelevane and Swillivawn. John Sullivan, father of General John Sullivan of the Revolution, appears in Dover, N. H., town records in 1723 as "Sullefund" and "Sullyfun," and one Donogh O'Sullivan who lived in Talbot County, Maryland, in 1675, was recorded "Donoch Osoulla."

diminutive, has a sound unfamiliar to the English ear; hence the terminations, *oway*, *away*, etc., found in the anglicised forms of many Irish names in the seventeenth century, may be satisfactorily accounted for.

CHAPTER V

Brian Murphy, an early Boston Irishman, in King Philip's War—Dermod O'Mahony in Essex County, Mass., 1639—mentioned many times in the Court records—Teague O'Mahony an interesting youth—Thaddeus and Florence MacCarty, prominent citizens of Boston—Charles McCarthy, one of the founders of East Greenwich, R. I., 1677.

THE proper name of "Bryan Morfrey," claimed to have been the only "genuine Irishman" mentioned in New England history of the seventeenth century, was Brian Murphy, and the "Margaret Mayhoone" whom he married was Margaret Mahony or O'Mahony. The entry of their marriage in the Boston town books [1] was as follows: "Bryan Morfrey, an Irishman, and Margaret Mayhoone, Widow, were married 20 July, 1661, by John Endicott, Governour." As "Bryan Murphey" he was listed among "Massachusetts Freemen, 1634-1655," [2] and as "Bryan Morphey" he was listed with a number of residents of Boston and vicinity who "took the Oath of Allegiance before Recorder Simon Bradstreet" on April 21, 1679; but as Brian Murphy his name was entered in a deed dated December 14, 1670, recorded at the Suffolk County Registery of Deeds.[3] Savage [4] also mentions him as Brian Murphy; under the same form of the name he appears in the lists of men recruited in Massachusetts for service in King Philip's War; but as "Bryan Morphy" he was credited

[1] Vol. 9, p. 82.
[2] List of Freemen, in *New England Historic-Genealogical Register,* Vol. 3.
[3] Lib. 8, fols. 299-301.
[4] *Genealogical Dictionary of the First Settlers of New England,* Vol. 3, p. 257.

with garrison duty at Mendon, Mass.[5] For his services in the war, and under the name "Bryan Merphew," he received a plot of land at a place called "Muddy River," now known by the more euphonious name of Brookline.

Mrs. Brian Murphy's maiden name was Margaret Norris. She was "admitted an inhabitant" of the town of Boston on July 26, 1658, on a bond for £7 given by David Faulkner, and was then described in its records as "an Irishwoman."[6] Her first husband was the Dermod O'Mahony, whose name appears in the appended list. As early as 1639 this Dermod O'Mahony and his family were residents of Essex County, Mass., and in the records of the Quarterly Court for that County his name was entered several times in connection with some legal proceedings. It is my belief that he came to Massachusetts about the year 1638 with his first wife, Dinah, and one son named Teague, and on May 9, 1639, he and Teague were indentured as servants to one George Strange of Salem for six years and ten years, respectively. In the Court records of October 27, 1642, he was referred to as "Dearman Mathew, alias Mahony"; on April 27, 1643, the "petition of Dearman O Mahonie" was recorded, and on the same date "Thomas Dexter confessed judgment in favor of Derman Mathew alias Mahownie." In the Essex County Court on June 27, 1643, he was described as "Derman Mahonie"; on December 27, 1643, he appeared as "Dierman O Mahonie"; on May 9, 1644, as "Derman O'Mahone," and on September 5, 1644, an entry in the records of the Salem Court said that "Goodman Harker and Dearmon O'Mahone undertake to pay Mr. Ralph Woory some mony."[7]

When his term of service had expired he seems to have

[5] *Critical Account of King Philip's War,* by Rev. George M. Bodge, p. 363, Boston, 1906.

[6] Boston Town Records, Vol. 2, p. 160.

[7] Records and Files of the Quarterly Court for Essex County, Vol. 1, pp. 47, 53, 57 and 64; Vol. 4, pp. 123, 153 and 185, and Vol. 5, p. 27.

removed to Boston, for in the year 1646 he was owner of a "house and garden," the location of which has been identified as part of the present block bounded by Court, Sudbury and Alden Streets.[8] His son, Teague, evidently was born in Ireland in 1630; the births of his children, Daniel and Honour, were recorded at Boston on October 4, 1646, and October 29, 1648, respectively; [9] he had a son, David, born in Boston in 1651, and a posthumous child, Margaret, was born in Boston on June 3, 1661. In 1657 he fell foul of a local law in Boston, under which householders were compelled to report to the authorities all "strangers" living with them, as in the "Minutes of the Meetings of the Selectmen of the Town of Boston," under date of "29: 10: 57," there is an entry to the effect that "Derman Mahoone is fined twenty shillings for intertaining two Irish women, contrary to a law of ye towne in that case provided, and is to quitt his house of them forthwith at his perill." [10]

He appears in many Massachusetts records,[11] where his Christian name was sometimes written "Dermondt," but never in its proper form of Dermod, and several times the surname was recorded "Mahowna," besides the forms of the name already mentioned.[12] His first wife signed her name

[8] John H. Edmonds, in a paper read before the Bostonian Society, May 23, 1916.

[9] Boston Town Books, Vol. 9, pp. 23 and 27.

[10] *Ibid.*, Vol. 2, p. 141. This law was aimed at all strangers, not specially at the Irish.

[11] Among them *Thomas Lechford's Note Book, Court of Assistants of the Colony of Massachusetts Bay,* Boston and Salem Quarterly Courts, *Aspinwall Notarial Records,* Suffolk County Deeds and Probate Records, Boston Town Books, *Massachusetts Archives, Calendar of State Papers, New Hampshire Province Papers,* and he is mentioned by Savage and the Prince Society.

[12] To those who have read Canon O'Mahony's history of the O'Mahonys, the names, Dermod and Tege, will look very familiar, because these names were much used by the Clan down to 1642, the year of its extinction by confiscation. The most common spelling of the surname in the English State Papers was Mahoon or Mahown, but every English writer in those days had a way of his own for spelling Irish names.

"Dina Mahowna," to a petition to the Court in 1650.[13] The Gaelic form of O'Mahony, when written in English letters, would be O *Mathghamhna,* which means literally "the grandson of Matthew";[14] it is pronounced as if spelled *o-ma-how-na,* which at once explains why the name was recorded in the different ways here described. The death of "Dorman Mahoon" was recorded at Boston on April 2, 1661,[15] and "administration to the estate of Dorman Mathue, als. Mahoone," was granted to Margaret, his widow, on May 17, 1661, and the value of his "goods and chattels" was appraised at £112. 1s.[16]

All entries in the records concerning Dermod O'Mahony and his sons are not here quoted; their names appear on record as many as sixty-five times between 1639 and 1661, and that being so, it is strange that our critic, who claims to be so "familiar with New England history," failed to find any information about this early Boston Irishman! After his death, his sons' names usually were recorded Mathews or Mathue, and all were described as mariners. At the Suffolk County Court on October 30, 1660, "Dermond Mahoone alis Mathews," as assignee of his son Teague or Thaddeus, secured a verdict against Joseph Armitage for wages due, but on February 25, 1661, Armitage filed "Reasons for Appeal against Dorman Mathews alias Mahonies."[17] His answer to the appeal closed as follows: "All of which I humbly leave unto the wise and godly consideration and determination of this honored Court and Jury, that I may have that which is

[13] *Massachusetts Archives*, Vol. 9, p. 14.

[14] In "The Apostasy of Myler Magrath, Archbishop of Cashel," a satirical poem written in Gaelic by Rev. Eoghan O'Duffy about the year 1577, the author referred to O'Mahony as "Matthew," and John O'Daly, the translator of the poem, explains in his "Notes" that "Mathghamhna" is Irish for Matthew.

[15] Boston Town Books, Vol. 9, p. 80.

[16] Suffolk County Probate Records, Lib. 9, fol. 342.

[17] County Court Files, 387, fols. 1, 2, 3, 4.

my just due to releive mee and mine now in my ould age when I have hardly eyes to see nor abbilitie to labor nor indeede a tongue to speake for myself as evidently may appeare and therefore doe humbly beseech this honored Court that in a way of Justis and Right you would releive the oppressed and dum."

In September, 1668, the Court[18] set off to Daniel Mahoone one-third of his father's estate, including a dwelling house at what is now the corner of Court and Sudbury Streets, Boston, then and until December, 1670, in the occupancy of Brian and Margaret Murphy. Daniel sold the property on October 23, 1668, to William Towers;[19] on October 29, 1672, by order of the Court, "the remaining part of the estate of Dorman Mahoone" was divided between his son, David, and daughter, Margaret.[20] David was then "of Block Island in New England, mariner"; in 1677, he was killed in Virginia; on November 20, 1679, the Suffolk County Court set off David's share to his brother, Daniel,[21] which the latter sold to William Clough on November 4, 1680.[22] On June 16, 1684, Margaret Mahoone sold to Henry Messenger her share of her father's estate.[23]

In June, 1675, Daniel enlisted in Captain Samuel Mosely's company of volunteers for service in King Philip's War and served as sergeant until March, 1676. Four years later, he was appointed "Deputy Searcher of Customs" at Boston, serving until July, 1683; and in that capacity, in August, 1680, he is on record as seizing in Boston harbor the "Ship *St. John* of Dublin" for "illegal trading."[24] In 1684, we find him as a

18 County Court Record, p. 86.
19 Suffolk Deeds, Lib. 41, fol. 94.
20 County Court Record, p. 90.
21 *Ibid.*, p. 621.
22 Suffolk Deeds, Lib. 12, fol. 218.
23 *Ibid.*, Lib. 13, fol. 343.
24 Records of the Court of Assistants, Vol. 1, pp. 170-2.

sheriff in New Hampshire, where he seems to have been constantly in trouble with the authorities, and eventually he was compelled to leave the Province.[25] He was mentioned nearly fifty times in all in Massachusetts and New Hampshire records.

Teague O'Mahony, son of Dermod, was recorded on May 9, 1639, in Essex County as "Teg Mayhoone, nine years old," when apprenticed to George Strange of Salem. On October 27, 1643, as "Tege O Mohoine, son of Dierman O Mahonie," he was apprenticed to Joseph Armitage, and since the latter agreed in the indenture "that Tege be taught the English tongue," [26] it is evident that the lad was conversant only with his native Gaelic. On the expiration of his term of service, he left Boston for Isles of Shoals, off the New Hampshire coast opposite Rye Beach, where his cousin, Matthew Colane, was engaged in the fisheries. As "Matthew Collaine" the latter was mentioned in the records of the Court on January 1, 1642, when he and two others were sentenced to be whipped "for concealing the plot of piracy" originated by one Peter Thatcher.[27] On December 4, 1649, Matthew Colane died, and the Aspinwall Notarial Records show that on June 1, 1650, testimony was taken at the Suffolk County Court in support of a claim that "Dermin Mahoone of Boston was his Cosen and only Cousen," and that he "had no more kinsmen in the land." [28] "Mahoone" applied for letters of administration on the ground that he was "next of kin and heir of Matthew Colane," and on March 11, 1651, the Court, then sitting at Kittery, appointed his son, "Teague Mahonies, fisherman, Isles of Shoals," administrator of the estate of Matthew Colane. It is evident Teague discontinued the Irish form of his

[25] Provincial Papers of New Hampshire, Vol. 1.

[26] Records and Files of the Essex County Quarterly Court, Vol. 1, p. 57.

[27] Records of the Court of Assistants, Vol. 2, p. 118.

[28] *Notarial Records of William Aspinwall, Recorder of Suffolk County Court,* p. 336, in Boston Town Books.

name, since in 1660 he appeared as "Thaddeus Matthews, mariner"; but thereafter his name disappeared from the records and nothing more is known of him.

Many readers of history seem to think that Lodge and Palfrey are infallible, and accept their statements with as much faith as Christian people accept the Gospel. That Lodge and Palfrey, in some respects at least, cannot be relied upon as impartial historians becomes perfectly clear when their work is analyzed and is put to the "acid test" of the official records. Neither of them makes any more allusion to a man of such prominence as Thaddeus MacCarty of Boston, than if he never existed! When history is written in this way, it is little wonder, once the truth becomes known, that there is a falling off of public confidence in its authors; perhaps even suspicion that men like Thaddeus MacCarty were deliberately omitted from their work, because of their name and race, may not be groundless. This Thaddeus MacCarty was born in Ireland, probably in the County of Cork, in 1640, and emigrated to Massachusetts sometime before 1664. The first mention of his name was on November 23, 1664, in the probate records of Suffolk County [29] as one of the creditors of Elkanah Gladman of Boston, when the latter's will was presented for probate. That he must have been a youth of no uncommon attainments for the time, is evident from the fact that in 1665 he was established as a merchant in Boston, and ten years later, as the records show, he imported goods in his own sailing vessels, thus indicating that he then occupied a prominent position in the life of the town. He appears regularly in Boston records between 1674 and the end of the century as a taxpayer, and sometimes in connection with deeds and conveyances of real estate. In 1691, he was surety

[29] Suffolk County Probate Records, in *New England Historic-Genealogical Register*, Vol. 16, p. 50.

on the bond for such an important official as John Usher, "Treasurer of New England."

One of the largest transactions in which his name figured was in a deed covering a tract of land laid out on the Merrimack River for prospective settlers about the year 1687. In the New Hampshire State Papers [30] there is a copy of the deed, dated April 15, 1686, by which "Robert Tufton Mason, Proprietor of the Province of New Hampshire," conveyed to "Thaddeus MacCarty of Boston, Merchant, and John Usher and Charles Lidgett, also Merchants of Boston," a tract of land described as "lying and being on ye Westerly side of the River of Merrimack, beginning at the East End of Soughegennock River, thence running Westward along the s^d^ Sou River six English miles and a halfe," etc. The deed was recorded at the Registry of Deeds for Suffolk County on November 10, 1686.[31]

Thaddeus MacCarty was a town magistrate and his name is associated in the records with some of the leading men of the Province, who are mentioned by the historians. He turns up frequently in State Papers of Massachusetts, New Hampshire and New York, in the "Minutes of the Meetings of the Selectmen of the Town of Boston," in papers of the Governors of Massachusetts and New York, in the *Old Colony Records* and the *Colonial Manuscripts of New York,* in papers preserved by the American Antiquarian Society, the Massachusetts Historical Society and the New England Historic-Genealogical Society, in the annals of "the Military Company of the Massachusetts," and in the annals of King's Chapel of which he was a founder in 1686. Yet it would seem to have been the opinion of Messrs. Lodge and Palfrey that he was not important enough to receive mention in their work, so that one cannot help wondering if their reason for omitting

[30] Vol. 29, pp. 138-141.

[31] Lib. 1, pp. 27-32.

him from history was because he was a "genuine Irishman" and bore one of the most ancient Irish names! Thaddeus MacCarty used as his seal the arms and crest of the Earls of Clancarthy, whose principal castles and estates were in County Cork, Ireland. His home in Brattle Square, Boston, was described by a chronicler of the time as "an elegant mansion."

Nor did Lodge or Palfrey consider Florence MacCarty, brother of Thaddeus, or any of their sons or daughters who married into prominent families, of sufficient importance to merit even passing notice. Florence was "a provision dealer and contractor in Boston"[32] and first appears in the records of the year 1680. He was recorded at the Essex County Registry of Deeds as the purchaser of lands and houses in Salem on March 17, 1698,[33] November 28, 1701,[34] and April 7, 1707.[35] He also owned much property in Suffolk County. Indeed, as late as the first quarter of the nineteenth century a tract of sixty acres of land which had originally surrounded the home of Florence MacCarty, through which High, Congress, Washington and other streets in Boston were afterwards laid out, was regularly referred to as "the Maccarty farm" in deeds and conveyances recorded at the Suffolk County Registry of Deeds. I submit that this one case alone of the MacCartys is a clear indication that Lodge and Palfrey cannot be depended upon by seekers of the truth of history. The interesting story of these families, with a reference to the authority for every statement concerning them, will be found in my book, *The McCarthys in Early American History*, which can be consulted at the leading public libraries.

There were several other McCarthy families in New Eng-

32 *Roxbury Town Records*, in Boston Town Books, Vol. 34, p. 370.

33 Deed Book, 13, fol. 213.

34 *Ibid.*, 15, fol. 7.

35 *Ibid.*, 20, fol. 27.

land, but there are no indications that they bore any relationship to Thaddeus and Florence of Boston. Charles McCarthy was one of a party of forty-eight settlers to whom a grant of five thousand acres of land, to be called East Greenwich, was made by the General Assembly of Rhode Island in May, 1677,[36] for services in King Philip's War. The town was incorporated on October 31, 1677. On May 6, 1679, "Charles Mecarte" was admitted "Freeman of the Collony." His will [37] dated February 18, 1682, the first to be entered in the probate record book of East Greenwich, shows that he resided in the Island of St. Christophers before coming to Rhode Island. He named "Richard Dunn of Newport" one of two "guardians" to carry out the provisions of his will, and mentioned his "brother from Kingsale," which would indicate that he came from Kinsale in County Cork, and he also referred to this brother as going from Ireland to Spain to take part in the wars.[38]

Thomas McCarty is mentioned as a participant in the overthrow of the government of Sir Edmund Andros in 1689, known as "The Revolution in New England"; and in 1691 a Thomas MacCarty was listed as a student at Harvard College.[39] Captain Thomas McCarthy was master of a Massachusetts vessel, as he was so mentioned in the "Letters of Samuel Sewall," Judge of the Massachusetts General Court, in 1695. Charles McCarty of Boston was a member of "The Military Company of the Massachusetts" under the command of Captain John Walley, and was badly wounded in the expedition against Quebec in 1690.[40] An Irishman named

[36] *Rhode Island Colonial Records*, Vol. 2, pp. 587-590.

[37] Copy in *Narragansett Historical Register* for April, 1891.

[38] "Charles McCarthy, a Founder of East Greenwich," by Thomas Hamilton Murray, in *Journal of the American Irish Historical Society*, Vol. 4.

[39] *New England Historic-Genealogical Register*, Vol. 32, p. 233.

[40] Savage, *Genealogical Dictionary of the First Settlers of New England*, Vol. 3, p. 139.

Daniel McCarthy was a resident of Boston in 1686. In the "Papers of Edmund Andros, Royal Gouvernour and President of Massachusetts,"[41] there is a record of a "Meeting of the Councill at Boston in New England the 22nd of January, 1687," in which the following item appears: "Before reading the petition of Daniell MacKarty setting forth that he had been a prisoner in his Matys Gaol in Boston and having been charged with felony and Burglary was tryed and acquitted by his Jury, but kept in prison for his fees, 'twas Ordered that upon payment of his fees he be forthwith discharged according to Law."

William McCarty was listed among "Leagell proprietors of ye Common and undevided Lands in ye Township of Salem" prior to 1661,[42] and a "William Carty," possibly the same man, served as a juror at Salem in 1672.[43] The marriage of "John Mecartey and Rebecka Meacham" was recorded at Salem on January 27, 1674.[44] They had eight children, born there between 1675 and 1690, and there is an entry in the parish register of the First Church at Salem of the baptisms of John, Jeremiah, Andrew, Peter and James "Makarta," all on the same day, November 16, 1687.[45] "John Mackartee" was on the Salem tax lists of the year 1700; Andrew and James "Mackarty" appear in a "List of Captain Thomas Laramore's Company raised in the Massachusetts Bay for His Majesty's special service in the West Indies, mustered by Governor Dudley, aboard the Gosper frigate, December 16, 1702."[46] Also, "John Mack Cartey of Salem" took out letters of administration to the estate of "Andrew Mack Cartey of Salem," at Newport, R. I., in the year 1703.

41 *American Antiquarian Society*, Vol. 13, p. 248.

42 *New England Historic-Genealogical Register*, Vol. 7, p. 152.

43 Town Records, Salem, Mass.

44 Vital Records, Salem.

45 *Ibid.*

46 *Calendar of English State Papers*, p. 38, Vol. 1702-03, London, 1913.

Captain Timothy McCarthy, a mariner, was at Newport in 1700. His marriage to Elizabeth Williams, daughter of John Williams, who in 1687 was Attorney-General of Rhode Island, is on record at Block Island under date of November 21, 1700, and the births of their four children appear in the town registers of New Shoreham, Block Island. In 1674 "John McCartey, a dyer" settled in Salem, and five years later he operated a fulling mill at that place and was then described as "John McCarty, clothier." [47] After eighteen years in business at Salem, he removed to Warren, R. I., but in 1699 "John McCartey, a dyer," is again found in Salem town records, and down to 1702, his name was on the tax rolls. Owen McCarthy was at New London, Conn., in 1673, and as "Owen McCarty" his name was entered in the town books under "New Inhabitants that appear between 1670 and 1700." "Kathrane Macarty" signed as a witness to an administration bond dated November 6, 1694, filed in the Bristol County Probate Court.[48]

[47] *Trades and Tradesmen of Essex County*, compiled by Henry W. Belknap, pp. 79, 83, Essex Institute, 1929.

[48] Probate Books, Vol. 2, p. 77A.

CHAPTER VI

The Fannings, Butlers and Bryans in New England—large number of Irish in Essex County, Mass.—among the earliest grantees of land at Exeter, N. H.—the "Irish Teagues" in New England—Teague Crehore, ancestor of numerous people of the name—Teague Barron from Ireland probably one of President Coolidge's ancestors.

THERE were several prominent families named Fanning in Connecticut in the seventeenth and eighteenth centuries. The first of the name in this country was Edmund Fanning, a native of Kilkenny, who served under the great Irish Chieftain, Owen Roe O'Neill, in the Rebellion of 1641. His father was Dominicus or Dominick Fanning, Mayor of Drogheda, who was executed by orders of Oliver Cromwell after the sack of that town in the year 1649. An account of the career of Edmund Fanning states that "he escaped from Dublin in 1641 in the time of the great rebellion, and after eleven years of wandering and uncertainty, he found a resting place in Groton, Conn., in the year 1652." [1] Thence he removed to Stonington, Conn., with which town the name has been associated for more than two centuries. He was the father of Thomas, William, Edmund, John and Mary Fanning, the first two born in Ireland. One of his grandsons, James Fanning, a Captain in the French-English war, 1755-1763, removed across the Sound and settled in Long Island, and was the forebear of numerous families of the name, not only in Long Island but in various parts of the country. From the inscription on the tombstone of Captain James Fanning in an

[1] Munsell's *American Ancestry.*

ancient cemetery at Riverhead, we obtain some interesting family history. The stone is a huge block of marble, said to be the largest in any burial-ground in the State of New York, and the inscription contains 1860 words, in part as follows:

"Captain James Fanning
Died 1776, in the 93d. year of his age.

He was the great grandson of Dominicus Fanning, who was Mayor of a City in Ireland, (under Charles I), was taken prisoner at the battle of Drogheda, 1649, all the garrison except himself being put to the sword; he was beheaded by Cromwell, his head stuck upon a pole, at the principal gate of the City, his property confiscated because when Charles I made proclamation of peace, as member of the Irish Council, he advised not to accept unless the British Government would secure to the Irish their religion, their property and their lives.

His son Edmund was born in Kilkenny, Ireland, married Catherine, daughter of Hugh Hayes, Earl of Connaught, and emigrated to this country with his family, consisting of his wife, two sons, Thomas and William, and two servants, Lahom and Orna, settled in Stonington, Ct. William, in a battle with the Indians, was killed by King William, who split his head open with a tomahawk. Thomas had a daughter, Catherine Page, and one son, James. This Capt. Jas. Fanning served under Great Britain, which government was at war with France; married Hannah Smith of Smithtown and had five sons and four daughters."

Much other genealogical data concerning the Fanning family is obtainable from this remarkable tombstone inscription. One of Captain James Fanning's sons, Gilbert, removed from Long Island to Stonington. Many of his descendants were sea-faring men and one of them, Edmund Fanning of Stonington, is noted in history for his discovery in the year 1797 of the group of islands near the equator, known as the Fanning Islands. Four of his descendants were officers in the Revolutionary Army; Nathaniel Fanning was with Captain

John Paul Jones on the *Bon Homme Richard* in the celebrated fight with the *Serapis*, and history states that "by his gallant conduct he contributed essentially to the brilliant result."

Andrew Fanning, who "came in the *Diligence*, February 6, 1679, as servant to Daniel Stanton," is also mentioned as of Stonington, and probably was of this family. There were at least two families of the name in Massachusetts. The births of four children of Thomas and Elizabeth Fanning were recorded at Watertown between 1656 and 1665; Thomas Fanning, probably the same man, served in King Philip's War; the town records show that Thomas Fanning was chosen "Tythingman" in the year 1679 and his death was recorded at Watertown on August 30, 1685.[2] William Fanning and Elizabeth Allen were married at Newbury on March 24, 1668, and they were the parents of five children born there between 1669 and 1681.[3] Evidently he was a mariner, and there was recorded at Boston a power of attorney dated November 26, 1692, from "William Fannen or Fanin of Newbury" to Thomas Harvey, authorizing him to collect his share "on account of ye prize now in Boston." His name was also recorded William Fanning.[4]

As early as 1653, John Butler, a native of Waterford, and a descendant of the Butlers of Kilkenny, one of the most eminent of the Anglo-Norman families of Ireland, was in business as a merchant both at Saybrook and at New London, Conn. In Saybrook town records he is described as "an Irish gentleman." He was the founder of the settlements known as Butlertown and Waterford, a few miles west of New London. Members of the family are mentioned in New London records of the year 1680, and Thomas Butler is said to have been one

[2] Town Records, Watertown, Mass.
[3] *Ibid.*, Newbury, Mass.
[4] Suffolk Deeds, Lib. 14, fol. 232.

of the leading men of the town in the early part of the eighteenth century. James Butler, a near relative of John, also came to Connecticut in the year 1653, but removed to Lancaster, Mass., where he received a grant of "a halfe home lott" in 1663, and his name appears in the tax lists of that town and also of Woburn and Billerica down to 1681. Although Billerica vital records contain an entry under date of March 20, 1681, of the death of "James Butler, Sr., Irishman," [5] the local historian quotes from the town records: "James Butler, Sen., Irishman, dyed 20, 01, 81." [6] He is said to have been "the largest landowner in what is now Worcester County." [7] His son, James, succeeded to this property and was mentioned in Lancaster town records in 1728.

A long account of the Butler family [8] concludes thus: "The Emerald Isle was undoubtedly the country from which their ancestors emigrated and the Irish the nation with whom they enjoy nationality." We are told that "James Butler came to the Colony when only four years old and knew nothing of his history, except that he came from a noble family in Ireland. He had a habit of enquiring of every emigrant from Ireland who came to the vicinity if they knew anything about the Butlers, and the frequency of his enquiries became a matter of much comment among the townspeople." Even on the day of his death (1681), "hearing that an Irishman had just arrived in town, it is said he had him summoned to his bedside and questioned as to whether the Butlers were not one of the noble families of Ireland, and when the newcomer informed him that he knew the Butlers of Kilkenny and that they were of the Ormond family, James Butler died in peace." His son, John, born July 22, 1677, was the father of

[5] Billerica Vital Records, p. 347.

[6] *History of Billerica, Mass.*, by Rev. Henry A. Hazen, p. 21, Boston, 1883.

[7] Letter dated April 21, 1897, from one of his descendants, Henry A. May, in *Journal of the American Irish Historical Society*, Vol. 2, p. 19.

[8] In *New England Historic-Genealogical Register*, Vol. for 1848.

ten children, all born at Woburn. In 1721, he removed to what is now Pelham, N. H., where a monument was erected to his memory, and on the occasion of its dedication, in June, 1886, it is said that 1200 of his descendants were present. John, son of John Butler, was a Captain in the Indian War in 1745, and David, son of John Butler (2), was an officer in the Revolutionary army. A Thomas Butler, born in Ireland in 1674,[9] came to Massachusetts in 1692 and settled at Berwick, Maine, and since he is mentioned by an historical writer as "of the ancient English House of Ormonde," we may safely say that he also was of the Butlers of Kilkenny. He had a son, Thomas, born at Berwick, in 1698.

Two Irishmen named Bryan were prominent merchants in Connecticut in the seventeenth century. The first of the name in New England, Alexander Bryan, a native of Armagh, Ireland, is described as "the great shipping merchant for thirty or more years from the settlement of Milford (Conn.) in 1639,"[10] trading chiefly with Barbados, which was then an important market for grain and other products. It is related that in 1661 he bought from the Indians "the last twenty acres of land they owned at Milford Neck" and paid for them, "six coats, three blankets and three pairs of breeches."[11] He died in 1679, and his tombstone and those of several other Bryans may still be seen in Milford's ancient cemetery. Richard Bryan, also from Armagh and a relative of Alexander, was one of Milford's pioneer settlers and one of the leading traders in Connecticut in his day. He lived at Stratford and is mentioned in connection with colonial events of the year 1679 as "a merchant in Stratford for more than half a century." It is said of him that "he bought and sold land in

[9] Mathews' *American Armoury and Blue Book.* Also *Genealogical and Family History of the State of Maine*, p. 131, by Dr. George T. Little.

[10] Munsell's *American Ancestry.*

[11] Ford's *Historical Sketches of the Town of Milford*, New Haven, 1914.

almost every town between New London and New York and it was he that furnished goods to pay the Indians for nearly all the townships of the region." He was one of a company of sixty-four men who went from Connecticut in the year 1666 and founded the town of Newark, N. J. Richard Bryan was also a shipbuilder and was the owner of several vessels trading with West Indian and European ports; indeed, "it is doubted if there were another merchant out of Boston on the American coast that did as large a business as the Bryans from 1639 to 1670." [12]

In the first century of colonial history, the Irish appear to have been in Essex County in greater numbers than in any other part of Massachusetts, with the possible exception of Boston. It is evident that a large proportion of the 550 Irish captives brought over in the *Goodfellow* in 1654 were landed at the port of Marblehead, and it is probable that many of those in need of farm laborers, who came to Marblehead to purchase their time and services from the captain of the vessel, were Essex County farmers. In the vital records of the townships of Beverly, Danvers, Gloucester, Ipswich, Lynn, Manchester, Newbury, Peabody, Rowley, Salem, Salisbury and Topsfield in Essex County, there are occasional references to these people. And in the files of the Quarterly Court, wills, deeds, and other records, may be found the names, not only of Irish "indentured servants," but in later years of former Irish "servants" engaged in various business callings, or cultivators of lands of which they themselves were the owners. Among the characteristic Irish names in Essex County records, including those mentioned in the first decade of the eighteenth century, were:

Barry	Carroll	Cody
Breen	Cartey	Coffeen
Burke	Casey	Collane

[12] Munsell's *American Ancestry.*

Collins
Comerford
Connally
Connor
Cotter
Crowley
Cullen
Currin
Curtin
Dalton
Daly
Deere
Dempsey
Dillon
Dolan
Donnell
Downing
Drisco(!)
Duffy
Duggan
Dunn
Dunnevan
Dwyer
Egan
Fanning
Flynn
Fitzgerald
Foley
Gilligan
Grady
Greeley
Harney
Hayes
Healy
Hickey
Joyce
Kelly
Kenny
Kinnacan
Larkin
Leary
Lunnagen
Lynch
McCarthy
McMullen
McShane
Magilligan
Mahony
Mooney
Moran
Murphy
Nealand
O'Brien
O'Dougherty
O'Mahony
Quinn
Reilly
Roche
Ryan
Sheahone
Strahan
Sullivan
Welsh

In 1664 a group of settlers came to Essex County, Mass., and located north of the Merrimack River, at Exeter (now New Hampshire). There were thirty-seven in all, and it is interesting to note that among them were Cornelius Leary, William Hacket, "Dany" Kelley, Teague "Drisco," Teague Cartey and "Jeremy" Connor. On October 10, 1664, the first three received grants of land at Exeter on condition that they remain and cultivate these lands; [13] and while Drisco, Cartey and Connor are not so listed, there are indications that they also received free grants, since they were residents and landowners at Exeter in 1674. Among grantees of land recorded by the Town Clerks at Exeter,[14] we find:

13 From lists of the early settlers, in Exeter, N. H., *Town Register,* and *History of Exeter,* by Charles H. Bell, pp. 135-146.

14 *Ibid.*

Grantee	*Acreage*	*Date*
Cornelius Leary	15	October 10, 1664
William Hacket	50	October 10, 1664
Dany Kelley	10	October 10, 1664
Philip Cartey	16	March 29, 1668
Teague Drisco	20	January 31, 1681
Jeremy Connor	20	January 31, 1681
Philip Cartee	20	January 31, 1681
Jeremiah Connor	30	February 3, 1698
Philip Dudy	50	February 3, 1698
Cornelius Conner	30	April 17, 1700
Jeremiah Conner	15	April 1, 1701
Cornelius Conner	30	April 1, 1702

That Cornelius Leary was in this country at least three years before his advent at Exeter, is evident from the record of the marriage of "Sarah, daughter of Cornelius Leary," to Matthew Moore at Newbury, Mass., on March 27, 1661. At a session of the Essex County Quarterly Court in April, 1669, a writ was issued in a case entitled "Roger Collins *vs.* Cornelius Lary"; [15] and an entry in the Court records in October of the same year says: "Cornelius Larie and Joseph Berrie acknowledged debt to Mr. Richard Cutt." [16] As Cornelius "Larey" he appeared in the "Provincial Rate Lists" of the town of Exeter, dated April 20, 1680; [17] Cornelius Leary, Edward Dwyer and Roger Kelly were listed among the men "on garrison duty" at the Exeter garrison during "King William's War" in 1696; [18] four years later Cornelius, Daniel and Thomas Leary, sons of the first named Cornelius Leary, served in an Exeter military company; [19] and in the roll of a com-

[15] Records and Files of the Essex County Quarterly Court, Vol. 4, p. 134.

[16] *Ibid.*, p. 184.

[17] Records of the Provincial Court, Vol. 1, in *Collections of the New Hampshire Historical Society*, Vol. 8.

[18] *History of Exeter*, by Charles H. Bell, p. 219.

[19] *Ibid.*, pp. 224-7.

pany commanded by Captain Nicholas Gilman, when on a "scouting expedition" against the Indians in July, 1710, there were listed

Cornelius Leary	John Drisco
Daniel Leary	Jeremiah Conner
Thomas Leary	Thomas McKeen

Throughout the eighteenth century, a large number of Cornelius Leary's descendants appear in the public records of Maine and New Hampshire, where the name usually is spelled "Lary." A Maine historian, in commenting upon the number of Larys who fought in the colonial and revolutionary wars, says: "The Lary family is co-existent with the early settlements of New England and the early military history of the colonies . . . that the family were patriots and of the fighting blood that has been the gift of Celtic ancestry is indisputable." [20]

The Jeremy or Jeremiah Connor and Cornelius Conner before referred to are supposed to have been brother and son, respectively, of Cornelius Connor, who came to Massachusetts as an indentured servant, and whose first appearance in the records was on June 23, 1659, when "Sarah, daughter of Cornelius and Sarah Connor," was born at Salisbury. On February 4, 1663, Cornelius Connor appears as a witness to the will of John Rolfe of Newbury; [21] on November 7, 1665, he was mentioned in Norfolk County records,[22] and "Richard Goodale, planter, of Newbury," in his will dated June 7, 1666, named among the beneficiaries, "Cornelius Conner, formerly my servant." On April 9, 1668, John Cluff brought suit in the Essex Court against "Cornelias Connor" for

[20] *Genealogical and Family History of the State of Maine,* by Dr. George T. Little.

[21] Probate Records, Essex County, Vol. 1, p. 439.

[22] Norfolk County Records, in *Essex Antiquarian,* Vol. 6, p. 41.

"defamation," but the case was withdrawn.[23] "Moses Worcester of Salisbury, planter," conveyed to "Cornelius Connor of Salisbury, husbandman," a six acre lot at that place for a consideration of £20. by deed dated June 24, 1673;[24] and in a deed dated July 8, 1678, covering the sale of lands at Salisbury by Richard Dole, the latter mentioned "Cornelius Conner, tenant to my uncle, Richard Goodale, several years."[25] Cornelius Connor and his wife, Sarah, were the parents of eleven children, whose births appear in the vital records[26] as follows:

Sarah, June 23, 1659	Ruth, March 16, 1670
John, October 8, 1660	Jeremiah, September 6, 1672
Samuel, December 12, 1661	Ursula, August 10, 1673
Mary, October 27, 1663	Cornelius, August 12, 1675
Elizabeth, December 26, 1664	Dorothy, November 1, 1676
Rebecca, February 10, 1668	

A Connecticut historian[27] mentions Cornelius Connor and links him with one Philip Connor, an emigrant from Ireland to Virginia in 1634, who became a man of great prominence in Kent County, Maryland, and according to some genealogical data furnished to me by one of Philip Connor's descendants,[28] "Philip Connor was of the O'Connors of Ardee Castle, County Kerry, Ireland." Jeremy Connor appears in Exeter town records on October 10, 1664, and probably received a grant of land on that date, although he was not so recorded until January 31, 1681. Three of the sons of Cornelius Con-

[23] Court Records, Essex County, Vol. 4, p. 22.

[24] Norfolk County Records, in *Essex Antiquarian*, Vol. 11.

[25] *Essex Institute Historical Collections*, Vol. 40, p. 148.

[26] Salisbury, Mass., Vital Records, pp. 58-59.

[27] *Catalogue of the Names of the Early Puritan Settlers of the Colony of Connecticut*, compiled by Royal A. Hinman, Hartford, Conn., 1852.

[28] Mr. Philip S. P. Conner, late of Rowlandsville, Md., son of Commodore Conner, commander of the American fleet at the siege of Vera Cruz in the war with Mexico.

nor of Salisbury also located at Exeter and one of them, Cornelius, received grants of land there in 1700 and 1702. Jeremiah Connor and Anne Gove were married at Exeter on July 3, 1696, and had four sons: Jeremiah, Jonathan, Philip and Samuel, and two daughters, Anne and Hannah, all born at Exeter between 1697 and 1709. The marriages of their four sons are also recorded; they were the fathers of twenty-eight children; and, as we are informed by the town historian, "the family has produced in several generations men of prominence." [29] In New Hampshire records twenty-nine Connors are listed among those who received grants of land, or whose names appear in the State Papers, at various times in the eighteenth century, and to the present day this family, which undoubtedly sprang from the Irish O'Connors, is well represented in New England. In this connection, it is of interest to note that another large family of New Hampshire Conners are descended from one David O'Connor, who with two brothers came from Ireland about the middle of the eighteenth century and settled in Exeter. David O'Connor served in the French-English war and his son, Captain James O'Connor, commanded a company raised in Henniker, N. H.[30]

Although it is evident that Teague Cartey came to Exeter in 1664, he does not appear on record until ten years later. At a session of the Essex County Court on August 14, 1674, a case was tried entitled "Teage Cartey, pltff *vs.* John Younge and Edward ——" [31] and "Teage Cartee of Exeter" was mentioned in the probate records of the year 1718.[32] By deed dated April 27, 1667, John and Mary Sinkler conveyed to Philip Cartey fifteen acres of land at Exeter, and the deed was "acknowledged in Court" on October 8, 1667,[33] and Cartey

29 Bell's *History of Exeter.*

30 *Biographical Review,* Vol. 22, p. 291.

31 Records and Files of the Quarterly Court, Vol. 5, p. 411.

32 Probate Records, Vol. 32, p. 31, in *Provincial Papers of New Hampshire.*

33 Norfolk County Records, in *Essex Antiquarian,* Vol. 6, p. 134.

and Dennis Seahone or Sheehan are also mentioned in Norfolk County records as of June 24, 1667.[34] Philip Carte and Elizabeth York were married at Exeter on September 23, 1668; in 1671 Philip Cartee was one of three surveyors employed by the town to lay out boundary lines; on October 24, 1676, Philip Cartey was credited with garrison duty in King Philip's War; [35] and since a John Cartee enlisted at Exeter in the War of the Revolution, it is apparent that Philip's descendants lived at Exeter for at least one hundred years.

Teague Drisco was not listed with the Exeter grantees of 1664, but his name is found among "Names First on the Town Books between 1640 and 1680," under date of October 10, 1664.[36] There can be no doubt that he was a Driscol, but although some of his descendants, even as late as one hundred years after his arrival in the Colony, used that form of the name, Teague invariably was recorded "Drisco." While the first recorded land grant in his name was on January 31, 1681, there is a record of a deed dated December 23, 1674, by which "Tege Drisco of Exiter" conveyed to "Philip Cartey of Exiter" "ten acres of upland granted by Exiter, bounded by land formerly Jeremiah Conaw's ye most way and land ye towne gave Cornelius Lare." [37] In October, 1673, Teague Drisco appeared as defendant in an action at law tried in the Essex County Quarterly Court,[38] and the record says: "Mr. Dalton was ordered to take security for Teague Drisco of 40li. and a mortgage on his land to answer an accusation made against him." On November 30, 1677, Teague Drisco, Philip Cartey and "Jerimie Coney" were listed among Exeter men who "took the Oath of Allegiance," and in the "Provincial Rate Lists" of the town of Exeter as of April 20, 1680,

[34] *Ibid.*, Vol. 8.

[35] Bodge's *King Philip's War*, p. 449.

[36] See list in Bell's *History of Exeter*, p. 59.

[37] Norfolk County Records, in *Essex Antiquarian*, Vol. 12, p. 182.

[38] Records and Files of the Quarterly Court, Vol. 5, p. 241.

there appear the names, Teague Drisco, Cornelius Larey, James Higgins and Philip Cartey.[39]

Teague Drisco had three sons, Lawrence, John and Cornelius. Lawrence removed to Boston, and as Lawrence Driscow he was on the Boston tax list of the year 1691.[40] John Drisco served in an Exeter military company in the year 1700, and Cornelius was one of a number of petitioners of the town of Dover in 1715, praying for the settlement of a minister. Cornelius was recorded both as Drisco and Driscol, and in 1725 he lived at Francestown, N. H., in a district known as "Driscoll Hill." James and Jeremiah Driscol, sons of Cornelius, seem to have adhered to the original form of the name; at least they once so signed, in a petition to the Legislature in 1749 with other residents of Rochester, N. H. Daniel Driskell, son of Cornelius, had seven children born at Isles of Shoals between 1737 and 1752; a James Driscoll, said to have been a great-grandson of Teague, lived at Portsmouth in 1775; in Point of Groves cemetery at Portsmouth there is a stone thus recording the death of another of his descendants: "Captain John Drisco, died March 8, 1812, aged 82"; and a "Mrs. Drisco, aged 86," died at Portsmouth on April 26, 1805.

Readers of Massachusetts history will recall, that in his defence of Captain Preston and the English soldiers who shot down the citizens in the streets of Boston, in what is known in history as "the massacre of 1770," John Adams told the Court that the "mob" that was fired on was comprised of "Irish Teagues." Whether or not John Adams's characterization of the members of the "mob" was intended as a reflection upon their racial origin, to prejudice the Court, is immaterial; it is certain that he picked a significant name and one that was sufficiently descriptive of the nationality of some of those

39 Records of the Provincial Court, Vol. 1, in *Collections of the New Hampshire Historical Society*, Vol. 8.

40 Tax Lists, in Boston Town Books, Vol. 1.

who comprised the patriot band. At any rate, the Irish in America have always accepted it as a compliment.[41] That suggests calling attention to a fact not generally known, that there were "Irish Teagues" in Massachusetts one hundred years before John Adams was born, and it is well known that many of the present residents of the "Back Bay" have the same ideas about the "Irish Teagues" that John Adams had, and probably would be shocked if they were told that Bostonians in the seventeenth century had to mingle with persons bearing such a name! Yet, it was so, as may be seen from the names in the appended list. Teague or Teige is Irish for Thaddeus or Timothy, and despite the way it is sometimes ridiculed by people who don't know any better, it is a perfectly "respectable" Christian name and for ages past it has been borne by members of Irish families of the highest standing in their own country. According to all the Irish glossaries, it signifies a poet. In New England in the seventeenth century there must have been many "Irish Teagues," but the only ones recorded were:

Teague Barron	Teage Daniell	"Teagu O'Crimi"
Teageo Barry	Teague Drisco	Tege O'Leary
Teague Brian	Teague Jones	Tege O'Mahonie
Teague Cartey	Teage Merrihew	Teage Rial
Teage Clark	Teague Nacton	Teague Williams
Teague Crehore	Teague O'Connell	

It is a matter of no little interest to find an Irishman, Teague Crehore, occupying a place of priority in the vital records of a very old New England town, Milton, Mass. He appears first at Dorchester about the year 1650. According to a tradition among his descendants, related by a local chronicler, "when a mere boy he was stolen from his parents in

[41] John Adams cordially disliked the Irish. That was shown several years later by his action in connection with the "Sedition Act."

Ireland during the troubles that followed the war of 1641 and was brought to New England and sold as a redemptioner." [42] That he redeemed himself from service is indicated by the fact that in December, 1660, he was mentioned in Suffolk County records as the purchaser of "a piece of salt marsh" from one John Gill. In 1665, he married Mary Spurr of Dorchester, and there are entries in the parish registers of the church at Milton recording the baptisms of four sons and four daughters of Teague and Mary Crehore, beginning with Timothy on October 18, 1666, and ending with Benjamin on July 22, 1689.

At the Suffolk County Registry of Deeds there is an entry of a conveyance dated January 21, 1670, from Robert Badcock to Teague and Mary Crehore, of a plot of land bordering on the Neponset River; and on November 10, 1671, "Tege and Mary Crohone" were so recorded as conveying lands at Milton to Robert Badcock.[43] It is probable that he was a carpenter or builder, for at "a publique towne meeting" at Dorchester on January 13, 1678, the town "granted to Teag Crohoar liberty for 7800 Clabord," [44] (clapboards for building purposes); as "Teage Corahone" he was listed among "persons in Milton who tooke the Oath of Allegeance in year 1679"; [45] in a deed covering a conveyance of land at Milton on January 8, 1682, one of the boundary lines was described as "the land of Teague Crohore"; [46] and in a "List of names of soldiers under the command of Captain John Whitington, October 3, 1690," [47] his son John was listed "John Crowhore."

[42] A. K. Teele, in *History of the Town of Milton, Mass.*

[43] Suffolk County Registry of Deeds, Lib. 7, fol. 281.

[44] *Dorchester Town Records,* in Boston Town Books, Vol. 4, p. 223.

[45] Boston Town Books, Vol. 29, p. 172.

[46] Suffolk Deeds, Lib. 12, fol. 319.

[47] *History of the Town of Dorchester,* compiled by the Dorchester Antiquarian and Historical Society, Boston, 1859.

According to the Milton parish register, Teague Crehore died at that place on January 3, 1695; on January 22nd of that year Mary Crehore took out letters of Administration to his estate; [48] and in 1714 there was recorded among Suffolk County deeds [49] a conveyance to Timothy Crehore, from Anne, Mary, Benjamin and Robert Crehore, of all their interest in "the estate of their deceased father, Teague Crehore." The Crehores were a prolific family. Sixty-three Crehores appear in the baptismal registers of the First Church at Milton in the seventeenth and eighteenth centuries; thirty-four of the name are in the probate records of Norfolk County, nineteen of whom were of Milton, and entries relating to no less than one hundred and twenty-two Crehores are in the vital records of that town between 1666 and 1835. For more than two hundred years the name has appeared in the vital records of towns in that vicinity,[50] and the last of the family at Milton, John Ames Crehore, died there without issue in 1877, in which year the original Crehore estate passed out of the family.

Teague's son, Timothy, born at Milton October 18, 1666, was a man of local prominence and the father of ten children; his grandson, Timothy Crehore, married Mary Driscoll at Dorchester on December 24, 1712, and in 1754 they lived at Ashburnham, Mass. In the records of this latter place there appear five generations of Crehores down to the middle of the last century. John Crehore was Captain of a Massachusetts military company in the French and Indian Wars; Benjamin Crehore, grandson of Teague, is said to have been "the maker of the first piano manufactured in this country"; and another grandson, Charles Crehore of Dorchester, was a famous clock-

[48] Suffolk County Probate Records, Lib. 10, fol. 723.

[49] Lib. 29, fol. 186.

[50] There is also a large number of Crehores in the probate records of Middlesex County, who lived at Waltham, Newton and Brighton, Mass., in the nineteenth century, who in all probability were descended from Teague Crehore.

maker at Roxbury in the eighteenth century.[51] In view of the record of this family, one would expect to find some reference to them in the State and County histories, where the names of other pioneer settlers of no greater importance are mentioned, but they were entirely omitted therefrom. While the town historian gives them due credit, he seems to have some doubt about the nationality of the progenitor of the family, and says that "although the name is said to be of Irish origin, it is probable that it was given an erroneous orthography." However, it is not the surname alone that stamps him as an Irishman, because his given name, Teague, is exclusively and distinctively Irish. One Cornelius Crehore was mentioned as in Essex County in 1670. Although an indentured servant, it is evident he served in a military company, for in the records of the County Court for October, 1673, an order was entered that "Cornelius Croho" be "discharged from all trainings and watchings," on condition that he "allow two day's work yearly to the military company of Exiter." [52] Possibly he was a relative of Teague Crehore, but in any event there can be very little doubt about his nationality.

Teague Barron appears in the Suffolk County tax lists, and on June 10, 1674, he was the grantee in a deed from Samuel Bennett covering the sale of thirty acres of land in Boston,[53] and he also appears in an undated "release" from John Bennett to Teague Barron.[54] "Teague Upbarron" was in a list of Boston tax payers dated December 15, 1681,[55] which form of the name is not understood, though it was meant probably for Teague Barron. As Thaddeus Barron he appeared in a

[51] Guild's *Geography of American Antiques*, p. 157, New York, 1927.

[52] Records of the Essex County Quarterly Court, Vol. 5, p. 240.

[53] Registry of Deeds, Lib. 8, fol. 420.

[54] *Ibid.*, fol. 342.

[55] Boston Town Books, Vol. 1, p. 76.

"List of Inhabitants of Boston, 1695,"[56] which indicates that he then used the anglicised form of his baptismal name. On November 15, 1657, Simon Coolidge, one of President Calvin Coolidge's ancestors in Watertown, Mass., married Hannah Barron, and there is a tradition in the Coolidge family that she was the daughter of a Boston Irishman; so it is quite possible that Teague Barron was a relative of Hannah (Barron) Coolidge. There were three Barron families in Ireland, one in Waterford, one in Tipperary, and another in Kilkenny. The latter were a branch of the Fitzgerald family, one of whom became Baron of Burnchurch in County Kilkenny; his descendants were popularly known as "the Barons," hence the name Barron.[57] One Peter Barron lived at Marblehead. On August 26, 1675, he was "prest to goe against the Indians," served under Captain Samuel Mosely and was "slain in the fight at Bloody Point on September 14, 1675."[58] The inventory of "the estate of Peter Barron of Marblehead, fisherman," was filed in Court in June, 1676.[59] Timothy Barron, son of Teague, and Rachel Jenison were married at Watertown, on March 10, 1689;[60] the births of their children, Timothy, Samuel, Peter and Hannah, were recorded there between 1700 and 1709, and down to 1711 Timothy Barron was listed among the town's taxpayers.[61]

In 1673, Teague Barry cultivated a farm in the vicinity of Boston. In a deed dated June 28th of that year, recorded in Suffolk County,[62] "the land of Tego Barrow" was described as one of the boundaries of a tract of land "at Rumly Marsh

56 *Ibid.*

57 *Irish Names and Surnames*, by Rev. Patrick Woulfe, p. 228, Dublin, Ire., 1923; and *Irish Pedigrees* by John O'Hart, Vol. 2, p. 35.

58 Essex Institute Historical Collections, Vol. 2.

59 Records of the Essex County Court, Vol. 6, pp. 111, 169.

60 Watertown, Mass., Vital Records, Vol. 4, p. 130.

61 Town Records, Vol. 4, pp. 23, 125.

62 Registry of Deeds, Lib. 8, fols. 181-190.

in the Township of Boston," and in a deed dated April 11, 1678, "the land of Teague Barrow" was again mentioned.[63] In 1687, "Teageo Barry" was listed among Suffolk County taxpayers, under the head of "Valuation of Rumney Marsh and the Islands"; and as "Teago Barry" he was assessed in 1688 for taxes upon "Arable Lands and Meadow, Pasture Land, Oxen, Bulls and Cowes, Heyfers and Steers, Ewe Sheep, Wethers and Swine." [64] At "a Court of Assistants houlden in Boston September 22, 1691," there was tried a case entitled "John Paul of Lynn Pl[t]. vers Tieg A Barrow of Boston def[t].," and the records of the Court say: "On Appeal from the County Court held at Salem June 30, 1691, where Judgement was for y[e] Pl[t]. Teig O Barrow, the land in controversy & costs. The Courts Judgm[t]. Reasons for Appeal & Evidences were read & comitted to y[e] Jury. The Jury find for the defend[t] Confirmation of y[e] former Judgem[t] & costs of Courts." [65] It is probable that Teague Barry died in 1691, since his widow was on the Rumney Marsh tax list in that year.

[63] Registry of Deeds, Lib. 12, fol. 178.

[64] Tax Lists, in Boston Town Records, Vol. 1.

[65] Records of the Court of Assistants, Vol. 1, p. 345.

CHAPTER VII

Darby Field, discoverer of the White Mountains, 1642—John Cogan called the "Father of Boston Merchants"—the Dexters from Ireland—John Kelly, one of the first settlers at Newbury, Mass., 1635—David O'Kelly of Yarmouth left numerous descendants—the Kellys in New England history.

TEAGUE BRIAN was a resident of Lynn, Mass. He was recorded under both the Irish and the anglicised forms of his given name, and he also appears as "Brann"; but whatever was the proper form of his surname, it is clear, from the fact that he was baptised Teague, that he was an Irishman. The death of "Elizabeth, daughter of Thaddeus Brian," was recorded at Lynn on October 26, 1675; "Mary, daughter of Thaddeus Brian," was born there December 27, 1675; "Sarah, wife of Thaddeus Bran," died at Lynn on December 31, 1675; [1] and as "Toodeas Brian" he was recorded on November 16, 1676.[2] In the records of the Essex County Court is found this entry: "Inventory of ye estate of Teague alias Thaddeus Brann, who was impressed a soldier of Lyn for the countrey's service and was sent forth from Lyn on ye 26 June, 1677, and slayne in the fight at Blackpoynt on ye 29 June, 1677." [3] The record says that "Teague Brian's estate was disposed of July 4, 1677," and one of the beneficiaries was "Macum Downing's wife," whose maiden name was Margaret Sullivan.[4] It is probable that Teague Brian had a son of the same given name, since a "Teage Bran" was a

[1] Lynn, Mass., Vital Records, Vol. 2, pp. 430 and 440.

[2] Records and Files of the Essex County Court, Vol. 6.

[3] *Ibid.*, Vol. 6, pp. 354-5.

[4] Lynn, Mass., Vital Records, Vol. 2, p. 123.

witness in a case tried in the Essex County Court on November 21, 1682.[5]

Teague O'Leary was one of the "elusive Irishmen" in New England of whom practically no information is now obtainable. He was recorded "Teg OLeare," but there can be no question as to his real name. The records are silent as to his history, except as to the fact that he came to this country as an indentured servant on the *Robert Bonaventure* from Plymouth, England, in 1633, and was then listed as "Tego Leare of Corke in Ireland, age 30." He was in Boston in 1634, or only four years after the founding of the town. Teague O'Connell must also be numbered among the "elusive" Irish in New England, since the only reference to him that can be found is an entry in the Boston town records [6] of his marriage to Philippa King on May 1, 1662, and his name was written in the register "Tego Ockonall" by the officiating minister. "Teage Rial, taxed 1661-1675 at Oyster River," appears in Dover, N. H. records; [7] in the tax list of 1662 he was recorded "Teage Reiall"; in 1669 he was listed as "Teag Royall of Oyster River"; [8] and on June 23, 1677, "administration to the estate of Teague Royall" was granted to John Woodman and Stephen Jones.[9] Teage Daniell testified in the Quarterly Court at Salem on April 30, 1678, in a dispute as to land ownership.[10]

Teague Nacton, whose correct name undoubtedly was Naughton, was listed in a quaint document entitled "Register of the names of all ye Passingers wch Passed from ye Porte of London for one whole yeare Endinge at Xpmas 1635," discovered at the Public Record Office at London by a repre-

[5] Records and Files of the Essex County Court, Vol. 8, p. 416.

[6] Vol. 9, p. 86.

[7] Dover tax lists, in *New England Historic-Genealogical Register*, Vol. 7, p. 356.

[8] Provincial Papers of New Hampshire, Vol. 1, p. 310.

[9] New Hampshire Deeds, Vol. 5, p. 243.

[10] Records and Files of the Quarterly Court, Vol. 6, p. 437.

sentative of the New England Historic-Genealogical Society, and published in its annual *Register*.[11] Teague O'Mahonie was the interesting youth before referred to, son of Dermod O'Mahony, whose descendants in New England call themselves Matthews. In this connection, the thought naturally comes to mind, that if the faintest spark of race pride could be kindled in the Matthews families, they might claim the right to resume their ancient name of O'Mahony.[12]

Teague Jones came to Massachusetts at a very early date, since he appears at Yarmouth in 1645 among soldiers "wch went forth wth the late Expedition against the Narrohiggansets and their Confederates," in October of that year.[13] He was several times a litigant in the Plymouth Court. On July 7, 1646, a case entitled "Teag Jones *vs.* Ralph Wheilden" was tried in that Court; [14] at a General Court held at Plymouth on October 29, 1649, "Teage Joanes complaineth against Edward Sturges in an action for slander to the dammag of an hundred pound," and a verdict was rendered for the defendant.[15] At the same Court on October 4, 1655, "Teage Jones accused Masshantampaine to haven stolen a gun from him," but the jury decided in favor of the Indian.[16] At the October session of the Court in 1660 he was fined £6. "for refusing to take the oath of fidelitie," but the fine was "abated"; [17] on October 3, 1662, he was fined fifty shillings

[11] Vol. 14.

[12] It may be of interest to recall that many years ago Rev. Thomas Hanlon, pastor of a Presbyterian Church at Lawrenceville, N. J., petitioned the Court at Trenton to change his name to O'Hanlon. He was several generations removed from his Irish immigrant ancestors, and in his application to the Court he stated that on reading an account of the career of the romantic character, Redmond Count O'Hanlon of Donegal, and learning that he was descended from the Rapparee Chieftain, he decided to resume the original family name.

[13] Plymouth Colony Records, Vol. 2, p. 91.

[14] *Ibid.*, p. 104.

[15] *Ibid.*, Vol. 7, p. 46.

[16] *Ibid.*, Vol. 3, pp. 88 and 200.

[17] *Ibid.*, Vol. 8, p. 103.

"for being overtaken in drink";[18] and on June 15, 1667, "Teage Jones was returned by the Selectmen of the Town of Yarmouth for not coming to meeting."[19] In 1675 Teague Jones, Jr., and his brother, Samuel, were enrolled for service in King Philip's War. In the next year a "rate" was struck to defray the expenses of the war, and Teague Jones, Sr., and "Teage Merrihew of Yarmouth" were assessed 2s. 4d. and 1s. 4d. respectively for their shares.[20] Jeremiah Jones, son of Teague, was sued by Thomas Sturges for debt in the Plymouth Court on March 15, 1684, and the marriage of Jeremiah Jones and Elizabeth Hall was recorded at Yarmouth on April 27, 1699. She was a daughter of "Thomas Folland," who was the Thomas Fallon of Yarmouth, later referred to. "Teage Williams, Irishman, 18," was listed among the "passengers on the *Margarett* from Plymouth," which arrived at Boston in 1633; and in 1681 Teage Clark of Wells, Maine, had land transactions with Thomas Brackett.[21] People bearing such surnames as Jones, Merrihew and Williams may not usually be considered Irish, yet the fact that these men were baptised Teague of itself warrants the conclusion that they were Irishmen.

So much for the "Irish Teagues" recorded in New England prior to the year 1700. Darby is another characteristic Irish Christian name which turns up occasionally in the records. It is an abbreviated form of Dermot or Diarmuid, a very old Irish name, wrongly supposed to correspond to Jeremiah, and signifies a freeman. There were a good many Darbies in this country in the seventeenth century, but the following appear to be the only men of the name recorded in New England in the period under discussion:

18 Plymouth Colony Records, Vol. 4, p. 29.

19 *Ibid.*, p. 153.

20 See list in Freeman's *Annals of the Thirteen Towns of Barnstable County*, Vol. 2, p. 194, Boston, 1869.

21 York, Maine, Deeds.

Darby Bryan
Darby Daniell
Darby Field
Darby Hurlie
Darby Maguire
Darby Mahoone
Darby Manning
Darby Makloney
Darby Morris
Darby O'Flynn
Darby Rylean

Of only one of these, Darby Field, is any detailed information available. Undoubtedly an Irishman, he seems to have been one of the most interesting characters in New England in his day, for he was a man of enterprise and intelligence, and, as the discoverer of the White Mountains in New Hampshire, he achieved considerable fame at a very early period of American history. The date of his arrival in this country cannot be ascertained, but according to Josselyn's *New England's Rarities Discovered*, printed in London in 1672, he was in the Colony as early as 1632. In that year Josselyn related that he and Darby Field and Captain Walter Neale "set out to discover the beautiful lakes" which "report placed in the interior," and in the course of their travels they viewed the White Mountains. An historical writer of this region says: "These mountains were first visited in 1632 by one Darby Field, whose glowing account of the riches he had discovered, on his return caused others immediately to make the same exploration." [22] Savage mentions "Darby Field, an Irishman, the first European probably who went up to the summit of the White Mountains," [23] and Belknap says "it is to Darby Field of Piscataquack that the credit is generally assigned of being the first explorer of the White Mountains." [24]

Darby Field lived at Piscatoquoke in 1638 and appears at Exeter, N. H., as one of the grantees in a deed dated April

[22] *Incidents of White Mountain History*, by Benjamin G. Willey, p. 15, Boston, 1857.

[23] *Genealogical Dictionary of the First Settlers of New England*, Vol. 2, p. 156.

[24] *History of New Hampshire*, by Jeremy Belknap, pp. 22-24, 31.

3, 1638, by which "Wehanownowit, Sagamore of Piskatoquake," conveyed to seven of the principal men of the colony, one of whom was Darby Field, immense tracts of land reaching "from Merrimack River to the Patents of Piscatoquake." [25] In the Provincial Papers of New Hampshire [26] there is a copy of a celebrated document, known as the "Combination Deed," dated April 5, 1639, signed by Darby Field and thirty-four others, and on April 10, 1639, he was one of two witnesses to the signature of the Indian Sagamore Watchanowet to a deed covering a tract of "meadows and grounds extending for the space of one English mile on the east side of Oyster River." [27] In 1645 Darby Field sold his lands at Oyster River to one John Bickford; and as "Darby ffeild" he was on the tax list of the town of Dover of the year 1648,[28] when he was possessed of "fyve hunddd acres of land uppon Pascatq River neere the Oyster River." [29]

We have no less an authority than John Winthrop, the first Governor of the Colony of Massachusetts Bay, for the information that Darby Field was the discoverer of the White Mountains. In his celebrated *Journal*, Governor Winthrop gave a long account of Darby Field's journey through the then wild and uninhabited country between Saco (now Biddeford), Maine, and the mountains to the north, evidently taken from the explorer's own written statement. On June 8, 1642, Governor Winthrop thus recorded the event: "One Darby Field, an Irishman, living about Pascataquack, being accompanied by two Indians, went to the top of the White Hill—(now known as Mount Washington). He made his journey in eighteen days. His relation at his return was that

[25] See copy of deed in Provincial Papers of New Hampshire, Vol. 1, p. 134.

[26] Vol. 1, pp. 132-3.

[27] Copy of deed in *History of Exeter, N. H.*, by Charles H. Bell, p. 14.

[28] *New Hampshire Genealogical Record*, Vol. 1, p. 178.

[29] Suffolk County Deeds, Lib. 1, pp. 97 and 106.

it was about one hundred miles from Saco," etc. Darby Field again made the journey one month later; and under date of October 6, 1642, Governor Winthrop thus wrote in his *Journal:* "The report brought by Darby Field of shining stones . . . caused divers others to travel thither, but they found nothing worth their pains."[30] What his purpose was in undertaking so hazardous a journey, through a territory trod only by roving bands of Indians, can only be conjectured; but evidently he was a bold and adventurous spirit and of a roving disposition, and for him this *terra incognita* had no terrors. Among those who followed the route laid out by Field three months later were two magistrates of the Province named Gorge and Vines.

A New England antiquary thus refers to him: "Darby Field, an Irishman; resident of Marblehead in 1637; removed to Exeter; signed the combination deed in 1639; traveled in Maine and went with two Indians up the Saco River Valley in 1642; was the first white man to visit and climb the 'White Hill,' one of the peaks of the White Mountains; wrote an account of his journey, which induced others to make the journey; was proprietor at Dover and was licensed to sell wine there, 1644."[31] Another Maine chronicler says that Darby Field was known as "an Irish soldier for discovery . . . he was a real explorer and left numerous descendants who settled on the bank of the river along whose course he made his way from Saco to the base of the mountains, and these related again and again the story of their

[30] *Winthrop's Journal,* 1630-1639, ed. by Dr. James K. Hosmer, Vol. 2, pp. 62 and 85, New York, 1908. Also *History of New England* by John Winthrop, Vol. 2, pp. 67, 107, 180, Boston, 1853. Other authorities for these statements are *Town Register of Exeter and Hampton, History of Exeter,* by Charles Bell; Merrill's *History of Coos County, N. H.;* Ridlon's *Saco Valley Families and Settlements; The Sokoki Trail,* by Herbert M. Sylvester, and *New England Historic-Genealogical Register,* Vol. 6.

[31] *The Pioneers of Maine and New Hampshire,* 1623 to 1660, by Rev. Charles Henry Pope, pp. 67-68.

ancestor's adventures at their firesides." [32] Francis Raynes, one of the "proprietors" at Dover, sold lands to Darby Field, and a suit at law involving successive transfers of these lands was tried in the York County Court on August 10, 1649. He died in 1650 and the record says that "administration to the estate of Darby Field was granted to Ambrose Gibbons" on October 1, 1651.[33] His son, Daniel, was on the Dover tax lists in 1659 and for several years thereafter; his grandson, Daniel Field of Scarboro, was a Lieutenant of Massachusetts troops at the siege of Louisburg, N. S., in 1745, and his great-grandson, also Daniel Field, was a soldier of the Revolution. Some of his descendants removed to Rhode Island; many persons named Field appear in eighteenth century records of that Colony, and it is probable that some of the present families of the name in the United States trace their line back to Darby Field.

A Gaelic scholar and authority, Mr. Charles O'Farrell of New York, in his compendium of John O'Donovan's work, *Origin and Meaning of Irish Family Names*, has given us the interesting information that Darby Field was a native of a place called Slieve Bawn, in Roscommon County, Ireland, and that it was he who named the White Mountains, after his Irish birthplace. Possibly, some skeptical persons may regard that as a far-fetched idea, but in view of the historic statements before quoted, there can be no doubt that the name originated with the discoverer, since the words, slieve bawn—(from *sliabh*, Gaelic for mountain, and *bhan*, white), mean literally "the white mountain." [34] In the region of the White Mountains are some of the most popular summer resorts in the United States, and each year thousands of vacationists

[32] *Saco Valley Families and Settlements*, by Rev. G. T. Ridlon, p. 7, Portland, Me., 1895.

[33] New Hampshire Court Records—Deeds, Vol. 1, p. 91.

[34] *The Origin and History of Irish Names and Places*, by Dr. P. W. Joyce, pp. 366 and 561. Dublin, Ire., 1871.

visit that territory and enjoy its salubrious climate. No tablet or monument perpetuating the name of this "Irish soldier for discovery" has been erected at the White Mountains; it is highly probable that few of the visitors to or residents of this region know that the first white man known to have set eyes on these picturesque mountains, nearly three centuries ago, and conquered Mount Washington, their loftiest peak, was the Irishman, Darby Field! His name and fame should be better known.

Darby Makloney lived at Charlestown in 1655 [35] and Darby Daniell was at Oyster River, N. H., in 1662.[36] The will of Thomas Daniel of Portsmouth, son of Darby, dated November 12, 1683, in which he named his wife Bridget, executrix and legatee, was proved in Court on November 19, 1683; [37] Bridget Daniel married Thomas Graffort of Portsmouth on December 11, 1684, and in the will of Bridget Graffort, dated April 1, 1701, she named among the beneficiaries her "cousins John Daniel and Bridget Vaughan." [38] Darby Maguire signed as witness to a deed dated April 17, 1676, between William Berkeley and Joshua Lamb of Boston, recorded on September 23, 1684, in Suffolk County.[39] Darby Mahoone was listed among "Massachusetts Freemen, 1634-1655." [40] Darby Morris served in King Philip's War; on September 21, 1675, he was listed among "soldiers credited with military service at the garrison at Marlborough," [41] and in July, 1676, he served in the garrison at Medfield, Mass.[42]

[35] *Charlestown Genealogies and Estates*, by Thomas B. Wyman, p. 646, Boston, 1879.

[36] Dover, N. H., Town Records, in *New England Historic-Genealogical Register*, Vol. 4, p. 250.

[37] Probate Records, Vol. 31, p. 266, in Provincial Papers of New Hampshire.

[38] *Ibid.*, pp. 473-75.

[39] Registry of Deeds, Lib. 13, fol. 18.

[40] In *New England Historic-Genealogical Register*, Vol. 3.

[41] *Massachusetts Archives*, Vol. 68, p. 222.

[42] Bodge's *King Philip's War*, p. 363.

Savage mentions him as "Dorman" Morris and says that he and his wife, Elinor, were the parents of Daniel and Honour Morris, born at Boston on February 13, 1672, and April 1, 1674, respectively.[43]

"Darby Bryan, residing in Boston," who is so mentioned in the "Records of the Court of Assistants of the Colony of Massachusetts Bay" in 1677, probably was an O'Brien. After the trial of a suit brought against him in the "Commissioner's Court" by John Soames, he filed an appeal, and under date of September 4, 1677, there is an entry in the records of the Court of Assistants: "Darby Bryan plaintiff ag[t] Jn[o] Soames deffend[t] in an Acon of Appeale from the Judgment of the last Commissioners Court in Boston. The Action & y[e] plaintiff was called three times y[e] plaintiff made default by non Appearance & was non suited."[44] Darby Manning was listed in the records of the Essex County Quarterly Court among residents of Lynn who took the "Oath of Allegiance" in 1678;[45] and Darby O'Flynn, a resident of Boston, was married there to Hannah Earl on March 26, 1700.[46] In the public records no reference to these men is made other than as here stated; they are not mentioned in local histories or genealogies; their descendants, if any, cannot be traced, and like the hundreds of their countrymen who were in New England in the seventeenth century, but of whom, as in these instances, we obtain only one fleeting glance, they are evidently lost to history for all time.

Referring to the statement in our critic's pamphlet, that John Cogan, Richard Dexter and John Kelly were Englishmen. While it is quite correct to say that all three "came to the colonies from England," that fact does not warrant the

[43] *Genealogical Dictionary of the First Settlers of New England*, Vol. 3, p. 235.

[44] Court records, Vol. 1, p. 98.

[45] Records and Files of the Quarterly Court, Vol. 7, p. 158.

[46] Boston Town Books.

assumption that they were English. However, let us see what are the facts of record concerning these three "Englishmen." John Cogan came to this country in the *Elizabeth Bonaventure* which arrived at Boston on June 15, 1633.[47] He was one of the first settlers at Dorchester, Mass., and on August 5, 1633, the town gave him a plot of land "in the necke southward of the plantation." [48] Governor Winthrop stated in his *Journal* that "Cogan was the first to open up a shop" in Boston, which, according to Drake,[49] was "at what is now the northeast corner of Washington and State Streets." He is referred to frequently as "the father of Boston Merchants," and might well be called one of the founders of Boston. For twenty-five years, he was identified with the Colony in no small way. He held several public offices, for he was a member of Boston's first Board of Selectmen, of the "Ancient and Honorable Artillery Company," and of its first Grand Jury. Besides, he was a constable and surveyor of highways. He owned much landed property and at one time he made a gift of seventy acres to Harvard College. Massachusetts historians are silent as to John Cogan's nationality, and contributors to the historical journals have had very little to say about him. While a historical writer of the Connecticut Valley states that "John Cogan's parents came from Cork, Ireland," [50] and some Irish writers have also asserted that he was an Irishman, they offer nothing to substantiate it, although his name unquestionably is Irish. As "John Coogan" he was chosen to serve as juror in the Court of Assistants in 1634, and on at least two other occasions he was so recorded.

Nowadays, hardly any one would question the racial origin of a man bearing such a name as Cogan or Coogan. The name

[47] *The Planters of the Commonwealth*, 1620-1640, by Charles Edward Banks, Boston, 1930.

[48] Dorchester Town Records, in Boston Town Books, Vol. 4, p. 2.

[49] *History of Boston*, p. 166.

[50] Edward A. Hall, in *Journal of the American Irish Historical Society*, Vol. 4.

is met with in Ireland as early as 1172, in the person of Milo de Cogan, one of Strongbow's "stalwarts" in the Norman invasion, and the "Huguenot family of Cogin" that is mentioned in Irish annals probably sprang from this Norman soldier. O'Hart lists two Cogan families, one in Cork and the other in Louth, among "Families in Ireland down to the fifteenth century"; [51] one branch he enumerates among "the principal families in County Cork" and another branch as "one of the principal families in Dublin," [52] and there were MacCogans in Queens and Tipperary Counties. The name originally was O'Cuagain, anglicised into its present forms, and the motto on the Cogan coat of arms is *Lamhh Dearg Eirin,* "the red hand of Erin." There are numerous persons in whose minds the thought is inconceivable that an Irishman could occupy so prominent a place in the business and social life of Boston as did John Cogan, and with that idea uppermost in their minds, they conclude that he must have been an Englishman; yet there is nothing to justify that conclusion and no historian makes the claim. The natural inference is that John Cogan was an Irishman.[53] He died in 1657, and in the will of "John Coggan," dated December 16th of that year, he mentioned his "wife, Martha Coggan," and brother, "Humphrey Coggan" of Boston.

Richard Dexter is called an Englishman, notwithstanding the evidence furnished by the genealogy of the Dexters that he sprang from an old Norman-Irish family. The first of the name in Ireland was Richard D'Exeter, who came from France and was made "Governor and Lord Justice of Ireland" after the Norman invasion in 1172. The family was closely identified with the history of Ireland for more than five hun-

[51] *Irish Pedigrees,* by John O'Hart, Vol. 2.

[52] *Ibid.,* Vol. 1, pp. 810 and 834.

[53] Patrick Cogan, an officer of the First New Hampshire Regiment in the Revolution, who served under General John Sullivan at Ticonderoga in 1777, was a native of Ireland.

dred years, and people of the name are found in ancient Irish records of the Counties of Cork, Dublin, Limerick and Meath, in which Counties they intermarried with some of the most prominent families of the ancient Race. On account of their adherence to the old faith and the fact that they aligned themselves with their countrymen against the common enemy, the Dexters suffered much at the hands of the English. When their estates in Munster were confiscated by the Crown they took refuge in Connaught.

In histories of the family,[54] it is stated that the pioneer of the American branch, "Richard Dexter, with his wife, Bridget, and three children came to this country from Ireland, where his fathers had lived for upwards of four hundred years." He was of the Meath branch of the family and is said to have been born at Slane in that County. They settled first in Boston, where Richard was "admitted Townsman" on December 28, 1641.[55] Later, they lived in Charlestown, but in 1663 they removed to Malden, and for more than a quarter of a century Richard and Bridget Dexter appear in town and church records of Malden and Charlestown. It would seem that Bridget Dexter was a leading woman in her day, since her name headed a petition of Massachusetts women to the General Court in the year 1650. She was born in Ireland in 1612 and died at Charlestown in 1675. Richard Dexter was the progenitor of a family that has been distinguished in New England for more than two centuries. The numerous references to the Dexters that appear in public records of the colonial and revolutionary periods and in town and county histories, show that they were people of considerable prominence in the communities where they lived. John,

[54] *The Dexters of New England*, by Orlando P. Dexter; "The Dexter Family" in *New York Genealogical and Biographical Record* for January, 1891, and *Journal of the American Irish Historical Society*, Vol. 5, pp. 28-31.

[55] Boston Town Records.

son of Richard Dexter, born in Ireland in 1639, was killed at Malden in 1677, and Richard's grandson, John Dexter, was the father of a celebrated New England physician, Dr. Richard Dexter, 1713-1783, who married a sister of General Israel Putnam of the Revolution. With these facts, I leave to the judgment of my readers the question as to whether it is proper to classify Richard Dexter, the first of this American family, as an "Englishman."

The last of this trio of "Englishmen" was John Kelly. On May 6, 1635, the General Court of the Colony of Massachusetts Bay appointed a Board of Commissioners "to set out the bounds between Ipswich and Quasacunquen" for a new settlement. In the same year a band of colonists, one of whom was John Kelly, came from Newbury, England, and settled on this tract of land. They called the place Newbury. Authorities on the early history of this territory inform us that John Kelly was a descendant of a celebrated Irishman known as "Fighting King Kelly," that "his father emigrated from Ireland to Newbury, England," where "he became attached to a lady of rank, and having on one occasion by his courage successfully defended her father's house when attacked by robbers, he obtained his consent to a marriage with his daughter." [56] His record, and that of his many descendants who fought in the colonial and revolutionary wars, was true to his name and race. The name, O'Kelly or Kelly, comes from O'Calleagh, formed from the Irish word *Ceallach*, meaning war or strife, and the pronunciation of the word (as if spelled *Kal-yĕ*) is the probable explanation for the reason why John Kelly (2) signed himself "John Kally" and why some of his descendants spelled their name in the same way. John Kelly was the son of an Irishman and came of a long line of Irish ancestors. He came to this country with an

[56] *History of Newbury, Mass.*, by Joshua Coffin, p. 394, Boston, 1845. Also *Genealogical and Family History of the State of Maine*, by Dr. George T. Little.

English colony, but he is now classified as an Englishman by one who claims to be "familiar with the facts." Even if we did not have the positive information that he was Irish, there is no evidence that he was other than his name implies.[57]

On March 17, 1642, John Kelly was "acknowledged to be a freeholder by the town of Newbury." As an indication of his sturdy character, we are told that "John Kelly's original land grant at Newbury being unsatisfactory to him, instead of using it he erected his dwelling on Oldtown Hill, some distance from the settlement, where he was exposed to the attacks of wild beasts and the savages. This action displeased his fellow colonists, who passed an act of remonstrance in town meeting, declaring that in case of disastrous consequences, 'his blood should be on his head.' " But, so like the Kellys of the "Fighting Race," "he insisted on remaining, depending on his ability to defend himself. It is related that when a wolf entered his home in the night, he attacked the animal with a club and killed it. There is a story current in the family that he was a man of considerable wealth." He died at Newbury on December 28, 1644. His son, John, born at Newbury in 1642, married Sarah Knight on May 25, 1663; they were the parents of five sons and five daughters, and from them descended numerous New England families. On March 26, 1694, John Kelly (2) petitioned the town "for liberty to keep a ffery on the river Merrimack in the place where he now dwells"; [58] in June 1695, he received the necessary approval, and the ferry then begun was operated by successive generations of Kellys for more than a hundred years. John Kelly (2) and his sons, John and Richard, were mem-

[57] About fifty years ago one of the family wrote an account of John Kelly and his descendants, in which he claimed that his immigrant ancestor was of English descent, and showed considerable disappointment at Coffin, town historian of Newbury, for stating that he was the son of an Irishman, who had emigrated to England.

[58] Proprietors' Records, Town of Newbury, Vol. 1.

bers of the "Newbury Watch" in 1691,[59] and John, Richard and Joseph Kelly were on the muster rolls of the forces raised in Essex County in 1706-07 for an expedition against the French in Nova Scotia. Joseph Kelly settled at Haverhill, and on an old house at that place there is a tablet, the inscription on which says it was "the home of Joseph Kelley prior to 1690 and always held by his descendants."

From the standpoint of numbers, the Kellys or O'Kellys are far in the lead among Irish families, as there were nine distinct families of the name in Ireland. So it is we find Kelly the most frequently occurring Irish name in this country. They began to come to the colonies as far back as three hundred years ago, and in Massachusetts, Maryland and Virginia the name is found on record as early as 1635, or only fifteen years after the coming of the Pilgrims in the *Mayflower.* At the present time there are Kellys in nearly every State of the Union, descended from pioneer settlers of the name in New England. The proper modern form of the name is O'Kelly, and I have no doubt that the David O'Kelly of Yarmouth and the Peter O'Kelly of Dorchester, hereinafter mentioned, came from one of the fighting O'Kelly clans in Ireland.

David O'Kelly rose from the obscure position of an indentured servant to a place of considerable local prominence on the Cape Cod Peninsula. One of his descendants writes: "there is a tradition in our family that when a mere boy in Ireland David O'Kelley and other youths were captured and placed on board a vessed for transportation to Virginia, but David was put ashore on Cape Cod by the heartless captain." The date is unknown, but circumstances indicate it was about the year 1652. He was first indentured as a servant to John Darby of Yarmouth; and in an inventory attached to the will of John Darby, dated February 22, 1655, proved in

59 *New England Historic-Genealogical Register,* Vol. 35, p. 140.

Barnstable County Probate Court on June 6, 1656, there was a list of persons to whom the testator was indebted, among them "Peeter, the Scotsman," and "David, the Irishman." The unexpired indentures seem to have been transferred to Edward Sturges, keeper of an "ordinary" at Yarmouth, who also was surveyor of highways and later Selectman. When entering his name in the Plymouth Colony Records on October 4, 1655, the clerk's best effort at spelling it was "David Ogillior," whom he described as "an Irish man, servant to Edward Sturges." [60] That the period of his service expired in or before 1657, seems certain, because in that year "David OKillia, Irishman," was recorded in a list of Yarmouth men who "tooke the oath of fidelitie," [61] and in the same year he was "admitted inhabitant" at Yarmouth, with the right to vote in town affairs, and was then recorded by the Town Clerk as "David O'Kelly, the Irishman." [62]

He married Jane Powell, and by her had sons, David, Jeremiah, Benjamin and John, and daughters, Sarah and Elizabeth. Thus he was the progenitor of the large families of Kelleys and Killeys who have been in Barnstable County for more than 250 years. His name usually was rendered "O'Kelia" or "O'Killea," and once only as "O'Kelly." An authority on local history informs me that "David O'Killea became a very prominent citizen of the town of Yarmouth, and his several sons and daughters intermarried with the old Plymouth Colony families in Barnstable County and from them descended some of the most prominent men in these parts." [63] He lived at Yarmouth for more than forty years and seems to have been engaged in the fishing industry with his four sons. Yarmouth records under date of April 29, 1676,

[60] Plymouth Colony Records, Vol. 3, p. 91.

[61] *Ibid.*, Vol. 8, pp. 185-6.

[62] Yarmouth, Mass., Town Records.

[63] Letter dated July 5, 1933, from Judge Charles C. Paine of Hyannis, Mass.

show that a "rate" was levied "towards the charge of the late war" (King Philip's war), and among the ninety-nine taxpaying inhabitants of the town then assessed was "David O'Kelia," whose share was fixed at £2, 6s., 9d.[64] In the entry of his will, dated February 10, 1696, in the probate book of Barnstable County on July 19, 1697,[65] he was called "David O'Killia." The beneficiaries were his wife, Jane, sons and daughters, and among these he distributed his "dwelling house, lands and meadows, farm stock and implements," and personal property.

For ten generations his descendants have appeared in Massachusetts town and county records, with the name spelled in many curious ways, and I have no doubt that a complete account of the family would make an interesting chapter in American family history. According to Barnstable County probate records, letters of administration to "John O'Killey's Estate" were granted to his widow, "Bathsua O'Killey," on December 14, 1683. This John is believed to have been the son of David. Yarmouth vital records show that "John O'Kelia," probably the grandson of David, and Berusa Lewes were "marry^{d} the tenth of August, 90"; "John OKelia, the Sonne of John and Bashrua (Berusa) Okelia, was Borne the twelve daye of October in the year 1692," but on his marriage to Elizabeth Crowell on February 24, 1714, he was described as "John O'Kelley, Jr."[66]

"Sarah O'Kellia, eldest daughter of David and Jane O'Kellia," was married to John Crowell; and while the date is unknown, they had eight children born at West Dennis,

64 Yarmouth Town Records. See also Freeman's *Annals of the Thirteen Towns of Barnstable County*, Vol. 2, p. 194.

65 Barnstable County Probate Records. There is a copy of the will in *One Hundred and Sixty Allied Families*, a genealogical work compiled by John Osborne Austin, Providence, R. I., 1893.

66 In "The Crowell Families of Yarmouth," by C. W. Swift, in the *Yarmouth Register* of May 9, 1850, he was called "John OKallia."

the first of whom was Thomas, born May 1, 1691.[67] "David O'Kille, Juny^{r}," son of David and Jane O'Kelly, and Anne Billes were "mary^{d} the tenth of March, 92"; "Elizabeth O'Killia,[68] daughter of David and Jane O'Killia," married Silas Sears at Yarmouth on May 1, 1707, and Benjamin O'Kelley, son of David and Jane O'Kelly, married Mary Lumbart at Barnstable on August 2, 1709. The birth of the first child of the latter couple was thus recorded: "Ruben Okilley, son of Benjamin and Mary Okilley, he was borne on ye 29th day of January in the yeare of our lord 1710"; but, when the father was registered in 1712 among those who drew shares in the "Division of the Common Lands" at Yarmouth, his name was spelled Benjamin O'Kelley. In Yarmouth records of the year 1739, among "Names of the Proprietors of the Common Lands in Crocket Neck," we find Amos O'Killey, son of Jeremiah O'Kelley; "Jonathan O'Killey, son of John O'Kelly or O'Kelia," was listed in the roll of "the town's company" which took part in the capture of Louisburg, Nova Scotia, in the French war (1745); and later, in a roll of Captain Elisha Doan's company of the Seventh Massachusetts Regiment, he appeared as Jonathan O'Kelley.

Jeremiah O'Kelley, son of David, was very active in local affairs and one of his descendants writes, "he was a man of considerable standing in the town of Yarmouth, owning much of the land between Bass River and West Pond River, including substantially all of the village of West Dennis. Apparently, he was a man of much prominence and he as well as his brothers, David, John and Benjamin, have very numerous descendants in this part of Barnstable County.[69] In the genealogy of the Twining family of Cape Cod, it is

[67] "Genealogy of the Crowell Family" in *John Crowe and his Descendants*, p. 23, published by Thomas Y. Crowell & Co., New York, 1903.

[68] In the genealogy of the Sears family, compiled by Samuel P. May, she was described as "Elizabeth O. Killey, daughter of David and Jane O. Killey."

[69] Statement of Judge Charles C. Paine.

shown that in 1688 "Jeremiah O'Kelley, son of David and Jane O'Keilia," married Sarah Chase; and the births and marriages of their children are listed as follows:

Sarah O'Kelley, born 1689; married Oliver Carpenter, 1721.
Jeremiah O'Kelley, born 1691; married Charity Pees, 1716.
Joseph O'Kelley, born 1693; married Tabitha Baker, 1717.
John O'Kelley, born 1695; married Hannah Eldridge, 1719.
Eleazar OKelley, born 1697; married Phebe Baker, ——.
Amos O'Kelley, born 1703; married Ruth Crowell, 1747.
Hannah O'Kelley, born 1705; married Elnathan Eldridge, ——.
Deliverance O'Kelley married Silas Baker, 1723.

Yarmouth vital records contain an entry which illustrates the manner in which the name was sometimes recorded. The following curious entry appears under date of July 3, 1707: "The naems and aege of the children of Jeremiah and Saray Oceley as followeth: Sarah Ocelley, the daughter of the above s^d^ Jerem and Sarah, she was borne the 17th day of Sept in the year 16—. Jeremiah Ocelley was borne the last day of June in the year —— and Joseph Ocelley, he was borne the 11 day of April in the year ——." [70] Notwithstanding these peculiar spellings, the father was recorded as "Jeremiah Kelle" in 1692, as "Jeremiah Kelley" in 1712 when he drew a twenty acre share in the "Division of the Common Lands," and the "will of Jeremiah O'Kelley" dated November 8, 1727, was proved in Court on October 23, 1728. The "Ocelley" was later changed to "Celley," and since in some cases it is known this name was pronounced with the soft sound of "C," we can understand at once what an extraordinary change was effected in that branch of the family! Indeed, at least two instances are found of the spelling, "Selley"! From all of this we see, that although the patrician prefix

[70] The year is so indistinct in each case that it cannot be determined.

"O' " was continued in some branches of the family for five generations, the O'Kelly name had a terrible struggle for existence. Eventually it succumbed, and its last appearance in Massachusetts public records was on December 3, 1793, when Ruth O'Kelley, daughter-in-law of Benjamin and Susanna O'Kelley, was married to Benjamin Bunker of Charlestown. Joseph, son of Jeremiah O'Kelley, who married Tabitha Baker, had:

Stephen O'Kelley, born 1718, who married Thankful Chase at Yarmouth, 1742.

Annah O'Kelley, born 1720, who married William Smith at Yarmouth, 1743.

Sarah O'Kelley, born 1721, who married Joseph Chase at Yarmouth, 1744.

Joseph O'Kelley, born 1728, who married Elizabeth Chase at Yarmouth, 1750.

Jeremiah O'Kelley, born 1730, died unmarried.

Notwithstanding that the name appears in these instances as O'Kelley, the following entries are also found in the vital records of the town of Yarmouth:

"David OKilley, son of John and Elisabeth OKilly, he was born on the 28th day of december in the year of our lord 1715"; "Stephen Okilly, the son of Joseph & Tabatha Okilly, he was born on the 22 day of September in the year 1718"; "Annah Okiley, she was born on ye 28 day of aprill in ye yr 1720"; "Sarah OKilley, the daughter of ye sd Joseph & Tabatha Okilley, was born on ye 21st day of february in ye year of our Lord 1721/2"; "Joseph Okiley, he was born on ye 20 day of march in ye year 1728," and "Jeremiah Okiley, the son of ye above sd Joseph and Thabatha, he was born on ye 8th day of may in ye year of our Lord 1730."

Other descendants of David O'Kelly, whose marriages were recorded in Barnstable County were:

Abigail Ockillee and Thomas Brown, at Eastham, July 30, 1730.

Benjamin O'Kelley and Susannah Davis, at Harwich, December 25, 1755.

Charity O'Kelley and Isaac Chase, at Yarmouth, June 28, 1727.

David O'Kilea and Elizabeth Nickerson, at Yarmouth, 1741.

Deliverance O'Kellia and Jasher Crowell, at Bass Ponds, April 30, 1752.

Eleazar O'Kelley and Hannah Baker, at Yarmouth, .

Hannah O'Killey and Rubin Eldridge, at Harwich, May 19, 1744.

Patrick O'Kelley and Bertha Baker, at Yarmouth, 1748.

Reuben O'Kelley and Mary Young, at Truro, May 28, 1733.

Ruth O'Kelley and James Covel, at Chatham, August 14, 1762.

Sarah O'Kellia and Abner Crowell, at Bass Ponds, June 1, 1752.

Few of the living descendants of the O'Kellys have been found in New England who are aware of the fact that theirs is one of the oldest Irish patronymics, and that the genealogical records of the family and its many branches run back fifteen hundred years to the princes and chieftains of *Ua Ceallaigh* in old Erin. Such a thing as "race pride" seems to be foreign to the mentality of many New Englanders of Irish blood, and this applies not to the Kellys alone, but to many other families of Irish descent. Their early training in school and college, and the influences to which they were subject in their maturer years, evidently have been such that they have no desire to investigate their line of descent, and some who are aware of it are reluctant to acknowledge it. Among David O'Kelly's direct and collateral descendants, however, there have been several exceptions. Osborne Howes of Boston and the Hon. Henry G. Crowell of South Yarmouth acknowledged "with pride" that they were "descended from David O'Kelley," [71] and both were members of the American Irish Historical Society for many years; Hon. Charles C. Paine of

[71] The genealogical records contain upwards of sixty entries of marriages of O'Kellys and Kellys with members of the Howes and Crowell families, down to the middle of the nineteenth century.

Hyannis, Mass., states that he is "descended from the very earliest of the Plymouth settlers and also a descendant of David O'Killea," and David Kelley, now living in South Yarmouth, writes that he is "of the ninth generation in direct descent from David O'Kelley of Ireland."

The Kellys in America have been a prolific race; the descendants of David O'Kelly generally were a hardy and long-lived people, and in the baptismal and death records are noted many instances of the Cape Cod Kelleys who lived for nearly a century. In every generation, members of these families followed the sea as fishermen or traders. At Harwich, Mass., there was a large family of the name, descended from Patrick O'Kelley, born at Yarmouth in 1723, a great-grandson of David. He was a miller at Harwich for many years, and his son, Patrick Kelley, a shipwright, was head of a family noted locally as the builders of several vessels engaged in the Cape Cod fishing industry. The name was well represented in all the colonies, and no less than 695 Kellys were enrolled in the Continental Army, the Navy and the Militia during the War of the Revolution,[72] of whom 213 were from New England. So numerous were the Kellys in New England, that the name occurs nearly a thousand times in the records of the following towns and cities in the seventeenth and eighteenth centuries:

Amesbury, Mass.	Chatham, Mass.
Barnstable, Mass.	Chester, Mass.
Beverly, Mass.	Danvers, Mass.
Boston, Mass.	Dennis, Mass.
Boylston, Mass.	Dorchester, Mass.
Bradford, Mass.	Dover, N. H.
Charlestown, Mass.	Exeter, N. H.
Charlton, Mass.	Gosport, Me.

[72] See list of their names in *A Hidden Phase of American History,* by Michael J. O'Brien, pp. 464 to 479, New York, 1919.

Granville, Mass.
Hartford, Conn.
Harvard, Mass.
Harwich, Mass.
Haverhill, Mass.
Hopkinton, Mass.
Jamestown, R. I.
Kittery, Me.
Lancaster, Mass.
Lexington, Mass.
Lynn, Mass.
Malden, Mass.
Marblehead, Mass.
Needham, Mass.
Newbury, Mass.
Newburyport, Mass.
New Castle, Me.
New Haven, Conn.
New London, Conn.
Newton, Mass.
Norton, Mass.
Northborough, Mass.
Oakham, Mass.
Oxford, Mass.
Paxton, Mass.
Portsmouth, N. H.
Providence, R. I.
Provincetown, Mass.
Rochester, Mass.
Rutland, Mass.
Salem, Mass.
Salisbury, Mass.
Sandwich, Mass.
Shrewsbury, Mass.
Shirley, Mass.
Taunton, Mass.
Truro, Mass.
Upton, Mass.
Warren, Mass.
Weymouth, Mass.
Worcester, Mass.
Worthington, Mass.
Yarmouth, Mass.
York, Maine.

CHAPTER VIII

Peter O'Kelly at Roxbury, 1668—Roger Kelly, Representative to the Massachusetts General Court, 1682—Irish in the Connecticut River Valley—Burke, Carroll, Driscoll, Dwyer, Fitzgerald, Hogan, Lynch, McMahon, O'Dea, O'Neil, Reilly and Sullivan among those recorded in Hartford County—how Cornelius Merry conquered Puritanical prejudices.

PRACTICALLY nothing is known of the history of Peter O'Kelly, and only the most meager scraps of information are on record. "Josiah, son of Petar O'Kally, was borne Novembar the 3^{d} 1668" at Dorchester, and "Peter O'Kelly of Roxbury" was listed in Boston Town Books [1] among those who took the oath of allegiance before Governor Simon Bradstreet on April 21, 1679. Under date of "27:7:96" (July 27, 1696), this entry appears in the records of the First Church at Dorchester: "Seaven of Peter O'Kelly's children baptised, Mary, Margarett, Mehetabell, Susannah, Henry, Josiah and Hephzibah," and "the family assignments in the church" were: "Peter O'Kelly the fifth Seat Mens below," and "Peter O'Kelly's wife the 7th Seat." In the church records of December 1696, there is a further entry: "Since August last unto this Instant December 1696 These following Persons (having been proved and approved by the Pastor and Ruling Elder as to knowledge and Experience and by ye Congregation as to Conversation) publickly took hold of ye Covenant." Then follows a list of sixty names, among them Margaret O'Kelly, Hannah O'Kelly, Mehetabel O'Kelly and "Peter O'Kelly's

[1] Vol. 29.

wife."[2] Because of some dissastisfaction in the church, a number of persons were "dismissed," among them "Peter O'Kelley, wife and six children," as a result of which they decided to leave Dorchester, and thus in the year 1700 the O'Kellys and two families named Sumner left for Berkeley County, South Carolina. On the Ashley River, about twenty-six miles from Charleston, they received a grant for a tract of land and established a settlement there which they called Dorchester.[3] That Peter O'Kelly was an Irishman, and originally a Catholic, there can be little or no question. There is no means of ascertaining when he came to this country on what his social standing was among his neighbors at Dorchester; but that he was a resident of the town 269 years ago is clear from the fact that he had a son born there in 1668. Twenty-eight years later, he seems to have renounced his faith when he and his family "took hold of ye covenant" and were received as members of the Puritan church at Dorchester. Many years afterwards people of the name turn up in South Carolina records, though there is nothing to indicate that they were descended from Peter O'Kelly. A Patrick O'Kelley of Charleston served with the South Carolina militia in the War of the Revolution, and a Methodist minister of the name was active in that State about a century ago.

William Kelly was a "Cunstable" at Boston in 1637.[4] One of the most frequently mentioned of the Clan in New England was Roger Kelly, who came from Ireland with his two brothers to the Isles of Shoals about the year 1653 and established their home on "Smutty Nose Island," afterwards and still called Haley's Island. The historian of the Isles informs us that "a group of brothers, William, Roger and John Kelly,

[2] *The Records of the First Church at Dorchester in New England,* transcribed from the originals by Rev. Charles Henry Pope, Boston, 1891.

[3] *New England Historic-Genealogical Register,* Vol. 2, p. 128.

[4] *Records of the Court of Assistants,* Vol. 2, p. 67.

made a considerable figure in the early records of the Shoals as men of energy and substance." [5] He refers to Roger as "the ancient mariner and taverner." At a Court of Assistants held at Boston on September 6, 1664, there was tried a case entitled "Benjamin Ward *vs.* Roger Kelly," for "imperiously & illegally withholding & improving & imploying without order his Catch (ketch) called the Hope," and there are forty separate papers in the Court files in connection with this litigation.[6]

In 1667, "Roger Kelly of Smutty Nose Island" was presented at Court "for selling wine without a license." [7] William and John Kelly are not mentioned in the colonial records, but judging by the number of references to Roger and his sons, they must have been very active in the public affairs of their day. The Isles of Shoals consist of six islands, a few miles off the New Hampshire coast opposite Rye Beach. "Smutty Nose Island," the largest of the group, had a considerable population before the close of the seventeenth century, and among its earliest settlers, besides the Kellys, were Matthew Colane, Teague Mahonie, the Cadogans, John McKenna and the Haley brothers, referred to elsewhere in this book. Roger Kelly was "Constable" and "Justice of the Peace" of the Isles in 1662. An entry in the Court records of March 17, 1679, says "Roger Kelly and Andrew Dyamont are empowered with any one of the Magistrates of this Province to hold Court on Isles of Shoals," [8] and at "a Court of Pleas houlden for the Province of Mayne at Yorke" on April 6, 1681, "Mr. Kelley and Mr. Dyamount, Commissioners of the Isles of Shoals," were empowered "to keep a Court for trial of actions as high as ten pounds."

[5] *Historical Sketch of the Isles of Shoals*, by John S. Jenness, p. 83, New York, 1873.

[6] *Records of the Court of Assistants of the Massachusetts Bay*, Vol. 3, p. 140.

[7] York County Records.

[8] Court Records, in *Maine Historical and Genealogical Recorder*, Vol. 2.

For several years Roger Kelly was the representative of the Isles at the Massachusetts General Court, and was known as "Captain of the Isles." As an indication of the prominent position which he held among the islanders, he was sometimes called "King of the Isles." He appears many times in the probate and administration and other records, always signing himself "Rog^r Kelly." The marriage of his son, Roger Kelly, and Mary Holdridge was recorded at Exeter, N. H., on September 28, 1681; and at "a Court of Sessions holden at Smutty Nose Island upon the Isles of Shoals," on November 9, 1681, one Robert Marr was "complained of by Mr. Kelley for abusing of said Roger and his wife," and the record says that "Robert Marr came into Court and owned himself bound in a bond of ten pounds to the Treasurer of this Province to be of good abearance and behaviour to Roger Kelley and Mary, his wife."

By deed dated July 20, 1698, Roger Kelly (1) bought lands at Kittery, Maine, from the heirs of George Lydden,[9] which apparently passed to his son, Roger; on May 24, 1707, Roger Kelley (2) executed a deed conveying to Elisha Kelley "all his estate on Isles of Shoals and houses and lands at Kittery";[10] and on April 4, 1709, there was filed in the Probate Court a "Bond of Roger Kelley of Newcastle" and two others, as "sureties for the proper administration of the estate of Andrew Kelley."[11] Robert Kelly was mentioned in York County records as "Commissioner and Justice of the Peace" between 1680 and 1694; Charles Kelley was "licensed to sell liquors out of dores" at the York Quarter Sessions Court on January 3, 1698,[12] and as Charles Kelly he signed

9 *Old Kittery and Her Families*, by Everett S. Stackpole, p. 79, Lewiston, Me., 1903.

10 York Deeds.

11 Probate Records, Vol. 31, p. 636, in *Provincial Papers of New Hampshire.*

12 York Court Records, Part 2, fol. 125.

as witness to the will of Edward Beall of Newcastle on September 27, 1706.[13]

"John Kelly, Attorney to Stephen Olivier of Exeter, merchant," is mentioned in the Aspinwall Notarial Records[14] as of June 19, 1648; in that year John Kelly witnessed several legal instruments at Boston, and one John Kelley witnessed a deed at Boston on November 7, 1681.[15] The latter is thought to have been the "John Kelly, an Irishman," against whom an action was brought for recovery of a debt by John Sparrey in the Court of Assistants in October, 1679. Kelly, being unable to pay, was imprisoned, and Sparrey petitioned the Court "for liberty to sell or dispose of him as a servant." James Kelly was mentioned in New London town records between 1652 and 1658; a James Kelley, possibly the same man, was there in 1682; and a John Kelly was at New Haven in 1662.

Michael Kelly of the island of Conanicut in Narragansett Bay was made a Freeman of Rhode Island in 1667. On August 26, 1669, the "Conservators of the Peace" were ordered by the Rhode Island Council to "assemble the inhabitants . . . for their defence and preservation of any mission or insurrection of the Indians," and two days later "the persons appointed to execute the Councill's order of the 26th inst. for the Island of Quononicut are John Homes, John Remington and Michaell Kelly." This indicates that Kelly must have been a man of considerable local influence. By deed dated July 30, 1673, the town of Newport conveyed to Michael Kelly "a house lott of forty foot square,"[16] and as "Michael Kaly" he was listed as one of the legatees under the will of former Governor Brenton in 1674, but in 1680 he was taxed as

13 Probate Records, Vol. 31, p. 564, in *Provincial Papers of New Hampshire.*

14 In Boston Town Books, Vol. 32.

15 Suffolk County Deeds, Lib. 12, fol. 145.

16 "Rhode Island Land Evidences, 1648-1696," Vol. 1, fol. 151, Rhode Island Historical Society.

Michael Kelly, in which year he died at Jamestown, R. I., without issue. A Christopher Kelly was mentioned in Dorchester records of November 25, 1694, and administration to the estate of John Kelly was granted at Providence in 1702.[17]

Two David Kellys, father and son, appear in Suffolk County records. By deed dated June 18, 1657, William Beamsley conveyed to David Kelly "marsh land on Hog Island"; [18] David Kelly sold "Marsh land on Hog Island" to Elias Maverick on August 17, 1662; [19] David Kelly and "David Kally, Jr.," joined in a deed dated November 18, 1666,[20] and David Kelley conveyed lands in Boston to Thomas Harvey on January 19, 1681.[21] "David, ye sonne of David Kelly and Elizabeth, his wife, was borne ye 18 of Decr 1647," at Boston, and under date of "22nd 8 mo 1662," there is an entry in the probate records to the effect that "Power of Administration to the Estate of the Late David Kellie is granted to Elizabeth his late (?) Wife in behalfe of herselfe and children." [22] By deed dated November 7, 1681, "Elizabeth Smith, formerly Kelley, the Relict of David Kelley of Boston," sold to Thomas Harvey "a parcel of wharfeing ground scituate at the north end of Boston, next adjoining to the land of her son, David Kelley," and "John Kalley" signed as a witness.[23]

Other families of the name were at Warren, Rhode Island, and for more than a century members of these families operated "Kelly's Ferry" across the Warren or Swansea River, between Warren and Barrington, R. I., at the place where

[17] Index to Probate Records, compiled by Edward Field, Providence, R. I., 1902.

[18] Suffolk County Registry of Deeds, Lib. 3.

[19] *Ibid.*, Lib. 4.

[20] *Ibid.*, Lib. 5.

[21] *Ibid.*, Lib. 12.

[22] Suffolk County Wills, transcribed for *New England Historic-Genealogical Society*, Register, Vol. 12.

[23] Suffolk Deeds, Lib. 12, fol. 145.

Kelley's Bridge now spans the river. This ferry was referred to at various times in town and county records of the early part of the eighteenth century, and in comments of travellers passing between Providence and Boston. It was first mentioned in 1681, when a petition was presented to the proprietors of Swansea "for a highway through Brooks' Pasture (now Warren) to Kelly's Ferry," and in 1688 a road was laid out "from Bristol Ferry to Kelly's Ferry." [24] The Kelly who then operated it is not referred to by name in the records and he is unknown to local chroniclers, and the first mention of its operator was in 1725, at which time and for many years thereafter it was owned by Duncan Kelley, who was succeeded by his son, John Kelley. This John Kelley apparently resumed the old family name. He was a soldier of the Revolution, and his name was entered as John O'Kelley, in the roll of Captain Ezra Ormsbee's company of militia of the town of Warren in 1776, and it again so appears in the records of the Rhode Island General Assembly in 1782, when permission to sell certain real property was granted to "Mrs. Elizabeth O'Kelley of Warren, widow and administratrix of John O'Kelley."

There are indications that in the second half of the seventeenth century many Irish came to the Connecticut River Valley who settled principally in Hartford County, Conn., and Hampden County, Mass. Comparatively few of them, however, are mentioned in the town or county records or in local histories, but, at various times during that period there are references in the records of the Valley towns to people bearing such names as:

Barry	Clary	Driscoll
Burke	Clesson	Dwier
Carroll	Cunningham	Fitzgerald

[24] *A History of Rhode Island Ferries*, by Anna Augusta and Charles V. Chapin, Providence, 1925.

Higgins	MacGill	Moore
Hogan	MackCranney	O'Dea
Kelly	MacMahon	O'Neil
Leary	Mahone	Reilly
Lynch	Merry	Sullivan
MacCoy		

Matthew Barry and Abigail Flood were married at Wethersfield, Conn., in 1689.[25] Thomas Burke was a resident of Middletown in 1670. Joseph Carroll seems to have lived at Hartford in 1687, as appears from an account of a journey through Connecticut in that year by Governor Andros,[26] in which he said that on his arrival at Hartford he "paid Joseph Carroll 16/- for Hyer of a Horse." The Clarys were among the pioneer settlers at Watertown, but, sometime before 1682 they removed to Northfield, Mass., where John Clary died on February 10, 1690, and his will was probated on September 30th in that year. John Clary, Jr., was married to Ann Dickinson on June 16, 1670; in 1682 he received a grant of "Clary's Island" in the Connecticut River, since known as Stebbin's Island, and three years later he built and operated a grist mill and also had a mill at Hadley. The genealogist of the family states that John Clary and his daughter were "two of six Christians killed by Indians on August 16, 1688," and his son, John, met a like fate at the hands of the Indians in 1709 at Brookfield, Mass.

Patrick Cunningham signed as witness to a deed for lands in Hartford township on December 3, 1685.[27] At Wethersfield and Windsor, Conn., are found traces of Florence Driscoll, whose marriage at Windsor was thus recorded: "ffluranc Drifcoll & mary Webfter both of Windfor ware maried by

[25] *Genealogical Dictionary of the First Settlers of New England,* by James Savage, Vol. 2, p. 175.

[26] *Colonial Society of Massachusetts,* Vol. 20, p. 277.

[27] *Connecticut Historical Society,* Vol. 15, p. 149.

capten Newbery aprel 24, 1674."[28] He died in 1678 and on March 6th of that year the Probate Court of Hartford County granted letters of administration to "the estate of Florence Driscoll of Wethersfield, deceased,"[29] and the record indicates that he owned property at that place and at Springfield, Mass. The baptismal register of the Second Church of Christ at Hartford shows that "Henry Dwier" had five children baptised there between 1696 and 1700, and although the name was also recorded "Duier," yet from the fact that two of the family appear as Dwyer in the burial register of the Ashford Congregational Church and the name reappears as "Dwier" in Hartford records of the year 1800, there can be little doubt that this man's proper name was Dwyer. An entry in the Connecticut Council Journal on April 2, 1664, shows that one Thomas Burnham of Hartford was called before the Council and "acknowledged himselfe bound to this Collony in the sume of Twenty Pounds that Gerald Fitzgerald shall appeare and answer what is objected against him when called by the Magistrates."[30] This is the only reference to Fitzgerald in the public records, but it is assumed that he was an indentured servant to Thomas Burnham. James Fitzgerald and Elizabeth Bullier were married at Saybrook, Conn., on April 28, 1678.[31]

Under "Settlers in Hartford between 1640 and 1670," with the years when they were "admitted as inhabitants," there were listed John Kelly 1655, Gabriel Lynch 1656 and "Pater" Hogan 1657, and all appear in a "List of Hartford taxpayers"[32] dated February 13, 1659. John Kelly was again recorded as at Hartford in 1662. He married a daughter of

[28] Colonial Land Records, Vol. 1, p. 46. Also *Genealogies and Biographies of Ancient Windsor*, by Dr. Henry R. Stiles, Hartford, 1892.

[29] Probate Records, Vol. 9, pp. 16-17.

[30] Public Records of Connecticut, Vol. 15.

[31] Genealogy of the Dawson Family.

[32] In *Connecticut Historical Society Collections*, Vol. 15, pp. 496-8.

Samuel Wakeman of Hartford and in the settlement of Wakeman's estate, "John Kelly receipted for his wife's portion, June 10, 1663." [33] "Grace, widow of John Kelly," purchased lands in Hartford township by deeds dated September 14, 1687, and April 28, 1691, and their three sons, Charles, John and William Kelly, also appear in the land records of the first quarter of the eighteenth century.[34] On February 25, 1656, there was recorded at Hartford a deed from Nathaniel Greensmith to Gabriel Lynch, covering "a dwelling house wth a small p'cell of land wch hee bought of Nat^{l} Greensmith," [35] and under head of "Sowth Side Rates Granted," in 1659, "Gab Linch" and "Pater Hogan" were taxed nine shillings and four shillings respectively. A Connecticut historian lists Hogan as "a Dutchman," the reason for which must be a mystery to everybody but himself! His name appears on record several times and always as "Pater Hogan." Such spellings as "Paterick," "Patterick" and "Pater^{k}" for Patrick are noted frequently in colonial records, and occasionally the abreviation "Pater"; yet while it is possible his given name may have been Peter, I am convinced that he was Patrick Hogan.

One John Higgins was mentioned among the "early grantees of land at Suffield, Conn.," in 1680, and in 1681 James, John and Thomas MacGill, or, as the name was sometimes spelled, "Mighill." The last mentioned married "Abigail Maclaflin," daughter of the Robert McLaughlin of Wenham, Mass., before referred to. Hugh MacCoy was a farmer at Wethersfield and after his death on July 31, 1683, letters of administration to his estate were granted to his widow, Alice MacCoy. John MacMahon was of Windsor and his marriage at that place to Elizabeth Stoughton was recorded under date of November 27, 1690, his name also appearing as

[33] *History and Genealogy of the Families of Old Fairfield*, ed. by Donald Lines Jacobus, Vol. 1, Part 2, pp. 631-2.

[34] Hartford Land Records, Vol. 4.

[35] *Connecticut Historical Society*, Vol. 14, p. 480.

"MacMan." The marriage at Springfield of Margaret Riley, daughter of the John and Margaret (O'Dea) Riley hereinafter referred to, and William MackCranney was recorded on July 8, 1685, and at a town meeting on May 10, 1711, the latter received a grant of "4 or 5 acres of Land to Ly Westerly of the Land he bought of Nathll Dumbleton." One of their sons, "Thomas McCranne of Springfield," was enrolled among the troops raised for the Indian War in 1709.

In April, 1664, the town of Hartford voted "that they would not receive Martin Moore an inhabitant of this town." In December, 1682, the Wethersfield Selectmen "warned John O'Neil out of town," as "not a lawful inhabitant." Edmund O'Neil was taxed at East Hartford in 1682, and Edward and Mary O'Neil executed a warrantee deed to Thomas Burnham on June 7, 1688.[36] The only other person of the name recorded in New England was "Daniell ONeale," one of the "Passengers aboard the *John and Sarah* of London," which sailed "for Boston in New England" on November 11, 1651.[37] Edward Mahone of Wethersfield was mentioned in Hartford County probate records in connection with the will of Daniel Bowen of Wethersfield, who died on September 15, 1683.

The town of Northampton, Mass., was settled in the year 1654, and the local historian in commenting upon the first Irish families who came to that place in 1658, says: "Little sympathy was wasted by the pioneers of Northampton upon the Irish. Willing that natives of the Emerald Isle should become residents, lands were granted to them on conditions expressly prohibiting them from gaining citizenship thereby." [38] He mentions only three of them by name, Cornelius

[36] Hartford Land Books, Vol. 2, p. 37.

[37] List of Passengers in Suffolk County Registry of Deeds, Lib. 1, fol. 5.

[38] *History of Northampton, Mass.*, by James R. Trumbull, Vol. 1, pp. 138-140, Northampton, 1898.

Merry, Matthew Clesson and David Frou, but adds, "there were more Irishmen in the town than those named, but none of them received direct grants." "Nearly all the emigrants from Ireland were children or young persons who came over for the express purpose of engaging as servants. Some made contracts for their services before embarking, accompanying their masters. Others of both sexes were sold for their passage money, that is, they agreed to serve someone who would pay their passage long enough to settle the account." [39] The search for information as to the careers of the three Irishmen here mentioned was highly interesting, because it shows that once they were freed from servitude and got a chance to work out their own salvation, they proved themselves worthy of the citizenship which for years had been denied them. And in due time, their sons and daughters were numbered among the "respectable" inhabitants of the communities where they lived; their names appear in the everyday transactions of life, and in Church, Court, land, military and other public records of their day as regularly as the descendants of the English settlers.

Cornelius Merry first appears at Northampton in 1658, when he was indentured as a "servant" to John Lyman, in whose service he remained for five years. On August 11, 1663, he married Rachel Ball, and on September 17, 1663, the town of Northampton gave him three acres of land, and the grant was thus entered in the Selectmen's records: "At a leagell town meeting there was then granted to Cornelius, the Irishman, three akers of land upon condition he build upon it and make improvement of it within one year, yet not so as to make him Capabele of acting in any town affairs no more than he had before it was granted to him."

From the language of the grant to Cornelius Merry, we obtain an idea of what the Irish of those days often had to

[39] *History of Northampton*, p. 139.

contend against in New England. The English element at Northampton were willing enough that "Cornelius, the Irishman," should reside among them and contribute to the development of the town and fight their battles when necessary, but they erected a social barrier against him, and this deprived him of the civil rights enjoyed by his fellow-townsmen, not of his race and blood! Nevertheless, Cornelius Merry eventually conquered their prejudices. He was an interesting character, and evidently he was one of those irrepressible Irishmen with no love for England, and in one respect he seems to have been a hundred years ahead of his time. In 1666, the General Court of Massachusetts "ordered Cornelius Merry to be whipt twenty stripes for abusing the authority in this country of the English by seditious speeches," which would indicate that, although originally a "servant," he must have been a man of no mean intelligence for the time, to be able to make "speeches" that brought down on him the penalty of the law!

On November 4, 1668, several inhabitants of Northampton sent a "petition against imposts" to the General Court, and among its signers were Cornelius Merry and Matthew Clesson,[40] and these two Irishmen with other inhabitants of Northampton joined in a petition to the Court on May 15, 1672, praying for "a convenient quantity of land at Skawkeage for a Village." This place is on the Connecticut River about thirty miles from Northampton and is now known as Northfield. In the next year Cornelius Merry removed there, became the owner of considerable land, and "Merry's Meadow" in that town preserved his name locally for more than 150 years.

There is a very complete account of the settlement in the town history of Northfield. Eight residents of Northampton

[40] Copy of petition in *New England Historic-Genealogical Register,* Vol. 9, p. 89.

first removed to Skawkeage, two of whom were Cornelius Merry and John Cleary, but when the Indian war broke out two years later they were obliged to abandon the settlement, and negotiations were not resumed with the Indians until 1686. By deed dated May 24, 1686, seven Indians ratified the original agreement of 1672, and conveyed 10,650 acres of land to "Micah Mudge, Cornelius Merry and John Lyman," representing "the rest of the inhabitants of Northfield." [41] That Cornelius Merry must have been a dominant personality, despite his previous condition of servitude, is evident from the fact that he was one of the boldest and most active spirits among the townsmen, determined to carry out the original agreement with the Indians, despite repeated warnings by the authorities about the danger of locating in that then remote territory. In almost every document concerning the settlement he appears with as much prominence as any of those who formerly contemned him. He and his son, John, served in King Philip's War and took part in an encounter with the Indians, known in history as the "Falls Fight," at what is now Bernardston, Mass., on May 19, 1676,[42] and on February 2, 1678, he took the oath of allegiance with other inhabitants of the township.[43]

Cornelius and Rachel Merry were the parents of seven children. They lived at Northfield for thirty-three years and Cornelius died there in 1716, "respected by all the people of the town," some of whom had formerly held themselves in arrogant detachment from their Irish neighbors. We are told that "several of his sons became prominent citizens at Northfield and Deerfield"; [44] Cornelius, the eldest, removed to

[41] Copy of deed in *History of Northfield, Mass.*, by J. H. Temple and George Sheldon, Albany, N. Y., 1875.

[42] Bodge's *King Philip's War*, pp. 250 and 253.

[43] Boston Town Books, Vol. 29, p. 180, and *New England Historic-Genealogical Register*, Vol. 4, p. 26.

[44] *History of Northfield* by James R. Trumbull.

Hartford and in 1698 he was recorded as the owner of lands at that place,[45] and John Merry settled on Long Island. The family scattered to various places in New England; there are five generations of Merrys mentioned in Massachusetts vital records, and the first born in each generation was named Cornelius. Thirty-three soldiers of the name served in Massachusetts regiments in the War of the Revolution, all of whom probably were descended from "Cornelius, the Irishman."

Now, the average person would be inclined to think that names such as Merry, Merryman and Merriman are not Irish, and American families bearing such names are usually regarded as of English descent. Merry was formed from the old Gaelic name, Mac-Giolla Meidhre[46] (pronounced as if spelled *moc-gilla-merry*), and it has a very beautiful conception, since it means literally "the son of the servant or devotee of (the blessed Virgin) Mary." One Brian MacGiolla Meidhre, a celebrated Gaelic poet, is known to the literary world as Brian Merryman. There have been many people named Merryman in New England, and we are told that "Walter Merryman, an Irishman kidnapped in Dublin and brought to Boston, was the ancestor of all of the name in that vicinity." And it is not at all improbable that this Walter Merryman was the "Walter Merry of Boston, shipwright," who was married at Boston to "Marry Dolens or Dowling" on August 18, 1653.[47]

Matthew Clesson also was an indentured servant and probably came to Massachusetts about the same time as Cornelius Merry, and the annals of the town of Northampton contain the following notation: "Matthew Clesson; from Ireland; settled at Northampton; took Oath of Allegiance February 8,

[45] Hartford, Conn., Land Books, Vol. 1, p. 181, and Vol. 7, p. 556.

[46] *Irish Names and Surnames*, by Rev. Patrick Woulfe, Dublin, Ire., 1923.

[47] *Genealogical Dictionary of the First Settlers of New England*, by James Savage, Vol. 3, p. 200.

1678; was Freeman 1690; made a will in 1713, which was proved November 7, 1716; removed to Deerfield, where his descendants live." He also had three acres of land "granted to him as the other Irishmen have it granted theme, not as a home lote," and according to the town historian "Matthew Clesson seems to have been something of a man, though the Town classed him with 'the other Irishmen.' He was quite prosperous and accumulated considerable property. His dwelling house was burned down by the Indians in 1675, and the town gave him other grants in compensation for his losses." [48] On December 22, 1670, he married Mary Phelps at Northampton and they were the parents of nine children, "several of whom became prominent citizens in this and other towns in the Valley." [49] They were of sturdy stock and a class of people who proved themselves a valuable acquisition to the colony. Sons and grandsons of the immigrant appear to have been substantial people and served their country well, and some of them receive frequent mention in accounts of the Indian warfare in New England.

Matthew's son, Joseph Clesson, when only fifteen years old, served in "King William's War," was in the "Pomeroy Pursuit" from the Deerfield garrison on July 14, 1698, was wounded in defence of the settlement at Deerfield on June 23, 1709, taken prisoner to Canada but escaped, and in 1713 was "Captain of the military forces at Deerfield." His brother, Matthew, also took a prominent part in the Indian wars and was mortally wounded in the fight of June 23rd. Three sons of Matthew Clesson (2), Matthew, Joseph and William, were officers in the French-English war, and Matthew (3) and Joseph died in the service in 1757 and were buried in the camp ground at Fort William Henry, N. Y. There were Clessons in the War of the Revolution, the name is found in

[48] *History of Northampton, Mass.*, by James R. Trumbull.
[49] *Ibid.*

vital records of Hampden County, Mass., towns down to the middle of the nineteenth century, and some descendants of the Irish immigrant still live in that part of the State.

In an order by the Selectmen of the town of Northampton in 1668, setting apart a plot of "two akers of land" for the use of David Frou, it was directed that it was to be "uppon the same condicions" as the grant to "Cornelius, the Irishman." The fact that this David Frou also was an Irishman may seem strange to some; yet he was so described in the town records.[50] There was an old family in Ireland whose Gaelic name, written in English letters, was *Froighthigh.* In the Irish language the "th" or dotted "t" has the soft sound of "h"; so therefore the phonetic sound of *Froighthigh* was as if it were spelled *Frohee* or *Frohy* (further changed to *Froo* or *Froe*). In modern times in Ireland the name is rendered into O'Free, and sometimes Free without the prefix "O." There can be no doubt that this was the origin of the name of David Frou of Northampton, and students of history might keep such things in mind, since they help to explain some of the apparent incongruities between surnames and nationality in this country's early days. David Frou removed to Springfield, Mass., where he married Priscilla Hunter on February 7, 1678; in the next year he removed to Suffield, Conn., and under the name, David Froe, the town of Suffield gave him a grant of forty acres of land.[51] He is mentioned as "an Irishman" in Suffield town records and died there in 1710, and upon the death of his wife in 1725 the name became extinct in New England. David Froe's grant at Suffield adjoined a tract known as "Ireland Plain," so named by John Reilly or Riley, who came there from Hartford, and "Riley Brook" in this vicinity is still known by that name.

[50] See also Savage's *Genealogical Dictionary,* Vol. 2, p. 213.

[51] Town Records, in *Documentary History of Suffield, Conn.,* by Hezekiah S. Sheldon, Springfield, Mass., 1886.

CHAPTER IX

Patrick Moran at New Haven, 1664—John Reilly, the first Irishman in Connecticut, 1634—Patrick and Bridget Riley—the Reillys in Massachusetts—the patrician prefix "O'"—the historic Leinster family of the Geraldines—Thomas Flynn and Rickard Burke, early landowners at Sudbury, Mass.

IN the proceedings of the New Haven Court under date of September 6, 1664, "Patrick Moraine, sometime servant to Mr. Purchase," was mentioned.[1] But apparently before a year had elapsed Patrick was in a position to hire his own "servant," for at a session of the Court held on August 22, 1665, "Giles Blach, servant to Patrick Moran, was Complayned of by his Master & accused for imbeizleing his goods." [2] In the same year, as we learn from New Haven town records, Patrick Moran was "Clarke to ye iron workes" [3] at New Haven and in 1667 "Michael Delaney died at the iron workes," said to have been the first enterprise of the kind established in Connecticut.[4] At the January, 1665, session of the Court there was tried a case of "Patricke Morran," in an action against three women for "slander and defamation," which resulted in a verdict for the plaintiff,[5] and on March 5, 1666, Nicholas Pinion, attorney for the defendants in that action, charged that "Patrick strooke him downe at ye forge," and the Court

[1] New Haven Town Records, Vol. 2, p. 99.

[2] *Ibid.*, p. 148.

[3] *Ibid.*, p. 117.

[4] *History of the Colony of New Haven*, by Edward P. Lambert, p. 84, New Haven, 1838.

[5] New Haven Town Records, Vol. 2, p. 122.

fined him "20/– and costs." [6] At a session of the Court at New Haven on February 5, 1666, "Patrick Moran and John Rose were called to give account of ye s^d Estate" (of William Shepheard, deceased), and "the s^d Patrick acknowledged y^t he had received ye Estate according to inventory." [7] In 1666 he was mentioned as a tavern keeper at New Haven; on May 7, 1667, Patrick Moran was up before the Court as defendant in an action brought against him by John Rylie and two others, and the case was dismissed,[8] and three years later he was still "Clarke of ye iron workes." After that time there is no reference to him in New Haven records.

An action for "slander," entitled "James Watters *vs.* Patrick Morrin," was tried at the Essex County, Mass., Quarterly Court on March 26, 1672, and the verdict of the jury was, that "Patrick Morrin make public acknowledgment in the first towne meeting in Topsfield." [9] As Patrick Moran he was mentioned in the records of the Court in 1673, and he probably was the Patrick Moran who served as a soldier in King Philip's War and was in the "Great Swamp Fight" on December 19, 1675. In February, 1676, under the names, "Patrick Moroone" and "Patraich Moraine," he was in a company commanded by Captain James Oliver, and as "Patrick Morren" he was on the roll of Captain Daniel Henchman's company in August, 1676.[10] As "Patrick Morrin" he was again mentioned in the court records in 1682.[11]

Among "Passengers for New England" who sailed in the *Bonaventure* from the port of London on January 2, 1634, were Thomas Murfie, John Dunn, Christopher Carroll, Garrett Riley and Miles Riley, of whom, however, there is no

[6] *Ibid.*, p. 201.

[7] *Ibid.*, p. 195.

[8] *Ibid.*, p. 204.

[9] Essex County Court Records, Vol. 5, p. 2.

[10] *Soldiers of King Philip's War*, by Rev. George M. Bodge.

[11] Court Records, Vol. 8, pp. 305-6.

mention in New England records. A writer on the early history of the Connecticut River Valley states that Garrett and Miles Riley were brothers of John Reilly, one of the pioneer settlers in the Valley, and that the latter came from Longford, Ireland. This John Reilly is believed to have been the first Irishman in the Province of Connecticut. His wife's maiden name was Grace O'Dea. He was a resident of Wethersfield as early as 1643, and he and his sons and nephews are mentioned many times in records of Hartford County and of the adjoining County of Hampden in Massachusetts. In the "will of John Riley of Wethersfield," proved in Hartford County on May 13, 1674, he divided his property among his wife, five sons and three daughters, and the inventory shows that he was one of the substantial men of the community.

His nephew, John Riley, settled further up the Connecticut River at Springfield, Mass., and the earliest mention of him there was on December 23, 1659, when he was assigned "a Seate in ye Meeting House," and in the next year he married Margaret O'Dea, a relative of the Grace O'Dea who married his uncle. At a "Gen^{ll} Town Meeting" on "ffebr (3) 62" he received a grant of a plantation, described as "lying on ye west side of ye great River by the great hill y^{t} is by the way to the playn called Chickuppe playne, this Lott thus granted on Condition y^{t} he build and Settle y^{t} upon within five yeares from this tyme," and on May 5, 1664, the town granted him "foure acres of meddow lying neere the great pond on ye back side of Chicuppe playne." [12] In 1671 he was made a Freeman by the Massachusetts General Court.[13] In 1683 he purchased lands from one Henry Chapin at West Springfield, now part of the City of Holyoke, and a local chronicler says: "It is said Riley was an Irishman, and with other settlers who came to that vicinity, gave the name of Ireland Parish to that part

[12] Town Records, Book 3, p. 165.

[13] Savage's *Genealogical Dictionary*, Vol. 3, p. 542.

of the town." [14] An historian of Springfield also states that "John Riley was from Ireland," [15] and from a series of historical articles on the Connecticut Valley,[16] we learn that "the territory now comprising Holyoke was originally a part of the town of West Springfield and in the early days of the settlement was styled Ireland Parish. Prior to 1745, an Irish family named Riley had located in the vicinity. Several other families of the same nationality came soon afterwards and it was from this little colony that the community took its early title." The name of "Ireland Parish" continued in local use down to about the middle of the nineteenth century, when it was changed to "New City."

Patrick Riley, nephew of John, and his wife, Bridget, settled at Hockanum, Conn.; others of the name were at Middletown, and so numerous were their descendants that the name turns up no less than 192 times in Connecticut eighteenth century records. As in many other cases, the spelling of the name was at the mercy of the recording clerks, which explains why the Connecticut Reillys were sometimes recorded in such forms as Riley, Righley, Righly, Ryly, Reyley and Royley, but most of them are believed to have been descendants of John, the original immigrant. The Middletown branches of the family were shipbuilders, and it is stated that there were more sea captains of this surname in command of vessels plying out of the Connecticut River in the eighteenth century than of any other name,[17] and three of them were masters of Connecticut privateers in the War of the Revolution. "Riley Brook" before mentioned perpetuates the name. They were people of some consequence, therefore, and are as fully entitled to a place in New England annals as any other colonial family, no matter of what race or blood.

[14] *Annals of Chicopee Street*, by Clara Skeele Palmer, Springfield, 1909.

[15] *History of Springfield*, by Charles H. Barrows.

[16] In *Springfield Union*, June 30, 1905.

[17] *History of Ancient Wethersfield*, by Dr. Henry R. Stiles, Vol. 1, p. 498.

The first of the name in Massachusetts records was Sarah Reiley, who married Nicholas Jackson at Rowley in May, 1646.[18] The Henry Reilly who appears in the list at page 298 was the village blacksmith at Rowley, and his name, spelled in several different ways, turns up frequently in town records of the years 1649 to 1710. In the tax lists he appears as "Henry Reyley" in 1649, as "Henry Riely" in 1662 and as "Henery Reiley" in 1665.[19] On August 12, 1656, the marriage of "Henry Reiley and Mary Eletrope" was recorded at Rowley,[20] and her death was thus entered in the town records: "Good Reila, wife of Henry Reila, died October 10, 1700." He signed his name "Henry Rielie" as witness to a deed dated February 14, 1665; as "Henry Reilie" he appeared at the Salem Court in September, 1668, and in September, 1672, his name was spelled "Henry Ryley." As Henry Reilly he testified in the Salem Court in an action at law between John Johnson and Thomas Remington in March, 1674; "Henry Riley" was mentioned in the records of the Court in 1681 as owner of "shares of Plum Island,[21] and as "Henry Riely" he was on the tax list of the town of Rowley in 1691.[22] The death of "Henry Reiley, aged 82," was recorded as of May 24, 1710, and his will was probated in Essex County on June 19th of that year.[23] John Rylie and two other residents of New Haven brought suit against Patrick Moran in the New Haven Court on May 7, 1667;[24] John Reylie served as a soldier of "the Ipswich company" in King Philip's War in 1675;[25] Jeremiah Reyley was at Ipswich in 1678; "John

18 Rowley, Mass., Vital Records, p. 385, and "First Book of Marriages of the Town of Rowley," in *Essex Institute Historical Collections*, Vol. 6, p. 37.

19 Town Records, Rowley, Mass.

20 Vital Records, Rowley, Mass.

21 Records of the Essex County Court, Vol. 8.

22 Tax lists in *New England Historic-Genealogical Register*, Vol. 15.

23 Essex County Probate Records, Vol. 10, p. 123.

24 New Haven Town Records, Vol. 2, p. 204.

25 Bodge's *King Philip's War*, p. 157.

Reyley, brother in law to Patrick Fassett, with wife and two children," came "from Eastward to town (Charlestown, Mass.) about October 21, 1689,"[26] and Boston records show that "Hannah, daughter of John and Bridget Rylee," was born there on April 22, 1697.[27]

Of names bearing the prefix "O," while many of them appear in the records of the colonies, only comparatively few turn up in New England in the seventeenth century. Besides O'Connell, O'Dea, O'Flynn, O'Leary, O'Mahony and the O'Kellys and O'Neills already referred to, there are mentioned in New England records men named O'Brien, O'Dougherty, O'Grady, O'Hogan, O'Shane and O'Shaw, and the curious name "Teagu O Crimi," appears in the records of the Court of Assistants for Massachusetts Bay under date of January 7, 1643. He appears to have been an indentured servant, but this is the only reference to him that can be found. Many others doubtless bore the "O" on their arrival, but they or their descendants evidently followed the usual custom of the time by dropping the prefix. Bryan O'Dougherty was at Salem in 1683,[28] and while William O'Brien, who also lived at Salem in 1669,[29] was the only man of the name so recorded in New England in this period, it is very probable there were others who, or whose forebears, originally were O'Briens. As, for example, the Darby Bryan already mentioned, Dennis Brian who lived at Oyster River (now Dover), N. H., in 1635,[30] Thomas Brian and Richard Brien, Massachusetts soldiers in King Philip's War,[31] and the Teague or Thaddeus

[26] *Genealogies and Estates of Charlestown*, by Henry W. Wyman, Boston, 1879.

[27] Boston Town Books, Vol. 9, p. 208.

[28] *Historical and Genealogical Notes and Queries*, ed. by Eben Putnam, Salem, Mass.

[29] Salem Town Records, in *Essex Institute Historical Collections*, Vol. 41, p. 301.

[30] Dover, N. H., Town Records.

[31] Bodge's *King Philip's War*.

Brian before mentioned. Apparently, the first of this name in New England was the Desmond O'Bryan mentioned in the shipping list at page 29, but of whom no trace can be found in the colonial records. "Thomas Brian, serv^{t} to Samuell Eedy," was brought before the Governor of the Plymouth Colony on January 10, 1633, because "the said Thomas had runne away and absented himself five daies from his master's service," and "for this his offence was privately whipped before the Govr and Cowncell." [32] "Barnabie Bryan, an indentured servant," witnessed a deed of conveyance on January 29, 1640, between Richard Parsons and John Turner, recorded in Suffolk County.[33]

One Charles O'Grady resided at Portsmouth, N. H., in 1685. In a deed for lands dated July 3, 1687, filed in York County, Maine,[34] from Robert Elliott to Nathaniel Kene, it was recited that part of the land was "sold by Ephraim Crockett to Charles O'Grado of Portsmouth, Yeoman," and was "afterwards sold by said Charles Ogrado to Robert Elliott"; but there is no further mention of O'Grady or "O'Grado" in the public records. Patrick O'Hogan lived at Boston in 1674. In a transcript of the records at the Suffolk County Registry of Deeds,[35] it is shown that "Patrick Chogon" and Rich. Henchman signed by their "marks" as witnesses to a deed dated October 3, 1674, covering the transfer of a town lot at Boston from Daniel Henchman to Edward Youring. But, on examination of the original entry,[36] dated June 14, 1675, recording the deed, it develops that the scrivener in drawing up the instrument spelled Patrick's surname "Ohogon" and wrote it indistinctly, with the result that the Register mistook the prefix "O" in the name for a "C," and

32 Plymouth Colony Records, Vol. 1, p. 7.

33 Lib. 1, fol. 50.

34 Court Records, Part 1, fol. 108.

35 Published by the Register of Deeds in 1897.

36 Registry of Deeds, Lib. 9, fol. 203.

transferred it to the deed book in that way. Consequently, this pioneer Hibernian has since appeared on record with the strange name of "Patrick Chogon"! O'Hogan died probably before 1694, and in Boston town records of that year there is an entry: "Relict of Patrick Ohogan died June 5." [37] These are the only references to this early Massachusetts Irishman that can be found in the records, except that he had a son named Daniel, who in all probability was the Daniel Hogan that was mentioned as a resident of Boston in 1685.

In New Hampshire records of the year 1693 Daniel Shaw was listed among residents of Newcastle. He died in 1715, and it is evident that his correct name was O'Shaw, since the "will of Daniel O'Shaw of Newcastle" was recorded on June 20, 1715.[38] Other entries in the records say that "John O'Shaw gave bond as surety to administer the estate of Daniel O'Shaw"; James, Daniel and Katherine O'Shaw were named among the beneficiaries,[39] and on July 15, 1716, administration to "the estate of James O'Shaw of Great Island" was granted to his brother, John O'Shaw.[40] A few years later, there were mentioned in the same records men named Samuel McNamara, Andrew and William Kelly, Samuel Hickey, Morris Shannon, William Cleary, William Daly and John Murphy,[41] though there is nothing to indicate that these men were in the colony in the seventeenth century.

The historic Leinster family of the Geraldines had representatives in New England in Gerald, James, David and Elephel Fitzgerald, the last mentioned being described as "an Irish lady of high birth." [42] Gerald Fitzgerald, an indentured

[37] Vol. 9, p. 219.

[38] Mentioned in New Hampshire Deeds, Vol. 31, p. 764.

[39] *Ibid.*

[40] New Hampshire Probate Records, Vol. 9, p. 14.

[41] *Collections, New Hampshire Historical Society*, Vol. 4, p. 503; Vol. 5, p. 86; Vol. 7, p. 158; Vol. 31, p. 578.

[42] *New England Historic-Genealogical Register*, Vol. 34, p. 394.

servant to Thomas Burnham, was mentioned in the Connecticut Council Journal of April 2, 1664;[43] James Fitzgerald was married to Elizabeth Bullier at Saybrook, Conn., on April 28, 1678, and according to Suffolk County, Mass., records, David FitzGerald signed as one of the witnesses to a deed dated June 6, 1682, between William Towers of Boston and Joseph Lynde of Charlestown.[44] Some information as to the history of these men has been sought, but none seems to be obtainable.

In the case of Elephel Fitzgerald, there is an interesting but all too inadequate account of her in the genealogy of the Slocum family, in which it is said that "about 1687, she married Eliezer Slocum of Dartmouth, Mass." (now New Bedford). Eliezer was a son of Giles Slocum of Portsmouth, R. I., who, on receiving a grant of a large tract of land in Dartmouth Township, removed to that place before 1682. Eliezer owned extensive properties at a place known as Slocum's Neck on Buzzard's Bay, and his will, dated March 1, 1727, still preserved in the probate office at Taunton, shows that he divided his estate, which was appraised at the immense sum for those days of £5790, among his "beloved wife, Elephel," and his sons, Eliezer and Ebenezer. The time of her arrival in this country is unknown, and among her New England descendants, there are partially conflicting opinions as to the circumstances of her departure from her native land. In one branch of the Slocum family, the tradition is, that although she was "a lady of high birth," she was "one of a number of young women who were forcibly brought to America and sold for wives to respectable purchasers, the purchase money in this instance amounting to about $600."[45]

Other branches apparently are unwilling to acknowledge

[43] In *Colonial Records of Connecticut*, Vol. 15, p. 537.

[44] Suffolk County Registry of Deeds, Lib. 12, fol. 224.

[45] *History of the Slocums*, by Dr. Charles E. Slocum, Syracuse, N. Y., 1882.

that she could have occupied so lowly a station in life as to be "sold" as a wife to their Slocum ancestor. These Slocums probably are unacquainted with England's methods of "governing" Ireland at that period, namely, in confiscating the property of the Irish and parcelling it out among the English adventurers and soldiers, rich and poor were treated with equal severity and some of the leading families of the island were thus reduced to the most extreme poverty. The tradition in these branches is to the effect that Elephel Fitzgerald was "a daughter of Earl Edmund Fitzgerald of Dublin, whose sister became affianced to an English officer against her father's will and eloped with him, taking with her a younger sister, this Lady Elephel, whom they brought to America, perhaps to further the success of their plans." [46]

In another account of the family, written by a descendant of Eliezer and Elephel Slocum,[47] it is stated that she lived as a domestic in the household of Giles Slocum at Portsmouth, that Eliezer was born at Portsmouth in 1664, he and Elephel Fitzgerald having been "married before they were twenty," and "with his wife, Elephel, he was living at Slocum's Neck prior to 1684." A romantic story has come down in the family of the courtship of Eliezer Slocum and the Irish maiden, but it has had no appeal for their descendant, and he not only treats it as a fable but seeks to cast ridicule on the tradition that she was of the noble family of the Geraldines. "In what manner," he relates, "our little Irish maid was separated from her sister and came to find a home in the simple household of Giles Slocum in Portsmouth, the tradition sayeth not. Irish maids were not commonly employed in those early days, and even in later times Irish maids were seldom Earl's daughters. None the less, it is probable that the Lady

[46] *Ibid.*

[47] Henry Howland Crapo, in *Old Dartmouth Historical Sketches*, Dartmouth Historical Society, No. 29, pp. 6-10.

Elephel did in fact serve in a domestic capacity in the household of Giles Slocum." Elephel (Fitzgerald) Slocum was the mother of seven children, all born in Dartmouth Township between 1689 and 1703, and her will, proved October 4, 1748, shows that she divided among them a considerable estate. Her daughter, Joanna, married Daniel Weeden of Jamestown, R. I., and many of the Weeden, Slocum, Carpenter and other families now in Rhole Island and Massachusetts trace their descent back to the gentle Irish girl, Elephel Fitzgerald.

The proprietors' records of Sudbury, Middlesex County, Mass., begin with a list of fifty-six "Grantees and Settlers who went to the Sudbury Plantation about 1638 or 1639," one of whom was Thomas Flynn, who received a grant of a town lot in that part of Sudbury now called Wayland in 1639. His name was recorded variously, Flynn, Flyn and Flinn and once as "Mr. Flint," but a local historian, apparently surprised at the fact that others besides Englishmen were in the settlement at that early day, "conjectures it may have been written by mistake for Thomas Joslyn or Islyn." [48] Yet, in a later work by the same author, entitled "*Annals of Sudbury, Wayland and Maynard*," [49] he reproduced the list of original grantees, in which both names appear as Thomas Joslyn and Thomas Flynn; and in the *History of Middlesex County*,[50] among the first settlers at Sudbury the names, Thomas Joslyn and Thomas Flynn, are also listed. Sudbury town records contain the original "Plan of Settlement," showing that "House Lot No. 4" was assigned to "Tho. Flinn, between John Loker and John Haynes"; the earliest known map of that region shows the location of "the first Roads and House-Lots in Sudbury," with the name,

48 *History of Sudbury, Mass.*, by Alfred S. Hudson, p. 26, Sudbury, 1889.

49 Sudbury, Mass., 1891.

50 By D. Hamilton Hurd, p. 378, Philadelphia, 1890.

"Thomas Flynn," next to the "Meeting-House Lot," and such careful chroniclers as those employed by the New England Historic-Genealogical Society also list him as "Thomas Flynn." [51]

There is no mistaking how the name was recorded; it is perfectly plain in each instance. It disappeared from the town records about 1645, indicating that Thomas Flynn removed from Sudbury, and it is possible that he relocated at Concord. The "will of Thomas Flynt of Concord" was proved in Middlesex County in 1654; in the eighteenth century probate records of that County there are numerous entries of people of the name and although it has been suggested that possibly this Thomas Flynt and Thomas Flynn were the same identical person, there seems to be no way of definitely proving that such was the fact. There was a Flynn family at Malden in Middlesex County, at which place the marriage of "Patrick Flinn and Mary Winsled" was recorded on July 2, 1713,[52] and in an old burying ground at that place there is a stone on which is engraven this inscription: "Mary Flyn, wife of Patrick, in her 27th year. Died May 24, 1720." The marriage of Patrick Flynn and Prudence Ward was recorded at Malden on July 20, 1721,[53] and in 1749 the Probate Court of Middlesex County appointed a guardian for "Joshua Flinn of Malden." Not until 1778 does the name again appear in the town or county records, in which year a "Patherick Flinn" enlisted "for the war" in Captain Nathaniel Maynard's company of the Fourth Middlesex County Regiment and was credited to the town of Sudbury. However, it is clear that he could not have been descended from Thomas Flynn, because Patrick Flinn's enlistment papers say that he was "a transient, late from Ireland."

[51] *New England Historic-Genealogical Register,* Vol. 60, p. 357.

[52] Vital Records, Malden, Mass.

[53] *Ibid.*

Flinns and Griffins appear in the vital records of the adjoining town of Wayland down to the early years of the last century.[54] The list of "Grantees and Settlers" before mentioned includes Hugh Griffin, who located at Sudbury in 1639, and although there is nothing said about his nationality, it is probable that he also was an Irishman. The name is very common in Meath and Clare and has an Irish root. The Meath Griffins are from O'Griobhtha (pronounced *o-greev-a*), anglicised Griffey and Griffin,[55] and the Clare Griffins are from O'Criomhthainn (pronounced *o-cree-av-aun*), anglicised Griffin and sometimes Cramton and Crampton.[56] Hugh Griffin was the first Town Clerk of Sudbury and the colonial records show that in 1645 he was appointed "Clerk of the writs, in place of Walter Haynes." He was one of the important men in the town and his name turns up in local records more often than that of any other of the pioneer settlers. He died in 1656, and one of his many descendants was Dr. Edward D. Griffin, born at East Haddam, Conn., in 1770, a distinguished president of Williams College. Another Hugh Griffin was at Stratford, Conn., in 1652, who is supposed to have been a relative of Hugh of Sudbury. He married Mary Norton, widow of Peter Norton who died in 1670, and they are mentioned in Stratford records as late as 1687. A great many Griffins are mentioned in Fairfield County, Conn., records.[57]

To Sudbury also came an Irishman named Rickard Burke. While nothing is known of his history prior to his advent in this country, his given name makes it reasonably certain that he was of the Clanrickard family of Burkes of Mayo and

[54] The marriage of Ann Flinn and Samuel Haynes was recorded at Wayland on October 18, 1804.

[55] *Irish Pedigrees*, by John O'Hart, Vol. 1, p. 857.

[56] *Ibid.*, p. 469.

[57] *History and Genealogy of the Families of Old Fairfield*, ed. by Donald Lines Jacobus, Vol. 1, part 3.

Galway, famous in Irish history. His descendants are of the belief that he was probably of the family of Ulick Burke, Earl of Clanrickard, who was driven out of Ireland in 1650 after his estates were confiscated by the English. He married Mary Parmenter at Sudbury on May 24, 1670,[58] and they were the parents of Richard, John, Joseph, Jonas, Thomas and Mary Burke, all born at Sudbury between 1671 and 1686. Originally, he was recorded Rickard, but the recording officers, not understanding the distinction between that name and Richard, usually spelled it Richard. He bought 130 acres of land from Henry and Hannah Loker at a place known by the Indian name of Pompassiticut, by deed dated October 24, 1670, recorded in Middlesex County,[59] and as Richard Burke he was recorded on March 1, 1685, as receiving from the town of Stow a grant of thirty acres of land, and the town made him a further grant on July 26, 1687.[60]

Rickard or Richard Burke was the progenitor of many American families of Burkes, and the names of his descendants may be found on record all over New England, especially in the Connecticut River Valley. He died in 1693 and the records of the probate office for Middlesex County show that on January 17, 1694, "Mary Burck, Relict widow of Richard Burck of Sudbury in ye County of Midd^x^, John Burck of said Sudbury, yeoman, Abraham Holeman of said Sudbury and Richard Burck of Stow" were appointed administrators of his estate. His son, Richard, appears in the "Proprietors' Book" at Northampton of the year 1700; one of his grandsons, Major John Burke of Bernardston, Mass., distinguished himself as a soldier in the Indian War in 1745 and in the French-English War, 1755-1763. It is said that much of the early history of Worcester County was obtained from

[58] Sudbury, Mass., Vital Records, p. 179.

[59] Registry of Deeds, Vol. 7, fol. 243.

[60] Town Records, Stow, Mass.

a diary kept by Major John Burke, and another of the family, Captain Burke, is mentioned as "a famous Revolutionary soldier and friend of Ethan Allen."

Of the other recorded Burkes, Edward Burk of Boston was appointed by the General Court one of "the administrators to the estate of Augustine Walker, deceased," on May 22, 1656,[61] and a case entitled "Walter Burke, pltff. vs. Michael White, deft," was tried before the Court on May 15, 1667.[62] Roger Burke and "Willyam Heally" of Cambridge, among others, signed a petition to the General Court on August 17, 1664; a Thomas Burke is mentioned as a resident of Middletown, Conn., in 1670; in the will of Walter Price of Salem dated May 21, 1674, he named his "daughter, Elizabeth Burke," one of the legatees; [63] Timothy Burke of Woburn and Richard Burke served in King Philip's War in 1676; John Burke owned lands in Weymouth, Mass., as stated in a deed dated February 9, 1676, recorded in Suffolk County; [64] Thomas Burke signed as witness to a deed in Essex County dated February 17, 1681, covering a transfer of lands at Rowley,[65] and Thomas and Stephen, sons of Thomas and Mary Burke, were born in Rowley in 1719 and 1721, respectively. "Edward, son of Edward Burke," was baptised at Salem on August 7, 1687;[66] a Captain Edward Burke was mentioned as of Salem about that time,[67] and Joseph Burke was listed among "persons (in Boston) who had their taxes

[61] *The Records of the Colony of Massachusetts Bay in New England*, Vol. 3, pp. 413-4.

[62] *Ibid.*, Vol. 4, part 2, p. 341, and *Records of the Court of Assistants*, Vol. 3, p. 180.

[63] Probate Records in *Essex Institute Historical Collection*, Vol. 2, p. 127.

[64] Suffolk Deeds, Lib. 12, fol. 300.

[65] Essex Deeds, Lib. 4, fol. 437, and Court Records, Essex County, Vol. 8, p. 269.

[66] Vital Records, Salem, Mass.

[67] Essex Notarial Records, in *Essex Institute Historical Collections*, Vol. 41, p. 381.

abated" in the year 1700.[68] Other Burkes appear in Massachusetts records in the early part of the eighteenth century, and generally appear to have been a class of men not unworthy of a place in histories of the State, if the compilers of those histories, in whose integrity the average reader seems to have such guileless faith, had any inclination to be fair and impartial.

[68] Boston Town Books, Vol. 10, pp. 99, 100.

CHAPTER X

The "Irish Donation"—Ireland the only country in the world to send relief to the suffering colonists in King Philip's War, 1676—Thomas Casey at Newport, R. I., 1658—the Caseys of East Greenwich a remarkable family—among the founders of Rhode Island's shipping industry.

ON October 11, 1676, Richard Burke and thirty-two other inhabitants of Sudbury petitioned the Massachusetts General Court to have part of "the large contribution sent out of Ireland" apportioned toward the relief of those who suffered losses in that town in the war with the Narragansett Indians, known as "King Philip's War."[1] The "contribution" here referred to was raised principally in Dublin, Ireland, and is known in history as "The Irish Donation" or "The Irish Charity," and when it was forwarded to Boston on August 28, 1676, the ship *Katharine* was chartered for the purpose and the Lord Mayor of the Irish Capital dispatched with it three "Commissioners" to supervise the distribution of the charity. A full account of this interesting but little known fragment of New England history can be found in the *New England Historic-Genealogical Register*,[2] the collections of the Connecticut and Massachusetts Historical Societies and in the Journal of the American Irish Historical Society,[3] with the facts properly authenticated by reference to the authorities.

Baylies in his history of New Plymouth says: "The City

[1] Massachusetts Colonial Records, Vol. 5, p. 124.

[2] Vol. 2, pp. 245-252, 398.

[3] Vol. 12.

of Dublin was the only place in the British European Dominions which bestowed any relief on the suffering Colony," [4] and Freeman says: "it is somewhat remarkable that from divers Christians in England and Wales no word of cheer greeted the suffering colonists, and no contribution, save that of Ireland, is recorded in this dark and perilous period!" Many references to "The Irish Donation" may be seen in Connecticut and Massachusetts records of the years 1676 and 1677, and in the *Plymouth Church Records* [5] there is an entry under 1677, reading thus: "The Chh (church) set apart April 26 to be kept as a day of Thanksgiving for peace, health, supplyes of corne & provisions by contribution from Connecticott & from Dublin in Ireland." "The shipload of provisions" sent from Dublin to Boston is mentioned also in Boston town records,[6] and in *Rev. John Eliot's Records of the First Church in Roxbury,* under the year 1676, he referred to "a gracious gift of charity to relieve such as suffered in our late warr," which had arrived "from Dublin in Ireland."

In the records of the Plymouth Colony we read about "the order and distribution of this collonies p^te^ of the contribution made by divers Christians in Ireland for the relieffe of such as are impoverished, distressed and in necessitie by the late Indian warr," and showing that thirteen towns in that colony received shares of the Irish Donation.[7] In the *Annals of Salem, Mass.,*[8] Rev. Joseph B. Felt gave due credit to "the Irish Charity," by which "sixty-one families at Salem, distressed by the war, were relieved by donations collected in Ireland," and another churchman, Rev. Enoch Pratt, in his

[4] *Historical Memoir of the Colony of New Plymouth,* by Francis Baylies, Vol. 2, p. 192.

[5] Published by the Colonial Society of Massachusetts, Vol. 22, p. 153.

[6] Vol. 5.

[7] Plymouth Colony Records, Vol. 5, p. 222.

[8] Vol. 2, pp. 130, 397, 635, Salem, 1849.

references to "the donation from Ireland," points to it as "a gratifying instance of the generous influence of Christian sympathies."[9] One hundred and seventy-one years later, the people of New England generously reciprocated, when they sent the *Jamestown* on her voyage of mercy to Ireland to relieve the sufferers in that country during the famine of 1847.

The name Barry turns up in New England at a very early date. Clement Barry was listed among the passengers in the *Margaret* which sailed for Boston from Plymouth, England, on March 1, 1633. William Barry was one of six settlers at Sandy Beach, Rye, N. H., who received grants of land at that place on March 27, 1653.[10] John Barry was at New London in 1659, in which year he signed as witness to a deed.[11] In 1669 John Barry bought lands at Ipswich from William Buckley, which he sold to John Wainwright by deed dated August 6, 1678,[12] and in that year "John Barry of Ipswich had rights of commonage as tenant to Samuel Bishop."[13] Ipswich vital records show that this John Barry and Hannah Hodgkins were married at that place on January 17, 1670, and according to the court files, "John Barry lived at Ipswich, sailor, 1670-1678, wife Hannah died May 29, 1676."[14] And since a John Barry and Mary Chapman were married there on January 24, 1676,[15] it is clear there were two Barrys of the same given name at Ipswich. In the will of Edward Chapman of Ipswich, proved in Essex County on April 30, 1678, he mentioned among the legatees "Mary,

[9] *History of Eastham, Wellfleet and Orleans, Mass.*, p. 44.

[10] *Early Portsmouth History*, by Ralph May, p. 151, Boston, 1926.

[11] *Genealogical Dictionary of the First Settlers of New England*, by James Savage, Vol. 1.

[12] Ipswich Deeds, Lib. 4, fol. 253.

[13] *The Hammatt Papers*, p. 43.

[14] Probate Records, quoted in *Essex Antiquarian*, Vol. 6.

[15] Ipswich Vital Records.

wife of John Barry,"[16] and on September 22, 1681, a case entitled "John Barry vs. Samuel Chapman," for recovery of "a legacy under the will of his father-in-law, Edward Chapman," was tried in the Essex County Court.[17] William Stoughton conveyed to John Barry a dwelling house and lot at Boston by deed dated November 2, 1682.[18] This John Barry was described as "an Irishman," and since he was "a mariner in the Colony service" it may be that he was the Ipswich sailor before referred to. Among those whose names are found in the Boston tax lists were John Barry, 1686-1688, Teage Barry in 1688 and "John Barry, Tanner," was taxed under "Countrie Rate" in 1691.[19] Peter Barry was a resident of Boston in 1685;[20] "James, son of James and Rachel Barrey," was born at Boston on January 8, 1688, and the birth of "James, son of James and Eliza Barry," was recorded there on June 14, 1692. James Barry was mentioned as a "huntsman" at one of the meetings of the Selectmen on June 27, 1707, when a complaint was made that "his dogs were suffered to go at large in ye Town and have done damage to the inhabitants in their pastures and gardens"; so James Barry was ordered to "shut them up" or "rid the Town of such Hounds or Dogges w[ch] are by him so kept."[21] Another James Barry lived near Pemaquid, Maine, 1674-1686.

The birth of "Samuel, son of Bryan Bradeene," was recorded at Malden, in June, 1671. "The land of Bryan Bradeene" and "the land of Tego Barrow" were described as the boundary lines of a tract of land "at Rumly Marsh in the Township of Boston," in a deed dated June 28, 1673, and again in a deed dated April 1, 1678, covering a transfer

[16] Ipswich Deeds, Lib. 4, fol. 169.

[17] Records and Files of the Quarterly Court, Vol. 8, p. 173.

[18] Suffolk County Registry of Deeds, Lib. 12, fol. 294.

[19] Boston Tax Lists, in Town Books, Vol. 1.

[20] Boston Town Books, Vol. 10, p. 61.

[21] *Ibid.*, Vol. 2.

of "lands in the bounds of Boston neer unto Lyn," the boundaries were "the lands of Teague Barrow and Brian Bradeen." [22] As of December 15, 1681, "Bryan Breedon" was on a list of tax-payers at Rumney Marsh; as Bryan Bradene he was taxed upon "Arable Lands, Pasture, Meadows, Bulls and Cowes, Hefyers, Steers and Sheep" in 1688,[23] and as Brian Bredon he was listed as an inhabitant of Boston in 1695. He had a son, James, who settled at Kittery, Maine. There are records there of the births of James and Bryan, sons of James and Priscilla Bradeen, in 1703 and 1707 respectively, and of the marriage of Bryan Breeden and Hannah Allen on December 17, 1733.

"Richard Bulger, bricklayer," was mentioned in Boston town records in 1632; in 1637 he received an allotment of thirty acres of land, located probably at Exeter, since he was a resident of that place in the next year, and in 1664 Richard Bulger was a town officer at Dover. William Bodkin served as a soldier in King Philip's War; [24] "John, son of William and Mary Bodkin," was born at Boston on March 15, 1680; Elizabeth Bodkin of the same parents on August 15, 1682, and Dominick Bodkin, a Boston merchant, sued Robert Brimsden for "libel," before the Court of Assistants on October 1, 1678.[25] John Bready or Brady was a farmer at Kittery, Maine, and in his will [26] dated August 30, 1681, probated in York County, he bequeathed "houses, lands, chattels," etc. to his wife, Sarah. "Patericke Boyce" was recorded as witness to the will of "Alexander Cooper at Barwicke in the Town of Kittery" on February 9, 1683. At Boxford, Mass., there seems to have been a family named Breen, and according to Lynn vital records, "Mary Breen of Boxford" was

[22] Registry of Deeds, Lib. 8, fols. 189-190, and Lib. 12, fol. 178.

[23] Tax Lists in Boston Town Books, Vol. 1.

[24] Bodge's *King Philip's War*, p. 55.

[25] Court Records, Vol. 1, p. 128.

[26] Recorded at York County Registry of Deeds, Lib. 5, fol. 13.

married to Dr. Ebenezer Tarbox at Lynn on April 5, 1700, and the town records inform us that "old Breen, the Doctor's wife's father, died at the Doctor's 29:5:1731."

Buckley is a frequently occurring name in New England records. While it is now, and has been for several centuries, common among the Irish, it is of English origin and there have been many English families of the name. For that reason it is impossible to state if any of the early American Buckleys were from Ireland, since their nationality is nowhere stated; so, they are not here claimed as "Irish." Edward Buckley sold lands to Robert Carver at Marshfield, Mass., on June 13, 1654. William Buckley was the grantee in a deed covering the purchase of a homestead and lands at Ipswich from Thomas Manning in 1657, and he evidently was the William Buckley who sold lots to John Barry at Ipswich in 1669. "Peter Buckley of Concord" is mentioned in Braintree town records as of January 2, 1670; Richard Buckley was a Boston police officer in 1678; William Buckley was on the Danvers tax list in 1682; Charles and Thomas Buckley were at Boston in 1685; Joseph Buckley was master of the ketch *Gabriel* of Boston in 1687, and David Buckley and Hannah Talley were married at Boston on June 3, 1697. There are numerous entries of the name in New England records of the eighteenth century.

Salem and Marblehead vital records of the past two hundred years show that many families named Boden and Bowden lived at these places, who doubtless descended from the brothers, Michael and Peter Bowden, who were in Essex County in the second half of the seventeenth century. "Mickall Bouden" was on the Topsfield, Mass., assessment roll of the year 1668; "Michael Bowden, planter," was taxed there in the following year;[27] the marriage of Michael Bowden and Sarah Nurse was recorded at Topsfield on March 24, 1669,

[27] Town Records, in *Topsfield Historical Society Collections.*

and in 1681 he was mentioned as "of Marblehead Plains." Peter Bowden was master of "the barque, John, lately of Dublin," which the records show he sold to "Thomas Gardner, merchant of Salem," on November 2, 1686, and the transaction was thus referred to in the records of the Essex County Registry of Deeds: [28] "Peter Bowden, protestant, merchant of the City of Wexford, Ireland, now living at Salem, sold shipp lately of Dublin, 1684-1686." Evidently, he removed to Boston, since a Peter Bowden appears in the tax lists of the town in the year 1687.[29] This name has been common in Ireland for several centuries, especially in Kildare, Carlow and Wexford. The family so called came into Ireland about the time of the Norman invasion (1172), and settled at Bodenstown in County Kildare, and the name was sometimes written "Bawdewyn" in the old Anglo-Irish records.[30]

A Samuel Casey who lived in Essex County, Mass., died there in 1670, and an entry in the records of the Probate Court of April 28th in that year says: "Samuel Casey, dying intestate, administration upon his estate was granted to Henry Skerry, Marshal." [31] John Casey lived at Muddy River (now Brookline) in 1675; on September 6th of that year he and Michael Martin signed as witnesses to a bill of sale at Boston, and on December 3, 1676, he was witness to a power of attorney, both recorded at the Suffolk County Registry of Deeds.[32] In 1675, John Casey enlisted for service in King Philip's War; "John Casey, servant to Thomas Gardiner of Muddy River," was among a "list of slayne and wounded in Captain Oliver's company, December 19, 1675," and he was

[28] Quoted in *Essex Antiquarian*, Vol. 11, p. 45.

[29] Boston Town Books, Vol. 1.

[30] *Irish Names and Surnames*, by Rev. Patrick Woulfe, p. 230, Dublin, Ire., 1923.

[31] Probate Records, Vol. 2, p. 195, and Records and Files of the Quarterly Court, Vol. 4, p. 272.

[32] Lib. 9, fols. 248 and 387.

also listed among the "wounded at Road Iland" [33] in an attack on an Indian fort in the "Great Swamp." The "estate of John Casey" was taxed £30 in 1676.[34] That a man of the name was in business in Boston three years later is evident from the following entry in the town records: "We John Turner Vintner and John Casey Taylor both of Bostone doe bind ourselves to Capt Thomas Brattle Treasurer of the Towne of Bostone in the Sum of ffortie pounds that Alexander Hamilton confectioner Shall not be Chargeable to the Towne, 30th day of January, 1679." [35] On November 14, 1678, Jonathan Casey of Roxbury took the oath of allegiance before Governor John Endicott; on April 21, 1679, John Casey subscribed to the oath before Governor Simon Bradstreet,[36] and in the next year John Casey of Boston was fined £15 for having "sold strong beer *sans* license."

In at least fifteen States of the Union there are families named Casey, all descended from Thomas Casey, a settler at Newport, Rhode Island, as early as 1658. From a short history of the Casey family,[37] written by Edward Pearce Casey, we learn that Thomas Casey was born in Ireland "about 1637." And according to a tradition handed down in the successive generations of the family, Thomas Casey's parents were killed during the Irish insurrection in 1641. The orphan child was carried by his nurse to England, whence he emigrated to this country at the age of twenty-one and located at Newport, of which community he became one of the leading business men and is mentioned as occupying a place of considerable social importance for many years. With other citizens

[33] Bodge's *King Philip's War*, p. 178. Also *History and Antiquities of the City of Boston*, by Samuel G. Drake, Vol. 2, p. 414.

[34] Tax Lists, Boston, in Town Books, Vol. 1.

[35] Town Books, Vol. 10, p. 65.

[36] *Ibid.*, Vol. 29, p. 68.

[37] *The Casey Family of East Greenwich, R. I.*, published in 1927 in connection with the celebration of the 250th anniversary of the founding of the town.

of Rhode Island, including the Charles McCarthy before mentioned, he was one of the founders of the town of East Greenwich in 1677, and twenty-five years later he was listed as "one of the proprietors of the common lands in Newport." He died in 1711, leaving three sons, Thomas (born 1663), Adam (born 1667) and Samuel (born 1675).[38] Thomas Casey (2) remained in Newport, where he inherited his father's estate, but Adam and Samuel struck out for themselves, settling at Warwick and Kingston, R. I., respectively, and these three were the ancestors of several Rhode Island families of the name. Thomas Casey (2) and his wife, Rebecca, had sons, John and Edmund, and daughters, Rebecca and Sarah, born at Newport between 1695 and 1704; Adam Casey and his wife, Mary, had Thomas, Silas, Edward, Mary and Sarah, born between 1706 and 1718, and Samuel Casey was the father of Thomas, John, Samuel and Gideon, whose births were recorded between 1716 and 1726.[39]

In many ways, the Caseys were a remarkable family, and in town books, probate and land records, parish registers, tax lists, military rolls and other public records, representatives of successive generations of Caseys appear for two hundred and fifty years after the original immigrant came to this country. Several of the Caseys are mentioned as successful merchants and shipping masters in command of vessels trading with Southern ports and the West Indies. Indeed, we are told that "Thomas Casey was one of those famous shipowners of Narragansett Bay whose enterprise laid the foundations of Rhode Island's industrial history." [40] They well preserved the record of the "Fighting Race," for in every generation of the Caseys there have been officers of the name in the army and the navy, beginning with the Indian war in the

[38] Austin's *Genealogical Dictionary of Rhode Island.*

[39] Vital Records of Rhode Island.

[40] *The Casey Family of East Greenwich,* by Edward Pearce Casey.

eighteenth century and down even to the present day. One of them, Silas Casey, born at East Greenwich in 1807, was a distinguished American soldier. He served with the United States Army in numerous Indian conflicts on the western frontiers, the Seminole War in Florida, the Mexican and the Civil Wars, and in two campaigns against the Indians on the Pacific Coast. It was he who led the "forlorn hope" at the storming of Chapultepec, in which he was severely wounded, and he gallantly defended with his division his position at Fair Oaks, Virginia. He retired in 1868, after forty-two years military service, with the rank of Major-General. Colonel Thomas Lincoln Casey, also a distinguished officer in the Civil War, Captain Silas Casey of the Navy and Edward P. Casey, architect of one of the handsomest public buildings in the United States, the Library of Congress at Washington, were also of this family. Much more can be said to show what an important American family the Caseys were, but one searches in vain in New England histories for any mention of the fact that their immigrant ancestor was an "Exile from Erin," as far back as 279 years ago!

In the seventeenth and eighteenth centuries numerous people named Collins came to this country, some of whom, notwithstanding their Irish name, seem to have been English. Originally, there were two distinct families in Ireland, O'Cuileann and O'Coilean, whose names were modernized into O'Collins, Collins, Collane, Culhane and Cullen. According to Irish annals and genealogies, a member of one of these families migrated to Cornwall, England, in the thirteenth or fourteenth century. In due course, his descendants so identified themselves with the English that they became "English" to all intents and purposes; in the same manner as the descendants of the English and the Normans who settled in Ireland became "Irish," and generally are so recognized. Therefore, when we find a man bearing this name in early

American records, it is a difficult matter to classify him; and while we know that many of them were Irish, since either they themselves said so or the records say they "came from Ireland," all of the name who settled in this country in the colonial period are not claimed as Irish.

The first Irishman of the name in New England seems to have been Henry Collins, who came with his family to Lynn, Mass., in the year 1635. In some references to Joseph Collins, an early settler on the Cape Cod Peninsula, a historian of that region says: "Joseph Collins was probably a son of Henry Collins, starch maker, who embarked June 17, 1635, with his wife, Anne, and children, Henry, Joseph and Marjery. They were from Ireland." [41] Henry Collins is said to have been "a member of the Salem Court," [42] and died at Lynn on February 20, 1687. Joseph removed to Eastham, and there married Ruth Knowles on March 20, 1672, and had sons, John, Joseph, Jonathan, Benjamin and James, all of whom married at Eastham. Their descendants, a numerous tribe, are mentioned in the vital records of various Massachusetts towns and cities. The historian of the town of Eastham informs us that "Joseph Collins came from Ireland and was here before 1670"; [43] and in Eastham vital records there is an incomplete entry to the effect that "Joseph Collins dyed the 18th 1723/4." [44] Timothy Collins served under Captain Joshua Scottow in King Philip's War,[45] and "Tim" Collins was a witness before the Salem Court on August 13, 1678.[46] Among Boston taxpayers between 1674 and 1687, there are listed

[41] "Annals of the Town of Eastham," in *Annals of Cape Cod*, by Frederick Freeman, p. 374.

[42] *Ibid.*

[43] *History of Eastham, Wellfleet and Orleans, Mass.*, by Rev. Enoch Pratt, p. 29, Yarmouth, Mass., 1844.

[44] Month omitted in the record.

[45] *New England Historic-Genealogical Register*, Vol. 43, p. 75.

[46] Records and Files of the Quarterly Court, Vol. 7.

Cornelius, Edward, Matthew and Thomas Collins,[47] and John Collins was the schoolmaster who taught the children of the little community of Guilford, Conn., in 1682.[48] A Captain John Collins, a native of Ireland, master of a trading vessel, died at Lynn on December 22, 1679, and an "agreement dated June 3, 1680," in settlement of "the estate of John Collins, who left a widow and twelve children," was filed in court in that month. A William Collins and his wife, Sarah, lived at Newport and the births of their children, William, Sarah and Anne Collins, were recorded there between 1698 and 1701.

[47] Boston Tax Lists, in Town Books, Vol. 1.

[48] *History of Guilford, Conn.*, by Ralph D. Smith, p. 81, Albany, N. Y.

CHAPTER XI

Many of the best known Irish names found in Massachusetts' records—Anthony Carroll of Topsfield and his descendants—the Dalys in Connecticut—"Richard Greeley, an Irishman," and "Mary Greeley, an Irishwoman," in Essex County, 1670—Andrew Greeley of Salisbury was ancestor of Horace Greeley, distinguished American journalist.

AS early as 1658, and possibly before that time, Anthony Carroll and his wife, Katherine, were residents of Topsfield, Mass. Since there is no entry of their marriage in Massachusetts vital records, it is probable they came to this country as "redemptioners"; but, that Anthony became a man of property, is clear from the records of several lawsuits tried at the Essex County Court between 1663 and 1668. In Topsfield town records of October 14, 1661, he was listed as one of thirty "Commoners," each of whom received an equal share in the division of the common lands.[1] In 1663 he appears as "Anthoone Carrell" under "Delinquent taxpayers"; as "Antoni Carol" in the tax list of 1664,[2] and as "Antony Carell" he was assessed for taxes under "County Rate made the 18 of November, 1668, for Topsfield." [3] In the vital records, however, are found the following entries covering the births of his children:

"Kathren Carroll, daughter of Anthony, born June 31 (?) 1658."
"Pricilah Carroll, daughter of Anthony, born March 19, 1660."
"John Carroll, son of Anthony, born October 19, 1663."

[1] Town Records, in *Topsfield Historical Society Collections*, Vol. 2, p. 6.
[2] *Ibid.*, p. 7.
[3] *Ibid.*, p. 51.

"Anthony Carroll, son of Anthony, born 1666."
"Mary Carroll, daughter of Anthony, born 1666."

"Antony Carrall, aged 30 years," was a witness in a case entitled "Allen Perley *vs.* Henry Bachelor," tried in the Essex County Court on November 25, 1662; and on March 21, 1663, a writ was issued in the case of "William Pritchett *vs.* Anthony Carroll" for "trespass and keeping a house and land of which Pritchett claimed ownership." A case entitled "William Pateson *vs.* Anthony Carroll" was tried in court on March 31, 1668, on a charge of "defamation spoken at Edward Dear's house," and a verdict was rendered for the defendant. In the record the name was spelled Carroll, Carrill, and Caryell, and the testimony indicates that both the plaintiff and defendant formerly resided in Barbados, from which it is assumed that Carroll was one of the Irish "captives," who, under the edict of Cromwell or his successors, were transported from Ireland to the West Indies, whence he came to this country.[4] On April 25, 1668, a writ was issued by the Court in an action brought by Anthony Carroll against William Patteson "for attaching his (Carroll's) estate and imprisoning him," but the case was withdrawn. "Thomas Baker *vs.* Anthony Carroll," was the title of a case tried in the Salem Court on September 28, 1669, "for not delivering a division of land," which resulted in a verdict for the plaintiff. A case entitled "Anthony Carroll *vs.* Thomas Baker," concerning "title to land which Baker pretended he bought from Carroll on the southside of Ipswich river," came before the Court on March 25, 1673. On the trial, a deed dated January 26, 1663, from "Anthony Carroll of Topsfield, tailor,

[4] In Hotten's *Original Lists of Emigrants* it is stated that between 1635 and 1680 indentured servants to the sugar planters in the West Indies were allowed, if they chose, to go to New England and other English colonies in America, and that many of them took advantage of the opportunity and became useful citizens of the colonies.

to Thomas Baker of Topsfield, husbandman," conveying "all right in the common belonging to the land I bought of Zacheous Gould in Topsfield on the south side of Ipswich River," and another deed dated May 21, 1663, from "Anthony Carroll and his wife, Katerane, to Luke Waklinge of Topsfield," covering the transfer of twenty acres of land in Topsfield, were produced in Court. There is a long account of the trial in the records of the Essex County Court.

Henry Leonard, owner of an iron forge, sued Anthony Carroll for debt on June 24, 1673; and on September 30th of the same year Henry Leonard sued "Anthony Carrill" for "refusing to give possession of a parcel of land and meadow bought of said Carroll for the term of eleven years by lease or deed dated June 19, 1673." But, as an offset to the claim Carroll produced a bond given to him by Leonard on March 22, 1672, for £13., "to be paid in bar iron," and a verdict was rendered in his favor. In the year 1711, Daniel Carroll, grandson of Anthony, and fourteen other men removed to Connecticut and became the proprietors of an immense tract of land in a district called Chestnut Hill, near Willimantic. Two sons of Daniel Carroll were officers of the Revolutionary army. Indeed, for more than a hundred years the descendants of Anthony are mentioned in the vital records of New England towns and several of them were physicians in Massachusetts and Connecticut. "Mary Carroll, age 35 in 1672," was listed among "Early Settlers of Essex and Old Norfolk";[5] Nathaniel Carroll was listed under the same head in 1682;[6] a "Mr. Carroll" was taxed at Boston in 1674, and he probably was the John Carroll who was listed as a resident of the town in 1685.[7] In 1685 Katherine, daughter of Anthony Carroll, married John Waite, a prominent man at

[5] *New England Historic-Genealogical Register*, Vol. 6, p. 246.

[6] *Ibid.*, Vol. 7.

[7] Boston Town Books, Vol. 1, and Vol. 10, p. 61.

Ipswich; [8] a Joseph Carroll was at Hartford in 1687; Thomas Carroll was at Salem in 1688; [9] Joseph and Edward Carroll were listed among Salem's taxpayers in the year 1700,[10] and in Salem birth and marriage registers of the eighteenth century there were recorded seventy-six Carrolls, whose names were spelled in eight different ways. No further information is available concerning these people, and with the exception of Daniel, they are not mentioned in any town or county history.

In June, 1635, the ship *Primrose* sailed from London, bound for Virginia, but her Captain was obliged to land his passengers at the port of New London. Among the passengers in the *Primrose* were Bridget Clifford and her two brothers, who, we are informed, "came from Ireland." [11] Bridget Clifford and John Huggins were married at Suffield, Conn., on July 26, 1635, and they were the parents of John, Nathaniel, Susanna, Ann, Mary, Martha and Bridget Huggins. In 1640, John Huggins received a grant of land at Hampton, N. H., and the family removed to that place. In John Huggins' will dated May 31, 1670, he bequeathed his property to his "deare and beloved wyfe, Bridget," and son, John, and directed that his "younger children receive a Christian education." [12] In the "will of Bridget Clifford, Relict to Jn° Huggens, Sen. of Hampton, deceased," dated September 1, 1679, she named her sons, John and Nathaniel, and daughter, Bridget, and the witnesses were Philemon and Elizabeth Dalton.[13] John Clifford, brother of Bridget, settled at Hampton and was re-

8 Ipswich, Mass., Vital Records.

9 *Genealogical Quarterly Magazine*, Vol. 1, p. 71.

10 Salem Tax Lists, in *Genealogical Quarterly Magazine*, Vol. 4.

11 Thomas A. Hall, in *Connecticut Historical Society Collections*, Vol. 2.

12 Norfolk County, Mass., Deed Book No. 2, p. 192.

13 Probate Records, Vol. 31, p. 234, in *Provincial Papers of New Hampshire.* Also Norfolk County, Mass., Deed Book No. 3, p. 28.

corded there in 1660;[14] and the marriage of his daughter, Hannah, and Luke Malone was recorded at that place under date of "20. 9 mo. 1667," and they were the parents of Luke, Nathaniel, Joseph, Samuel and Elizabeth Malone, all born at Hampton. Hendrick Malone is mentioned as at Dover, N. H., in 1660,[15] and Luke Malone appears several times in the records as a resident of the town. He was "taxed at Bloody Point, 1667-1672";[16] in the 1670 tax list he was recorded "Lucke Malowne,"[17] and as "Luke Maloone" he was listed among the men who enrolled for service in King Philip's War in 1675. Several of his descendants are mentioned in Massachusetts and New Hampshire records of the eighteenth century, and one of them, Captain James Mallone of Methuen, Mass., was a famous soldier of the Revolution.

Several Crowleys appear in New England records. "Percy Kinge, a maide servant to Mr. Robert Crowley," arrived at Boston in the *Elizabeth and Ann* on April 15, 1635.[18] Robert Crowley is assumed to have been a resident of Boston, though there is no mention of him in the town books. Thomas Crowley was listed among the "original settlers at Exeter"[19] in 1639; a Thomas Crowley and his wife, Joanna, were living at York, Maine, in 1668;[20] the will of David Crowley was admitted to probate at Boston in 1690,[21] and Gilbert Crowley

14 *New England Historic-Genealogical Register*, Vol. 25, p. 60.

15 Savage's *Genealogical Dictionary*, Vol. 3, p. 145.

16 Essex County, Mass., Probate Records, in *Provincial Papers of New Hampshire.*

17 Dover Town Records, in *New England Historic-Genealogical Register*, Vol. 7, p. 256.

18 *Ibid.*, Vol. 9, p. 250.

19 Pope's *Pioneers of Massachusetts*, p. 270, and *New England Historic-Genealogical Register*, Vol. 14, p. 310.

20 York Records, in *Maine Historical and Genealogical Recorder*, Vol. 2.

21 Probate Records, transcribed by Elijah George, Register of Probate, Boston, 1896.

was listed among "persons (at Boston) who had their taxes abated" in the year 1700.[22]

Savage mentions "Abraham Conley or Connelly of Kittery, 1640," who "took the oath of allegiance in 1652 and was constable, 1647-1659,"[23] and the "will of Abraham Coneley of Kittery," dated March 1, 1674, was recorded in York County, Maine. At the Salem court on September 29, 1653, a case was tried entitled "William Phillips *vs.* John Child and Patrick Conaway," for "attaching his goods in the hands of Mr. William Browne,"[24] and a Jeremiah Connaway was appointed "Tythingman" at Charlestown in 1677.[25] Robert and Mary Conway had a son, Matthew, born at Ipswich on October 22, 1687. "David Conway, servant to William Beamsley," was "censured to be whipped" at the Court of Assistants at Boston on August 27, 1642, for "resisting his master."[26] On September 2, 1679, Morris Conway was charged before the Court with "Inticeing others to steale a boate & turn pyrate," and he was sentenced "to be whipt fifteen stripes" and to "pay chardges of prosecution & ffees."[27]

Ann Callahan and John Masson were married at Charlestown on November 30, 1658.[28] "Hugh Collohane of Dedham," or Hugh Collane, as he was also recorded, was listed among the troops raised for service in King Philip's War in 1675,[29] serving in a company commanded by Captain Samuel Mosely. In Dedham records of the year 1676 his name was spelled "Hugh Collohue"; as "Hugh Gollihu" he appeared in

[22] Boston Town Books, Vol. 10, p. 104.

[23] Savage's *Genealogical Dictionary*, Vol. 1, p. 443.

[24] Essex County Court Records, Vol. 8, p. 320.

[25] Savage, Vol. 1, p. 443.

[26] *Records of the Court of Assistants*, Vol. 2, p. 127.

[27] *Ibid.*, Vol. 1, p. 144.

[28] *Charlestown Genealogies and Estates*, by Thomas B. Wyman.

[29] Bodge's *King Philip's War*, pp. 71 and 477.

a return of Captain Mosely's company in the same year, and as "Hugh Goliko" he was listed among "Hattfield's Souldiers" in Captain William Turner's company. Robert Cotter was at Charlestown in 1653 and was then mentioned as "a surveyor";[30] William Cotter, described as "a farmer at New Haven," married "Eleanor, servant to John Winthrop," on March 12, 1657,[31] and in 1661 he received "a house-lot grant of six acres" at New London, where he brought up a large family. John Cotter was witness to a "letter of Attorney" dated March 15, 1680, filed in the Essex County Court,[32] and Philip Cotter was one of the signers to an address to the Massachusetts General Court by the "Inhabitants and Train Soldiers of New Hampshire" on February 20, 1689.[33] Other signers were Roger Kelly, Richard Shannon, William Moore, Anthony Hern, Nicholas Dunn, Thomas Lucey, John and James Derry and John Hayes.

"Matthias Currin" was listed as a resident of Ipswich in 1634; three years later "Matthew Curren" was mentioned as owner of lands at that place,[34] but in 1640 he removed to Southold, Long Island. An historical writer on the Connecticut River Valley says that "James Coggin and John Cogan from Dublin, Ireland, settled at Windsor, Conn., and removed to Hartford in 1641," and that "John Connor, whose parents, Philip and Mary Connor, came from Cork, Ireland, was born in Middletown, Conn., on June 15, 1686."[35] However, neither in local annals nor in the public records of the colony can verification be found for these statements.

[30] Charlestown Land Records, in Boston Town Books, Vol. 3, p. 69.

[31] New Haven Town Records.

[32] Court Records, Vol. 8.

[33] *Provincial Papers of New Hampshire,* Vol. 2, p. 34.

[34] *The Ancient Records of the Town of Ipswich,* compiled by George H. H. Schofield, Ipswich, 1899.

[35] Edward A. Hall, in *Journal of the American Irish Historical Society,* Vol. 4, p. 51.

James Conniers and Naomi Harman were married at Boston on August 15, 1696; a Richard Conniers was listed as a resident of Boston in 1698, and as "richard conners" he had his taxes abated on July 27, 1702.[36] "Richard Cadogan, fisherman, Isles of Shoals," bought land there on June 24, 1650; he took the oath of allegiance on November 20, 1652;[37] he was in a lawsuit at York, Maine, in 1656, and "Philip Cadogan of Isles of Shoals" signed a petition there on March 13, 1653.[38]

Thomas Cullen was mentioned in the records of the Salem Court[39] in 1675, and James Cullen served under Captain William Turner in King Philip's War in 1676.[40] David Cummins took the oath of allegiance at Boston on November 11, 1678;[41] Boston Town records[42] show that Matthew Collins and John Carney served in "Captain Daniel Hinksman's military company" in 1681; John Carney was taxed at Boston in the same year;[43] "James Carne and Shopp" were taxed there in 1687, but Savage refers to him as "James Carney, Boston, 1686, a surgeon."[44] David Cremin was mentioned as at Dorchester in 1700.[45]

Thomas Connell bought a "house, gardens and eighty-six acres of land in Mount Willystone" from William Baulston, by deed dated August 5, 1638,[46] and Thomas Connell and his wife, Mary, sold this property on July 7, 1645.[47] "Sarah

[36] Boston Town Books, Vol. 10, p. 88.
[37] *The Pioneers of Maine and New Hampshire,* by Rev. Charles Henry Pope.
[38] *Massachusetts Archives,* Vol. 3, p. 215.
[39] Vol. 6.
[40] Savage's *Genealogical Dictionary,* Vol. 1, p. 482.
[41] Boston Town Books, Vol. 29.
[42] *Ibid.,* Vol. 1, p. 70.
[43] Tax Lists in Town Books, Vol. 1.
[44] Savage's *Genealogical Dictionary,* Vol. 1, p. 335.
[45] Dorchester Town Records.
[46] Boston Town Books, Vol. 2, p. 38.
[47] *Pioneers of Massachusetts,* by Rev. Charles Henry Pope, p. 114.

Connell, servant to Walter Abbott" of Strawberry Bank, now Portsmouth, N. H., when testifying in a suit tried in the York County Court on August 16, 1655, said that she had "told her countrymen about the case"; [48] Mary Connell was married in Boston to Johannes Demosmaker on January 4, 1664; Timothy Connell enlisted under Captain Joshua Scottow for King Philip's War on January 15, 1676; "William Connell, son of Tymothy Connell," was mentioned in Boston town records as "apprentice to John Eaton of Readinge" in 1680; [49] Philip Connel and Elizabeth Atwood were married at Malden in 1688; and "Timothy Connel of Oyster River," son of William Connell, signed a petition to the New Hampshire Legislature on May 5, 1716, for a grant of land. A Thomas Cooke was a resident of Boston in 1679. By deed dated June 20, 1681, Anthony Haywood conveyed to John Spread "a parcel of land and flatts scituate at the northerly end of the town of Boston," for a consideration of £472, "for Acco^tt^ of Thomas Cooke of Corke in the Kingdom of Ireland, merchant, now resident in Boston, to the onely use, benefit and behoof of Thomas Cooke, his heirs and assignees for ever." [50] There is nothing in the records to indicate that Cooke was an Irishman.

In the probate book at Plymouth, Barnstable County, Mass., there is an item reading thus: "Inventory of a certain Irishman named Cornelius, who died at Barnstable 15 December, 1664, £1, 18s, 6d. Debts £1, 12s, od." It is probable, from the manner in which he was referred to, that he was an indentured servant, and since the death of one Cornelius Croggin was recorded at Barnstable on December 15, 1664, it is clear that the "certain Irishman" here mentioned was Cor-

[48] *Pioneers of Massachusetts*, by Rev. Charles Henry Pope, p. 45.

[49] Boston Town Books, Vol. 7, p. 142.

[50] Suffolk County Registry of Deeds, Lib. 12, fol. 74.

nelius Croggin. A Thomas Croggin was at Taunton in 1643,[51] and he may have been the Thomas Croggin who died at Barnstable on February 26, 1658. John Creagan was a resident of Woburn in 1662; a John Craggin was mentioned in Concord town records on February 25, 1692, and a number of Cragins and Craggons appear in the vital records of that town in the early part of the eighteenth century. These are common names in Ireland and are from the original O'Criochain or O'Crehan, once a numerous family in County Fermanagh.[52]

From the colonial records of Connecticut we learn that one Nicholas Daly was made a Freeman of the Colony by the General Court in the year 1663; but as to what place he occupied in the life of the day or whence he came, search fails to disclose. He lived at Colchester, and at Woodbury, Windham County, and is mentioned in a work by Royal R. Hinman,[53] a former Secretary of State, who says the Daly family had "three Coats of Arms, all Irish." If the inference is correct, that he used these "Arms," it would appear that Nicholas Daly must have been a man of some importance; yet there is not the slightest mention of him in any town or county history. In Colchester town records of December 10, 1708, there is an entry of the birth of "John Daley, son of Joseph and Patience Daley," and it is thought this Joseph was a son of Nicholas Daly. People of the name turn up frequently in Connecticut eighteenth century records, especially in Windham County; also in the rolls of the Connecticut troops raised for service in the colonial wars, there were listed Cornelius, Daniel, Eben, Jacob, James, Jeremiah, John, Justus, Nicholas and Samuel, whose surnames were spelled variously,

[51] Plymouth Colony Records, Vol. 8, p. 195.

[52] *Irish Pedigrees*, by John O'Hart, Vol. 1, p. 618.

[53] *A Catalogue of the Names of the Early Puritan Settlers in the Colony of Connecticut*, Hartford, 1852.

Daly, Dailey, Dayly and Dayley; but there is no assurance that any of these men were descendants of the original Nicholas Daly.

Braintree, Mass., vital records contain an entry under date of "6th mo. 18, 1669," covering the birth of "Samuel, son of John and Elizabeth Daly." Thomas Daley was married at Salem on September 16, 1682, and in the town records there is an entry of the birth of "Mary, daughter of Thomas Daley," at Salem on July 6, 1685.[54] In Mendon, Mass., vital records there are entered the births of Joseph, John, Benjamin and Abigail, children of "John and Elizabeth Dayly," the earliest on March 25, 1679, and the last on January 30, 1694. Joseph Dailey bought lands at Providence from James Phillips on August 27, 1689, which he sold to his son, Joseph, by deed dated April 13, 1703, and both appear in the tax lists of the town.

Patrick Daniell was listed among "Massachusetts Freemen, 1634 to 1655";[55] William Dempsey took the oath of allegiance before Governor Simon Bradstreet at Boston on April 21, 1679,[56] and on December 4th of that year William Dempsey signed as witness to a deed between John Glover of Dorchester and John Glover, Jr.[57] John Downey was a witness in a case tried in the Ipswich Court on April 27, 1665;[58] William "Douney" was mentioned in the same record and a William Downey was on "Rumney Marsh Tax List" in 1691.[59] "John Donogen, servant to Nathaniel Treadwell," was mentioned as in Essex County in 1677.[60] "Jude Donley, a servant" came to Boston in "the *Confidence* of London" in

54 Salem Town Records, in *Essex Institute Historical Collections*, Vol. 2, p. 42.
55 List of Freemen in *New England Historic-Genealogical Register*, Vol. 3.
56 Boston Town Books, Vol. 29, p. 169.
57 Suffolk County Registry of Deeds, Lib. 11, fol. 258.
58 Essex County Court Records, Vol. 3, p. 255.
59 Boston Town Books, Vol. 1.
60 Essex County Court Records, Vol. 7, p. 267.

July, 1638,[61] and Edward Dulen was among the "passengers aboard the *John and Sarah* of London" which sailed "for Boston in New England" on November 11, 1651,[62] but in Massachusetts records there is no indication of his whereabouts in the Colony.

It is interesting to observe that the Dongan family of County Kildare, Ireland, one of whom was Thomas Dongan, the distinguished Colonial Governor of New York (1683-1688), was represented in New England. Frances, widow of William Dungan, a brother of Sir John Dongan of Castletown, County Kildare, married Jeremy Clarke in London, England, and sometime before the year 1655 they emigrated to Rhode Island with her children, Thomas, William, Frances and Barbara Dungan. The family settled at Newport, and Thomas Dungan first appears on record there, in a "Roule of ye ffreemen of ye Colonie for everie Towne" of the year 1655. He and Charles McCarthy, supposed to have come from Kinsale, County Cork, appear among the patentees in the charter of the town of East Greenwich, R. I., dated October 31, 1677, and in the next year he was elected a Representative from that town to the Rhode Island Assembly. In 1684, he sold his property in Newport and removed to Cold Spring, Bucks County, Pennsylvania, where he became a Baptist Minister and established there a church of that denomination. His daughter, Sarah, married James Carroll, and his daughter, Rebecca, married Edmund Doyle, both in Bucks County. We are told that "Edmund Doyle emigrated from Ireland in the year 1683, on the ship *Lion* of Liverpool as an indentured servant to Joseph Fisher of Stillorgan, near Dublin, and arrived in the Delaware River on August 14, 1683. The term of service was four years, he to receive £4. 10s. and fifty acres of land. He was free August 14, 1687,

61 *New England Historic-Genealogical Register*, Vol. 14, p. 310.

62 List of passengers in Suffolk County Registry of Deeds, Vol. 1, fol. 5.

and probably married Rebecca Dongan shortly thereafter.[63] Edmund was the grandfather of William Doyle, founder of Doylestown, Pa.

All of this branch of the Dongan family, as well as their American descendants, spelled the name Dungan. Gilbert, in his *History of Affairs in Ireland,* states the family patronymic was O'Donegan, but after the "O" was dropped, sometime in the sixteenth century, the name was variously spelled, Donegan, Dongan, Dungan, Donaghe, Donagane, Dunghen and in other forms. "Hannah Dongan of Oyster River" was listed as one of several "prisoners in hands of the French in Canada" in October, 1695,[64] but her relationship to the Dungans or Dongans of Rhode Island has not been ascertained. In 1696, Barbara Dungan became the wife of James Barker of Newport, Deputy Governor of Rhode Island for fourteen years. Her name appears in the parish register as "Barbara Dugan, daughter of William and Frances Dugan."

One Thomas Dunn came to Massachusetts in the *Defence* in July, 1635;[65] a Thomas Dunn of Weymouth, Mass., believed to have been the same man, was made a Freeman by the Massachusetts General Court on May 6, 1646, but two years later he removed to New Haven, Conn., "bought an estate at Fairfield and died there in 1660."[66] A case entitled "Willm Dunne *vs.* William Halloway," on a charge of "trespass," was tried before the Court of Assistants at New Plymouth on August 3, 1641,[67] and in 1675 "William Dunn was one of the first purchasers of land at Taunton."[68] In 1655

[63] *Ancestry of Jeremy Clarke of Rhode Island and Dungan Genealogy,* compiled by Alfred R. Justice, p. 121, Philadelphia, 1927. There is a very long account of the Dongans and Doyles and their descendants for ten generations in this work, pages 115 to 530.

[64] List in *New England Historic-Genealogical Register,* Vol. 6, p. 87.

[65] *Pioneers of Massachusetts,* by Rev. Charles Henry Pope, p. 147.

[66] *New Hampshire Genealogical Record,* Vol. 1, p. 148.

[67] Plymouth Colony Records, Vol. 7, p. 22.

[68] *New Hampshire Genealogical Record,* Vol. 1, p. 148.

Richard Dunn was made a Freeman of the Colony of Rhode Island; in 1661 he was a resident of Newport, and was taxed there down to the year 1680, was a "Deputy to the General Court" in 1681, and was the father of Richard, Samuel and Nathaniel Dunn, all born at Newport. Joseph Dunn was at Salem in 1663;[69] John Dunn was mentioned as at New Haven in 1657;[70] Nicholas Dunn was at Cochecho, N. H., in 1689, and on February 20th of that year he signed an address of "The Inhabitants and Train Soldiers of New Hampshire."[71] Hugh Dunn was listed among New Hampshire landowners in the Piscataqua region in 1663; in that year he was made a Freeman, and in 1664 he received grants of land in the towns of Dover and Durham. Because of some "disquietude in property holdings and unsettled land titles," he sold his property in New Hampshire and removed to New Jersey. A marriage license was recorded at Piscataway, N. J., on December 19, 1670, between Hugh Dunn and Elizabeth Drake, a native of Drakesworth, County Meath, Ireland, who is said to have been related to the Dongans of Kildare. Hugh Dunn was "one of the original patentees in 1666 of the large township of New Pascataway,"[72] and became a very prominent man in the Province.

In a list of "men who took the oath of fidelity in Scituate from 1633 to 1668,"[73] appears the name, Richard Dogan, but this is the only mention of him. Christopher Dolan was mentioned in the records of the Essex County Quarterly Court in 1681.[74] In 1633, "Richard Duffy, servant to Richard Saltonstall" of Ipswich, was sentenced by the Court "to be

69 *Ibid.*, p. 319.

70 New Haven Town Records.

71 Provincial Papers of New Hampshire, Vol. 2, p. 34.

72 *New Hampshire Genealogical Record*, Vol. 1, p. 149.

73 In *History of Scituate, Mass.*, by S. Deane, p. 155.

74 Court Records, Vol. 8, p. 452.

whipped for misdemeanor toward his master";[75] and on March 29, 1645, John Duffy of Exeter signed a petition to the Provincial Court in relation to "disputed bounds."[76] The marriage of "Andrew Devin and An Donstall" was recorded at Dedham on September 10, 1652, and Richard Deven was a resident of the town in 1679.[77] William Dillon was listed among "Early Settlers of Essex and Old Norfolk Counties" in 1659, and John Dillon was appointed "Constable of Monhegin" (Maine) by order of the General Court on March 7, 1673.[78] Mary Dinan was one of the "Early Settlers of Essex and old Norfolk Counties" in 1665,[79] and in the same year the marriage of Jonathan Wilt and Mary Dinan was recorded at Lynn.[80] Dennis Darley is mentioned by Farmer[81] as "an early settler at Braintree, Mass." Robert Doyle and Johanna Farrar were married at Woburn on September 30, 1680;[82] the death of two children of Robert and Johanna Doyle appears in Woburn vital records in 1698 and 1700; at Westerly, Rhode Island, "William, son of William and Elizabeth Doyle," was born on August 2, 1698;[83] and in the eighteenth century vital records of that town there are entries of the births of eleven grandchildren of William Doyle.

"Crobar Dunnavan" was defendant in an action brought against him by Henry Dearing for recovery of a debt, and the case was tried in the Essex County Quarterly Court on

[75] Ipswich, Mass., Town Records.

[76] Provincial Papers of New Hampshire, Vol. 24, p. 847.

[77] Boston Town Books, Vol. 10, p. 63.

[78] Records of the Court of Assistants, Vol. 1, p. 12.

[79] *New England Historic-Genealogical Register*, Vol. 7.

[80] *Ibid.*, Vol. 6, p. 253.

[81] *Genealogical Register of the First Settlers in New England.*

[82] "Memoir of the Farrar Family," in *New England Historic-Genealogical Register*, Vol. 6, p. 319.

[83] *Vital Records of Rhode Island*, Vol. 5, p. 100.

August 26, 1675.[84] On March 21, 1684, Daniel Duggan was one of a number of "petitioners" who appeared before the Council of New Hampshire; in 1685 he joined other inhabitants of Portsmouth in a petition to the King, praying for relief from certain conditions "brought about by Robert Mason, the proprietor," [85] and Daniel Duggan was named as one of the creditors of James Jones of Portsmouth, N.H., in the inventory of the latter's estate, filed in Court May 4, 1686.[86] As "Daniel Duggins," he was listed on May 11, 1693, among a number of persons who were fined five shillings each "for not appearing with their arms"; [87] and on August 10, 1694, the New Hampshire Council ordered "that Daniel Duggan be paid for 36 days work at fourt Wm. & Mary." Samuel Duggan, "servant to Richard Martyn of Portsmouth," was named in the latter's will dated January 7, 1693, [88] and in 1702 letters of administration to "the estate of Samuel Dugan" were granted by the Suffolk County Probate Court.

Edward and James Dwyer were at Exeter, and in 1695 Edward Dwyer appears in the roster of Captain Kingsley Hall's Exeter military company.[89] Downing is a frequently occurring name in early New England records. Derman and John Downing, brothers, were mentioned in a deed dated July 5, 1648, as owners of lands at Braintree; [90] "Dennis Downing, blacksmith at Kittery," is mentioned in 1650; in November, 1652, he "swore allegiance to Massachusetts"; he sold lands at Kittery to Joane Dyamont on June 20, 1679, and signed the deed "Dinnis Downeing." [91] The last mention

[84] Court Records, Vol. 6, p. 140.

[85] *Provincial Papers of New Hampshire,* Vol. 1, p. 559.

[86] New Hampshire Probate Records, Vol. 1, p. 296.

[87] Provincial Papers of New Hampshire, Vol. 5, p. 106.

[88] Probate Records, Vol. 2, p. 296.

[89] *Provincial Papers of New Hampshire,* Vol. 2, p. 662.

[90] Suffolk Deeds, Lib. 5, fol. 456.

[91] York Deeds, Book 3, fol. 47.

of him was on July 4, 1697, when he was "killed by the Indians" at Kittery.

New London was the gateway through which many of the early settlers entered the country, and at various times in the seventeenth century a number of persons, who in all probability were natives of Ireland, are mentioned in New London records. In April, 1635, one Philemon Dalton, described as "a lynnean weaver," with his wife, Hannah, and one son arrived there in "the ship *Increase* from London," accompanied by Daniel Buckley, Thomas Barrett, and "William White, age 14, his servant." Also, between 1652 and 1658, James Kelly and Thomas Mullen were mentioned in the town records. William Collins was a resident of the town between 1654 and 1663, and Peter Collins, who died there in 1655, was listed as one of "the early grantees of town lots." Philemon Dalton removed to Dedham, Mass., and on March 3, 1636, he was made a Freeman by the Massachusetts General Court. Three years later Philemon and Timothy Dalton went to Hampton, N. H., with a band of settlers from Essex County and on December 24, 1639, the town of Hampton gave Philemon a grant of 100 acres, and Timothy 300 acres of land.[92] In the will of Timothy Dalton dated March 8, 1657, he named his wife, Ruth, brother, Philemon, and cousin, Samuel Dalton;[93] and Timothy Dalton, son of Timothy (1), was mentioned in Salem court records in October, 1677.[94] Nicholas Dalton took the oath of allegiance at Boston on November 11, 1678;[95] Michael Dalton took the oath on April 21, 1679, and John Dalton was one of the legatees under the will of Henry Palmer of Haverhill, dated July 10,

92 Town Register, Hampton, N. H.

93 Essex County Probate Files, in *Provincial Papers of New Hampshire,* Vol. 31, p. 36.

94 Records and Files of the Quarterly Court, Vol. 6.

95 Boston Town Books, Vol. 29.

1680.[96] There is nothing on record, or in any of the references to these Daltons in the journals of the historical societies, stating definitely what their nationality was, but Dalton is such a frequently occurring name among the Irish as to justify the assumption that these early New Englanders were of the old Norman family of that name that has been in Ireland for more than six centuries. The name is very common in the midland counties of Ireland.

"John Eagon from Boston" was mentioned in Charlestown records on October 6, 1674, and "John Egan and his wife were disallowed to be inhabitants" on December 15, 1674. They had a son, Hugh, and a "Dr. Hugh Agan of Andover" who was married to Elizabeth Giddings at Ipswich on June 2, 1737, is believed to have been one of their descendants. "Thomas Farrall of Cohannett" was listed among "persons proposed to be Freemen" at the Plymouth Court on September 3, 1669; [97] Farmer mentions "John Farell, a Freeman at Dedham in 1654"; [98] Savage lists "Benjamin Farrell, a soldier in Lathrop's company" in King Philip's War,[99] though he expresses some doubt as to whether his name was Farrell or Farwell, and the historian of the war lists this man as "Benjamin ffarnell." He was "killed at Bloody Brook, September 18, 1675." At a session of the Court of Assistants on October 14, 1685, "Mr. Jn° Bisco Appeared and Complayned again^st^ his servant James Farrell with John Macolly servant to m^r^ Joseph Sherman that Gott into the cellar," and they were admonished by the Court.[100]

Edmund FitzMorris was one of a number of persons recorded as arriving in Boston on January 29, 1676, who were

[96] Essex Probate Records, Vol. 3, p. 382.

[97] Plymouth Colony Records, Vol. 1, pp. 128 and 132.

[98] *Genealogical Register of the First Settlers of New England*, p. 340.

[99] *Genealogical Dictionary*, Vol. 2, p. 145.

[100] Records of the Court of Assistants, Vol. 1, p. 286.

"returned to ye court,"[101] and as "Edward Ffeitzmorris" he was again listed in the town records under date of January 29, 1677.[102] A power of attorney from Thomas Foley and others to William Tyng, dated September 10, 1652, was recorded at the Suffolk County Registry of Deeds,[103] and a similar instrument from Thomas Foley to John Becx dated February 25, 1658.[104] A Thomas Foley appears in the records of the Essex County Quarterly Court under date of September 29, 1655, in legal proceedings against John Gifford,[105] and on March 11, 1660, Thomas Foley and "other inhabitants of the Province of New Hampshire" signed a petition to the "Council for Foreign Plantations."[106] This Thomas Foley is said to have been "one of a company of Englishmen who owned the iron works at Lynn in 1657."

A very large number of Farleys appear in Billerica, Mass., vital records, all descended from Timothy Farley who settled at that place some time in the seventeenth century. He served as a soldier in King Philip's War and was "slaine by ye Indians at Quaboag"[107] (now Brookfield, Mass.). His son, Timothy, married Abigail Foster on November 1, 1704. There is no mention anywhere of the nationality of the first of the family, and although people of this name are now generally regarded as Irish, some of Timothy Farley's descendants are of the belief that he was an Englishman, which is quite possible because the name occurs among English families of the period. Michael Farley was at Ipswich in 1675, and "Michael Farley, a corn miller at Rock Falls, uppon Ipswich River," was mentioned in 1682. At a session of the Essex Court at Salem in

[101] Boston Town Books, Vol. 7, p. 107.
[102] *Ibid.*, Vol. 10, p. 57.
[103] Lib. 1.
[104] Lib. 3.
[105] Court Records, Vol. 8, p. 173.
[106] *Provincial Papers of New Hampshire*, Vol. 23, p. 24.
[107] Billerica, Mass., Vital Records.

March, 1676, there was tried a case entitled "Edward Lomas *vs.* Michaell Farley," [108] and "an action for appeale from the Judg^t of the County Court at Salem," entitled "Michael Farley against Edward Lummas," was tried at the Essex Court in 1681.

Thomas Finnan received a grant of land from the town of Ipswich on April 20, 1635, described as "beyond Chebocca creeke." [109] "Thomas Fallan" was appointed surveyor of highways at Yarmouth on June 8, 1655. His son, "Thomas Fallon, Jr.," was on the Plymouth County Grand Jury in 1681,[110] and as "Thomas Fallen" he brought suit against William Nickerson in the County Court in 1686.[111] He appears to have been a man of some local importance, and while his name and that of his father was recorded as here stated, he also appears several times as "Thomas Folland." In 1677 Patrick Flannery was mentioned as an indentured servant to John Holbrooke of Scituate. The guardians of the law hailed master and servant before the Plymouth County Court on June 3, 1679, charging them with the offence of "playing at cards," and Holbrooke was "fined one pound" and "his man, Patrick, at the same time, ten shillings." [112]

A Patrick Fassett, who appears frequently in Massachusetts town records, is believed to have been an Irishman, and judging by the references that are made to him, he seems to have been a sort of roving mechanic, going from place to place with his tools and equipment. His wife's name was Sarah Reilly. As "Patriach Mackfassy" he was recorded on October

[108] Court Records, Vol. 6, p. 119.

[109] *The Ancient Records of the Town of Ipswich,* ed. by George A. Schofield, Ipswich, 1899.

[110] Plymouth Colony Records, Vol. 3, p. 79, and Vol. 6, p. 60. See also *Civil, Military and Professional Lists of the Plymouth and Rhode Island Colonies,* compiled by Ebenezer W. Peirce, Boston, 1881.

[111] Plymouth Colony Records, Vol. 6, p. 197.

[112] *Ibid.,* Vol. 8, p. 152.

3, 1670, on which date "John, son of Patriach & Sarah Mackfassy," was born at Charlestown, and in the next year "Patrick Fassett, brother in law of John Reyley," was listed as a resident of the town.[113] He was taxed at Malden in 1672, and on June 2, 1679, Patrick Fassett was "admitted an inhabitant" at Billerica; but as "Patrick ffacit" he appears in the tax records of that year. He had seven sons and two daughters, the births of four of whom appear in Billerica vital records between 1679 and 1685; and down through the eighteenth century there are numerous entries of the name in Massachusetts town records. He died on November 7, 1713, and in the next year "Letters of Administration to the estate of Patrick Fassett of Billerica" were granted by the probate Court of Middlesex County.[114] His grandson, John Fassett of Bennington, Vt., has been described as "a leading man in that company of wise and brave pioneers who resisted the encroachments of New York and laid the foundations of Vermont, making the name Green Mountain Boys famous." [115]

The records of the Essex County Court show that John Garvin was "fined for abusing Richard Middleton" on May 20, 1658; [116] Salem town records inform us that "John Garven was drowned 5: 12: 61"; [117] and in March, 1662, the Court appointed George Corwin "administrator of the estate of John Garven, cast away at sea." [118] Andrew Greeley and his wife, Mary, ancestors of Horace Greeley, founder and editor of the *New York Tribune*, settled at Salisbury, Mass.,

113 *Genealogies and Estates of Charlestown*, by Thomas B. Wyman.

114 Many Fassetts appeared in the probate books of this County throughout the eighteenth century.

115 "Genealogical Register" in *History of Billerica, Mass.*, by Rev. Henry A. Hagen, Boston, 1883.

116 Court Records, Vol. 2, p. 107.

117 Salem Town Records, in *Essex Institute Historical Collections*, Vol. 2, p. 148.

118 Court Records, Vol. 2, p. 369.

about 1640, in which year Andrew first appeared in the town records as building "a tide mill for the grinding of corn on Kane's River." They were the parents of Andrew, Philip, Joseph, Benjamin and Mary Greeley, born at Salisbury, between 1644 and 1654.[119] He was described variously as "a surveyor" and "a shoe maker," and on December 27, 1653, he was appointed town constable.[120] In 1664 Andrew Greeley and John Osgood were joint owners of a sawmill at Haverhill, and at the annual town meeting in 1668 "the town did make choice of Andrew Greeley, Sen, to keep the ferry at Haverhill." [121] In 1677 Andrew Greeley and Michael Emerson were appointed "joint sealers of leather" at Haverhill, and the County historian expresses it as his belief that "Michael Emerson was an Irishman." [122] An elaborate genealogy of the Greeleys was published by one of their descendants, but, as in so many other cases of early New England settlers bearing Irish names, there is not the slightest reference in this work to the nationality of the immigrant ancestor of the family. "Mary Greeley, an Irishwoman," who is supposed to have been the wife of Andrew, was mentioned in the Essex County Court records in 1670,[123] and "Richard Greeley, an Irishman," was so mentioned in the Court records in 1673. John Greeley and his wife, Elizabeth, were at Newbury in 1695. Andrew Greeley (2) married Sarah Brown and had Andrew, Henry, Mary, Abigail, Sarah, Rachel, Hannah and Judith, born at Salisbury between 1674 and 1696. Andrew and his son, Andrew, junior, were listed among the taxpayers at Hampton Falls, N. H., in 1709; according to the probate

[119] Salisbury, Mass., Vital Records.

[120] *Trades and Tradesmen of Essex County*, compiled by Henry W. Belknap, The Essex Institute, 1929.

[121] *History of Essex County*, by D. Hamilton Hurd, Vol. 2, p. 1931, Philadelphia, 1888.

[122] *Ibid.*, Vol. 2, p. 1938.

[123] Records and Files of the Quarterly Court, Vol. 3.

records the Greeleys operated a "mill in ye township of Salisbury"[124] in 1713; and on July 27, 1721, "Andrew Greelee and Henry Ambrose, borderers upon the partition line between N Hamp^{r} and Mass," were brought before the Council at Portsmouth because of their refusal to pay their taxes.[125] By deed dated November 18, 1701, James Treworthy sold to Thomas Greeley lands near Mast Cove in the town of Kittery, and also "all fences erected and improved by my predecessor, John Bready"; and John McGoune was one of the witnesses to the deed.[126] Bryan Gilmore and Mary Rucker were married at Boston on August 2, 1701, and in that year "Briant Gilmore" received an abatement of his taxes.[127]

[124] New Hampshire Probate Records, Vol. 31, p. 703.

[125] *Provincial Papers of New Hampshire,* Vol. 2, p. 742.

[126] York Deeds, Lib. 6, fol. 115.

[127] Boston Town Books, Vol. 10, pp. 141, 144.

CHAPTER XII

Gleasons, Gilligans and Gearys—Hayes and Higgins frequently recorded—William Heffernan an important man in Rhode Island—Ann Miles from Tipperary at Lynn, Mass., 1681—Mary Jordan from Cork at New London—Joyce a common name in the Cape Cod Peninsula, 1637 to 1755.

PEOPLE named Gleason appear in the town records of Charlestown, Cambridge, Sudbury, Framingham and Oxford, Mass., but there is nothing to indicate their racial identity. The Irish origin of the name Gleason has been disputed by a Massachusetts historical writer, yet the Gleasons, originally O'Glasain or O'Gliasain, a name common in the south of Ireland for centuries, are listed among the "ancient Irish families" as chiefs of the Barony of Imokilly in the County of Cork,[1] and the motto on their coat of arms is in the Irish language, *Lamb Laidir An Uachdar,* meaning "the strong hand uppermost." "Mary, daughter of Thomas and Susanna Gleason," was born at Cambridge on October 31, 1657, and other children mentioned in the records of Middlesex County [2] were Thomas, Joseph, William and John. In 1663, Thomas Gleason (1) leased a farm from a Captain Scarlett at Charlestown. His sons, Thomas and John, located at Sudbury and Thomas bought a tract of land "on Gleason's Pond" near Framingham, from Benjamin Rice by deed dated September 29, 1673; [3] and according to the genealogy of the

[1] *Irish Pedigrees,* by John O'Hart, Vol. 1, p. 808.
[2] Vol. 1, p. 158, and Vol. 6, p. 13.
[3] Middlesex Deeds, Vol. 6, p. 378.

Gleasons [4] his descendants lived there for at least four generations. John and William Gleason and Philip Gleason served in King Philip's War, and Thomas Gleason and his son, Thomas, were listed among the thirty incorporators of the town of Framingham in 1692. John Gleason had land assigned to him at Sherburne, Mass., in 1682, and he was the father of eight children born at that place between 1680 and 1700.[5]

Alexander Gilligan and his wife, Frances, received mention several times in the records of the Essex County Court between 1667 and 1670, and in June, 1679, a "Mrs. Magilligon." He was master of a vessel registered at Marblehead, and was listed in the town records among the 114 "householders" who comprised the whole population of the town in the year 1674, to whom "privileges of commonage were granted and conferred by the General Court on October 5, 1674." [6] The name was recorded variously Gilligan, Gelligin, Gillican, and Gilliginn. At the Suffolk County Registry of Deeds [7] there was recorded a deed dated November 27, 1683, by which "Mary English, the Relict widdow and Sole Executrix of William English, late of Boston," conveyed "a dwelling house, with an orchard, yard and garden" in Boston to "Ferdinando Gilligan of Belfast in ye Kingdom of Ireland, at present residing in Boston, Merchant," and Nicholas Lynch signed as one of the witnesses.

"Denis Geary of Lynn came from London in the *Abigail* in 1635, and his wife, Elizabeth, and two daughters, Elizabeth and Sarah," and William Geary of Salem was made a Free-

[4] In *History of Framingham*, by William Barry, and "Genealogical Register" in *History of Framingham*, by J. H. Temple.

[5] *Genealogical Register of the Inhabitants of the Towns of Sherborn and Holliston*, compiled by Rev. Abner Morse, Boston, 1856.

[6] *Maine Genealogist and Biographer*, p. 55.

[7] Lib. 13, fol. 190.

man on June 2, 1641.[8] Arthur Geary was mentioned as of Roxbury in 1638; on March 14, 1639, he was made a Freeman by the General Court and his death at Roxbury was recorded on December 17, 1666. "William Garey of Roxbury" was made a Freeman on May 7, 1651, and on April 11, 1679, Nicholas and William Garey appeared before the Governor and took the oath of allegiance. Thomas Geary was on the Charlestown tax list of the year 1688; a "Thomas Geary of Stoneham" was listed among the men enrolled for King Philip's War, and local records show that seven Gearys from that town were soldiers of the Revolution.[9]

A Daniel Hanbury came from London to Massachusetts in the *Planter* in 1635; Luke Hanbury was in the Colony in 1637, and at "a Quarter Court held at Newetowne" on March 6, 1638, Luke Heneberry was convicted of "theft," and was "censured to bee severely whiped & for runing away." [10] William Hanbury was at Duxbury in 1639, and Peter Hanbury was mentioned in the town records of Sandwich, Mass., in 1643. The name was sometimes rendered in Massachusetts records "Henbury" and "Henebury," and since it is evident it was so pronounced, it is probable that these people were of the old family of Henebry or Henneberry, a common name in Waterford, Ireland. One Edward Harnett and his son Ed-

[8] *Genealogical Dictionary of the First Settlers of New England,* by James Savage, Vol. 2, p. 240.

[9] Nearly all their descendants in the male line now spell the name "Gary" and pronounce it *Garry,* notwithstanding that for two hundred years it was recorded in the Irish form, Geary, or by its phonetic spelling, Garey. Many of the name are mentioned in Massachusetts town records. For example, in 1741 Benjamin Geary of Reading was "surety on the guardianship bond of John Geary of Stoneham, guardian of David Geary, son of Thomas Geary of Stoneham, deceased." Edward Geary and Phebe Holden were married at Lynn on December 9, 1750; administration to "the estate of John Holden" was granted to "Edward Geary of Lunenburg" on April 19, 1756; "Thomas Geary of Lunenburg" married Elizabeth Farwell on February 21, 1760, and so on down to the end of the eighteenth century.

[10] Records of the Court of Assistants, Vol. 2, p. 72.

ward, received grants of land at Salem in the year 1639;[11] in 1645 Edward Harnett was mentioned in the records of the Essex County Court[12] and Thomas Harney in 1674;[13] and a Peter Harney appears at Salem as of February 11, 1676.[14] Thomas Hyland was listed among inhabitants of Scituate who took the oath of allegiance on February 1, 1638;[15] in 1646 he was a member of the "Grand Inquest," and on June 7, 1648, he was appointed "Constable for Seteaat."[16] On June 7, 1653, "Thomas Hieland" and his son, Thomas, were fined at the Plymouth Court, and "Thomas Hieland, Jr.," was the town constable in 1683.[17] The name Hyland receives frequent mention in seventeenth and eighteenth century records and four Hylands from Scituate served in the War of the Revolution. William Hearne witnessed a bill of sale dated March 8, 1676, filed in Suffolk County, on a vessel named *Thomas and Mary,* covering security for "debts due Thaddeus Mackarty of Boston" by persons in Jamaica.[18]

Robert Hayes was listed among the "First Settlers of Ipswich" in 1635,[19] where he received a grant of land on February 5, 1637, and on March 2nd of the same year "the company of ffreemen gave Robert Hayes a house lott and one acre, and six acres for planting ground."[20] Edmund

11 *Genealogical Dictionary of the First Settlers of New England,* by James Savage, Vol. 2.

12 Court Records, Vol. 1, p. 92.

13 *Ibid.,* Vol. 5, p. 340.

14 O'Hart (*Irish Pedigrees,* Vol. 1, p. 809) states that the Harnetts were originally O'Harneys, one of the "Clans of note in Kerry."

15 Plymouth Colony Records, Vol. 1, p. 110.

16 *Ibid.,* Vol. 2, pp. 102 and 104.

17 *Ibid.,* Vol. 3, p. 46, and Vol. 6, p. 107.

18 Suffolk County Registry of Deeds, Lib. 14, fol. 113.

19 *Ipswich in the Massachusetts Bay Colony,* by Thos. F. Waters, p. 490, Ipswich Historical Society, 1905.

20 *The Ancient Records of the Town of Ipswich,* ed. by George A. Schofield, Ipswich, 1889.

Hayes was a merchant at Kittery, Maine, in 1665,[21] and the probate of his will dated July 2, 1675, was recorded in York County on March 9, 1676.[22] Christopher Hayes and Sarah King were married at Charlestown on October 2, 1669;[23] Sylvester Hayes was there in 1668,[24] and as "Sylvester Haies of Charlestown," he was listed among Massachusetts soldiers in King Philip's War (1676). The marriage of John Hayes and Mary Horne was recorded at Dover, N. H., on June 1, 1686; John Hayes signed as witness to a release executed by John Ham of Dover dated January 24, 1689;[25] on February 20th of that year he signed an address of the "Inhabitants and Train Soldiers" of New Hampshire;[26] and a "Quitt clame to John Hayes and Peter Hayes" was mentioned in the will of John Tuttle of Dover, dated December 8, 1717.[27] "Eliza, daughter of Thomas and Bridget Hayes," was born at Boston, on July 25, 1690; Patrick Hayes and Mary Kibbee were married at Reading, Mass., on March 26, 1685;[28] "Mary, daughter of Patrick Hay," was born at Lynn in 1686;[29] but on her marriage at that place in 1705 she was recorded "Mary Hayes."

A family of the name was at Norwalk, Conn., in 1655, and Samuel and Nathaniel Hayes, brothers, were listed among Norwalk freemen in 1669. Samuel married Elizabeth Moore of Farmington about 1665; Nathaniel married Mary Kimberley, and in the will of her father, Thomas Kimberley, in 1672, he named his grandchildren, Nathaniel, Mary and Elizabeth

[21] York Deeds, Vol. 1.

[22] York County Records, Part 1, fol. 10.

[23] Charlestown, Mass., Vital Records.

[24] Selectmen's Records, p. 93.

[25] New Hampshire Deeds, Vol. 5, p. 88.

[26] *Provincial Papers of New Hampshire,* Vol. 2, p. 34.

[27] Probate Records, Vol. 31, p. 814.

[28] Reading, Mass., Vital Records.

[29] Lynn, Mass., Vital Records, Vol. 1, pp. 74 and 185.

Hayes. In November, 1706, "Mary Bouton chose James Hayes as her guardian," and in her will, dated July 16, 1720, she named her "grandchild, Mary Hayes." Luke Hayes, schoolmaster at Farmington, married Maudlin Fountain of Greenwich, and on May 3, 1716, she married Dennis Hogan, described as "Dennis Hoogin of Ireland," [30] and while the latter's name also appears as "Dennis Higgins," his son, James, was baptised "James Hogans" in 1743. In the will of Rachel Messenger of Norwalk, dated April 17, 1738, she mentioned her "cousin Thomas Hayes" and Samuel and James Hayes. Although no information is obtainable as to the history of these various people, and in no case is there any mention of their nationality, the fact that Hayes is such a common Irish name justifies our placing them in that category. The Gaelic of the name is *O'h-Aodha* (pronounced *o-hay*), derived from Aodh, meaning Hugh. It was anglicized O'Hea, Hay, and sometimes Hughes. The custom of referring to members of the family as "the O'Heas," explains why in course of time Hayes became the permanent form of the name in some branches.

Families named Heffernan are met with frequently in early Rhode Island records, all descended from William Heffernan, who first appeared in 1661 at Scituate, Mass., as "William Hiferney." On June 10th of that year a complaint was made to Governor Prence of the Plymouth Colony by "William Hiferney, Irish Man, servant to John Hollot of Scituate," between whom there was a dispute over the period of the former's indentures. On behalf of the complainant it was said "hee is bound to his said master the tearme of twelve yeares, having bin stollen away out of his owne countrey and engaging for soe long a time when hee was unaquainted with the English tongue"; and thereupon the Governor adjusted the dispute by "remitting two yeares off the time of his serv-

[30] *Schools and Schoolmasters in Farmington,* by Julius Gay, in Connecticut Historical Society Collections.

ice."[31] Three years later he was released, and "William Heffernan and Susanna Groce" were married at Scituate, and then removed to a place known by the Indian name of Pittaquamscutt in Rhode Island. In a deed dated April 3, 1665, recorded in Suffolk County,[32] there was mentioned the will of Edmond Groce, in which he named as legatees his "daughter, Susanna, and her husband, William Heiffernan of Petoquamscot," to whom he gave "tenn acres of upland and sixe acres of meadow or marsh" at Rumney Marsh in the township of Boston, which Heffernan and his wife conveyed to Isaack, son of Edmond Groce.

The former Irish servant seems to have been a man of intelligence and in time he attained a position of some local importance. The Rhode Island colonial records show that on May 19, 1671, he was appointed "Clerk to the Train Band,"[33] and on the same date "His Majestie's Court of Justices" ordered "that a warrant bee issued out to William Hefernan to warne in the inhabitants of this Plantation to attend on tomorrow, at six of the clock, at the house of Mr. Jireh Bull"; and when the people assembled, "Mr. William Heffernan was chosen and engaged to the office and place of a Conservator of the Peace in jointe commission with Mr. Samuel Wilson and Mr. Jireh Bull."[34] On September 25, 1671, "William Herfernan" was appointed "tax assessor for Pettacomscutt."[35] In 1674, Heffernan and his family, consisting of his sons, John, William, Robert and Samuel, and a daughter, Joanna, resided at Wickford, R. I.; in 1676 he appears to have been at Newport, where he died in 1680, and his estate was administered on February 28, 1681. For several generations his descendants were mentioned in Rhode Island records.

[31] Plymouth Colony Records, Vol. 3, p. 220.

[32] Registry of Deeds, Lib. 4, fols. 285-7.

[33] *Civil and Military List of Rhode Island*, 1647-1800, Vol. 1, p. 7.

[34] Records of the Colony of Rhode Island, Vol. 2, p. 390.

[35] *Ibid.*, p. 413.

By deed dated May 12, 1692, Samuel Sewall and others conveyed to William Heffernan (2) 300 acres of land, called "Share in Pitticomcutt to William Heffernan (1)."[36] On February 2, 1697, John Heffernan married Mary Bockaway at Portsmouth, and some of their descendants were recorded "Heffernand" and "Hefferland." In Boston town records on September 21, 1692, there is an entry of the marriage of Christopher Vale and "Joanna Heifernan,"[37] probably the daughter of William Heffernan; and Stephen Heffernan and his wife, Abigail, had four children born to them at North Kingston, R. I., after 1711. Three of the family were Freemen of the Colony. In 1724, William Heffernan (2) was admitted Freeman, another William in 1746 and John Heffernan of Newport was admitted Freeman in 1759. William Heffernan (3) was a Justice at Newport in 1751 and Jeremiah Heffernan was a resident of the town in 1750.

Families named Higgins have been numerous in New England for more than two centuries. The earliest of the name in Massachusetts was "Richard Higgins, one of the first seven settlers of the town of Eastham," and several town historians are in agreement as to his racial origin.[38] Freeman, in his *Annals of Eastham,* states that "he was of Celtic ancestry," and that "he came to Plymouth soon after the town was settled, as his name appears in the list of Freemen in 1633; went to Eastham in 1644 and became one of the prominent men of that town and held the highest offices."[39] He was mentioned in the colony records as "Richard Higgins of Plymouth,

[36] "Rhode Island Land Evidences, 1648-1696," Vol. 1, fol. 415, Rhode Island Historical Society.

[37] Boston Town Books, Vol. 9.

[38] In an address at the 250th anniversary celebration of the founding of the town of Sandwich, Mass., in 1889, Rev. N. H. Chamberlain, a Cape Cod antiquary, said "the Higgins and Kellys were Irish." The Kellys here referred to were the descendants of David O'Kelly of Yarmouth.

[39] *Annals of Eastham,* by Frederick Freeman.

Taylor."[40] He married (1) Lydia Chandler on November 23, 1634, and (2) Mary Yates in October, 1661, and was the father of six sons and four daughters. He is described as "a man of giant strength and integrity of character," and we are told, "he was the ancestor of nearly all the Higgins's in Maine, Massachusetts and Rhode Island." Another New England historian says: "Richard Higgins, the ancestor, was of Celtic origin, but seems to have emigrated to America from England, though some of his descendants claim he came from the North of Ireland."[41] Some of them settled in the Saco Valley, and an historical investigator of that region in commenting upon an assertion by a member of the family that his ancestor "came from England" and presumably was an Englishman, remarks that the Higgins families of Saco "all smack of old Ireland," and he asks, "did they come from Belfast, Dublin or Cork, via Liverpool, and is this the way they came from England?"[42]

John Higgins received a grant of land at Hampton, N. H., in June 1640.[43] "John, son of John and Susanna Higgins," was born at Boston on February 15, 1655; Robert Higgins was at Boston in 1660; James Higgins was at Exeter, N. H., in 1680, and Providence town records show that in 1682 Cornelius Higgins bought ninety-eight acres of land from Andrew Harris "at Scituate in ye precincts of ye said Towne of Providence," and Cornelius Higgins was on the tax list of the town in 1688. Richard and Elizabeth Higgins were the parents of eight children, born at Newport, the first of whom was Richard, born on December 12, 1697; Owen Higgins was a resident of Newport in 1699, and in 1701 his son, Richard, was made a Freeman of the Colony; Thomas Higgins

40 *Plymouth Colony Records*, Vol. 1, p. 37.

41 *Genealogical and Family History of the State of Maine*, by Dr. George T. Little.

42 *Saco Valley Families and Settlements*, by Rev. Gideon T. Ridlon, p. 727.

43 Town Register, Hampton, N. H.

is mentioned in Boston records in 1699 and in 1702 the town granted him an abatement in his taxes.[44]

In 1679, one John Humphrey died intestate at Lynn, Mass. At the Essex County Probate Court on June 28, 1681, Griffin Edwards, attorney for Ann Myles of Swanzey, Mass., made application for her appointment as administratrix, and "to have the estate settled upon her as the rightful heir." He presented two documents, one "a certificate from the Mayor of Clonmell in Ireland, that Ann was the only surviving child of John Humphrey," the other "a Letter of Attorney," dated January 15, 1680, "given by John Myles of Swanzey and Ann Myles, his wife," in which it was stated that her first husband was "William Palmer, late of Ardfinan, County Tipperary, Ireland, Gentleman." [45] While the documents here quoted do not establish definitely an Irish nationality for John Humphrey, it is evident that, prior to his emigration to this country, he resided in Tipperary, Ireland, and that his daughter, Ann Myles, was born there. Humphrey is more often met with among the Irish as a baptismal name, though there are also Irish families of this surname, and O'Hart lists them among "the landed proprietors resident in County Cavan since the reign of James the First." [46] The name Myles, or Miles, is also very common in Ireland.

The will of William Wodell of Pocasset was proved in the Bristol County, Mass., court on May 3, 1693, and in an "Account of the estate presented to John Saffin, Judge of Probate," on October 18, 1697, the executor included among "debts paid" an item due to Thomas Hickey.[47] Darby Hurlie was listed among the "passengers in the *Margaret* from Plymouth," which arrived at Boston in 1633. Matthew Hur-

[44] Tax List, in Boston Town Books, Vol. 1, p. 141.

[45] Essex County Probate Records, Vol. 3, pp. 366-7.

[46] *Irish Pedigrees*, by John O'Hart, Vol. 1, p. 828.

[47] "First Book of Bristol County Probate Records."

ley, also recorded Mortho Hurley, enlisted for service in King Philip's War on March 24, 1676, under Captain Samuel Wadsworth, and was listed among the casualties at the battle of Sudbury. There is no other reference to him, but it is thought he lived at Boston, or Cambridge, and a Sarah Hurley, probably his daughter, was married in Cambridge to Richard Ferguson on July 31, 1690. "John Hanagine, a Taylor," came to Boston from the Island of Nevis, and on October 31, 1681, he made application to the Selectmen "for admission as an inhabitant," but was refused and he "was given libertie till next month," but seven years later "John Hannagen, tailor," was one of the taxable inhabitants of the town.[48] "Mary Jordan, daughter of Jeffry Jordan of Ireland," and James Rogers were married at New London on November 5, 1674. She is supposed to have been a native of Cork. A New London historian informs us that Rogers was master of a vessel that "brought over from Ireland a number of redemptioners, among them the Jordan family," and "in after life he was accustomed to say sportively, that it was the richest cargo he ever shipped and she (his wife) the best bargain he ever made." [49]

Several families named Joyce are mentioned in Barnstable County seventeenth century records, all believed to have been descended from John Joyce, who about 1637 came to Lynn, Mass. In the same year he removed to Sandwich, and a Cape Cod historian refers to him as one of "the first settlers of the town of Sandwich," [50] where he received a grant of "a p'cell of land" on August 7, 1638.[51] An action for "trespass" entitled "John Joyce *vs.* Walter Deuell," was tried before the

[48] Tax Lists, in Boston Town Books, Vol. 10, p. 90.

[49] *History of New London, Conn.*, by Frances M. Caulkins, p. 202, New London, 1852.

[50] *History of Cape Cod*, by Frederick Freeman, Vol. 2, pp. 17 and 37.

[51] Plymouth Colony Records, Vol. 1, p. 93.

General Court of Assistants on June 17, 1642. In the next year John Joyce settled at Yarmouth, and he appears in the town records of 1643 among "persons capable of bearing arms,"[52] and in 1652 as "Surveyor of Highways."[53] He is described as "a man of wealth, residing in the village of Hackanom,"[54] where he died in 1666, and letters of administration to "the estate of John Joyce of Yarmouth," were granted to his widow on March 5, 1666.[55] Walter Joyce was recorded at Marshfield in 1668;[56] John, Samuel and Thomas, sons of John Joyce, were among those who drew shares of twenty acres each in the "Division of the Common Lands" at Yarmouth in the year 1712, and the will of John Joyce (2) dated December 28, 1714, was proved in Barnstable County on April 6, 1715.[57] Although the town historian states that "the family name of the Cape Cod Joyces became extinct with the death in 1755 of Jeremiah Joyce," grandson of the immigrant, there are many of the name mentioned in Barnstable County records subsequent to 1755, as well as in vital records of Boston, Braintree, Scituate and Weymouth.

[52] Town Records, quoted in *History of Old Yarmouth*, by Charles F. Swift, p. 66, Yarmouthport, 1845.

[53] Plymouth Colony Records, Vol. 3, p. 9.

[54] Town Records, Yarmouth, Mass.

[55] Plymouth Colony Records, Vol. 4, p. 141.

[56] *Ibid.*, Vol. 4.

[57] Probate Records, Vol. 3, p. 344.

CHAPTER XIII

Numerous Kennys and Larkins in Massachusetts and Rhode Island—the "Mac" families well represented—"Guires" or McGuires in Fairfield County, Conn.—Daniel McGinnis, pioneer of Woburn, Mass., 1675—Irish soldiers in King Philip's War—"Dorman, ye Irishman," taxed at Brookline 263 years ago.

NICHOLAS HOYT and Susanna Joyce were married at Windsor, Conn., on July 12, 1646.[1] "William Joyce, seaman, of Boston," was paid his wages by order of the Court on June 6, 1648,[2] and in the same year letters of administration to the estate of William Joyce were granted by the probate court of Suffolk County. Another William Joyce was on the Boston tax list in 1687; Christopher Joyce was a land owner at Kittery, Maine, in 1682; [3] and a James Joyce was a resident of New Castle, N. H., in 1693.[4] Joyce is one of the most numerous names in the Province of Connaught, and there is a large territory in Galway called "Joyce's Country" inhabited almost exclusively by families of the name. Authorities state they were of Welsh origin, descended from "a De Jorse who came from Wales to Galway in the reign of Edward the First, and having formed an alliance with the O'Flahertys, Chiefs of West Connaught, got large possessions in Connemara, in the Barony of Ross, and towards the borders of Mayo, a territory which is called 'Joyce's Country.' These De Jorses changed their name to Joyce." [5]

[1] Stiles' *Ancient Windsor.*

[2] Records of the Colony of Massachusetts Bay, Vol. 3, p. 18.

[3] York County Court Records.

[4] Provincial Papers of New Hampshire, Vol. 2, p. 90.

[5] *Irish Pedigrees,* by John O'Hart, Vol. 1, pp. 854-5.

Mary Keefe became the wife of Henry Thomson at Boston on August 5, 1693,[6] and the birth of "Christopher, son of Christopher and Elizabeth Kehoe," was recorded at Dorchester on January 25, 1695. Daniel Keniday or Kennedy served in a Boston company under Captain Henchman in King Philip's War and was in the "Great Swamp Fight" on December 19, 1675. William Kennedy came to Boston with his parents from Ireland with a number of other emigrants, after the defeat of the Irish army at the battle of the Boyne in 1690.[7] The Kennedys settled at Middleboro, Mass., where they received a grant of land. The name was generally recorded "Kanedy." In 1722 William Kennedy was captain of a company of militia raised at Middleboro to resist a threatened Indian attack, and the town historian relates that on Christmas Day, in 1723, Kennedy's company repulsed a force of French and Indians with great loss. Among the men in the company are noted Philip Butler, William Kelley and John Murphy.[8]

Henry Kenny was at Salem in 1653 and was the father of John, Mary and Sarah Kenny, born at Salem, between 1654 and 1662,[9] and at the November, 1670, session of the Essex County Court "Sarah Kenny, ex^{tx} under the will of John Kenny, deceased," presented the will for probate. This family lived at Danvers, at which place Henry, John and James Kenny, sons of John and Sarah Kenny, were listed among the town's taxpayers in 1682. Henry Kenny (2) married Priscilla Lewis at Salem on May 14, 1691, and they were the parents of Priscilla, Jemima, Dinah and Mary Kenny, born at Salem between 1693 and 1701.[10] Others of the name in

[6] Boston Town Books, Vol. 9.

[7] *History of the Town of Middleboro, Mass.*, by Thomas Weston, p. 91, Boston, 1906.

[8] *Ibid.*

[9] Salem Church Records, in *Essex Institute Historical Collections*, Vol. 7.

[10] Salem Vital Records.

Massachusetts were John Kenny, whose daughter, Hannah, was baptized at Salem on March 8, 1657,[11] Thomas Kenny of Gloucester in 1664, Andrew Kenny of Malden in 1690,[12] and a Richard Kenny was mentioned as in New Hampshire in 1680.[13] Henry and John Kenny and Thomas Kenny were listed among the men who served in King Philip's War under Captain James Gardiner in 1675,[14] and there was a John Kenny at Boston in 1672.[15]

The old Irish name Larkin is more numerous in New England colonial records than many of the English names now prominent in the vicinity of Boston. Larkin originally was O'Lorcain, derived from the Gaelic word, *lorc* (meaning fierce), anglicised O'Larkin, Larkin and sometimes Larcon, and the motto on their Irish coat of arms is *fortiter et fideliter,* "brave and faithful." There were several distinct families of the name in Ireland, in Wexford, Meath, Armagh, Galway and Tipperary Counties, and the territory adjacent to Carnsore Point in Wexford was for centuries known as "O'Larkin's Country." Richard and Thomas "Larkyn" were included in a "Register of the Names of all ye Passingers wch passed from ye Porte of London for one whole yeare Endinge at Xp^{mas} 1635," a curiously worded document in the Public Record Office at London, reproduced by the New England Historic-Genealogical Society.[16] Their destination was Boston, but no trace of Richard or Thomas "Larkyn" can be found in the public records. On October 30, 1647, a "Thomas Larckin" was a witness in a case tried at the Quarterly Court for Essex County, Mass.,[17] and a Thomas Larkin served as a

11 *Ibid.*

12 Malden Vital Records.

13 Savage's *Genealogical Dictionary,* Vol. 3, p. 10.

14 Bodge's *King Philip's War,* pp. 88, 166 and 452.

15 Suffolk Deeds, Lib. 6, fol. 280.

16 *Register,* Vol. 14.

17 Court Records, Vol. 1, p. 134.

juryman in the Court of Assistants at Boston in September, 1677.[18]

The first of the name recorded in Massachusetts was "Edward Larkin, wheelmaker," who was "admitted an inhabitant" at Charlestown on May 30, 1638, and in that year he was the owner of lands and houses "scituate within Charletowne limites." [19] On September 29, 1647, "Edward Larkin of Charletowne, Turner," sold to John Gove a "house, yeard and garden" at "Charletowne," [20] and on November 26th of the same year Francis Willoughby sold to Edward Larkin "a parcell of ground on the Charles River in Charletowne." [21] Joanna Larkin, widow of Edward, married Moses Newton, and land records show that she was the owner of a considerable estate. Her son, John Larkin, married Joanna Hale at Charlestown on November 9, 1644,[22] and on April 15, 1694, Joanna, widow of John Larkin, became the wife of Joshua Dodge at Salem.[23] Edward, son of the first Edward Larkin, married Elizabeth Hall at Charlestown, and his brother, Thomas, married Elizabeth Miles at that place on June 8, 1674.[24] Edward, John and Thomas Larkin appear in the records of the First Church at Charlestown between 1639 and 1675, and down to the end of the eighteenth century there are approximately one hundred entries of Larkins among Charlestown births and marriages. In Wyman's *Genealogies and Estates of Charlestown,* there is an extensive genealogy of the descendants of Edward Larkin, which brings the family records down to the early part of the nineteenth

[18] Records of the Court of Assistants, Vol. 1, p. 95.

[19] *Charlestown Land Records,* in Boston Town Books, Vol. 3, p. 43.

[20] *Ibid.,* p. 106.

[21] *Ibid.,* p. 112.

[22] *Genealogical Dictionary of the First Settlers of New England,* by James Savage, Vol. 2, p. 330.

[23] Salem, Mass., Vital Records.

[24] Savage, Vol. 2, pp. 580 and 591.

century, and which also shows that many of them were prominent and substantial people.

Henry Larkin was at Braintree, Mass., in 1670 and in a deed for lands dated March 25th of that year from Marjery Howard to Jeremy Fitch, "Henry Larkin of Braintry" was mentioned as the owner of the adjoining lands.[25] There was at least one family of the name in Essex County, Mass. In the records of the Quarterly Court under date of June 28, 1659, there is an entry of a case entitled "Henry Herrick, administrator of the estate of Hugh Larkin, deceased, *vs.* Elyas Stileman," and Robert Larkin, probably a son of Hugh, and Jane Pitman were married at Marblehead on March 27, 1661.[26] John and Edward Larkin were settlers at Newport, Rhode Island, in 1655,[27] and Edward appears in a quaint record of that year, entitled "Roule of ye Freemen of ye colonie of everie Towne." In 1663 he was commissioner from Newport in the "General Court of Commissioners," held at Providence; in 1669 he was an inhabitant of Westerly; and in "A List of all ye Freemen of Westerly Town from the first settlement thereof to 1727," [28] there appear the names, Edward Larkin, Edward Larkin, Jr., John Larkin and Roger Larkin. There was a reuniting of the Irish strain when Edward Larkin, Jr., married Mary, daughter of Nicholas Cottrell of Newport, and in 1671 this Edward Larkin and John Mackoone were "called on to see how they stand as to their fidelity to his Majestie and this Colony." Edward Larkin (1) of Newport left many descendants. For two centuries men and women of this name appear in Rhode Island records and were people of consequence.[29]

25 Suffolk County Registry of Deeds, Lib. 7, fol. 155.

26 Marblehead, Mass., Vital Records.

27 Austin's *Genealogical Dictionary of Rhode Island.*

28 In Cole's *History of Washington and Kent Counties.*

29 See "The Early Larkins of Rhode Island," by Thomas Hamilton Murray, in *Journal of the American Irish Historical Society,* Vol. 4, pp. 110-2.

An Edward Larkin from Connecticut was a soldier in King Philip's War and his name is on a "List of Volunteers who drew Cedar Swamp Lots" at Voluntown, Conn., in 1676.[30] Timothy Larkin served with the Massachusetts troops, and "Tim ° Larkin," doubtless the same man, was on "Salem Tax Lists of 1700." [31] Thomas Larkin was taxed at Boston, 1685-7,[32] and the births of Jane and Sarah, children of Thomas and Jane Larkin, and of Thomas and Elizabeth, children of John and Sarah Larkin, were recorded at Boston between 1676 and 1688.[33]

There were several families of the name in Worcester County, Mass., and their genealogy states that they were "descended from one of three brothers named Larkin who came from Ireland," and that they were a branch of "the O'Larkins of Lagenia." The period of their emigration is not stated, but since we are told that Peter Larkin was born at Lancaster, Mass., "about 1700," it is probable that the original emigrants were there in the late years of the seventeenth century. Peter purchased a tract of land at Lancaster, which came to be known as Larkindale. He is said to have removed to Poolville, Maryland, where there was a Catholic settlement, but it is evident that his family remained in Massachusetts. He had five sons, and they were the fathers of twenty-five children, all born at Lancaster in the eighteenth century. They were a patriotic family and very active in town affairs, and the records show that John, Peter, Matthias, William and Edmund Larkin, all of Lancaster, served in the French-English War, and several of the name from that town were in the War of the Revolution.

Sarah Larey was "admitted to ye Church" at Charlestown

[30] Bodge's *King Philip's War.*

[31] In *Genealogical Quarterly Magazine,* Vol. 4.

[32] Town Books, Vol. 1, pp. 81, 89 and 116.

[33] *Ibid.,* Vol. 9.

on February 7, 1639;[34] "Katherine Lary of Lynn" was a witness in a case tried at the Ipswich Court on March 31, 1657;[35] and Sarah, daughter of Cornelius Leary, and Matthew Moore were married at Newbury, Mass., on March 27, 1661.[36] John Leare was arraigned in the Essex County Court "for being drunk" on October 11, 1669, and a case entitled "Philip Cromwell *vs.* John Leerey" for debt was tried in Court on June 5, 1671. Gerrard Lawler was mentioned as at Boston in 1649.[37] At the October, 1666, session of the Essex County Court, there was tried a case entitled "Edw Goodwin *vs.* George Linche,"[38] and on October 12, 1683, a case entitled "Launcelott Smith *vs.* Nicholas Lynch" was tried before the "Court of Assistants of the Colony of Massachusetts Bay." In the quaint language of the day, the record says: "Ye plaintiffe Launcelott Smith Appeared & presented his libel ye deffendant Nicholas Lynch Appeared & put in his Ans^{r}. and after their Libell & Answ^{r} wth ye Evidences p'duced and pleas made by both partyes the Court on a full hearing of the partyes declared they found for the plaintiffe eighty pounds mony of the Countrey & Costs of Courts two pounds sixteene shillings." The marriage of James Townsend and Mary Lynch was recorded at Boston on November 7, 1693.

There were several families named Lyons at Roxbury. "Joseph Lyons, sonne of William Lyons," and "Sarah, daughter of William Lyons," were baptised there on October 3, 1654, and August 1, 1656, respectively,[39] and on February 29, 1667, "William Lyons was ordered to answer the presentm^{t} of the defect of the high wayes to Roxsberry" at

[34] *Charlestown Genealogies and Estates,* by Thomas B. Wyman.

[35] Court Records, Vol. 2, p. 35.

[36] Newbury, Mass., Vital Records.

[37] Boston Town Books.

[38] Court Records, Vol. 3, p. 364.

[39] Roxbury Church Records, in Boston Town Books, Vol. 6.

"the next County Court at Boston." [40] John Lyons and Abigail, his wife, were mentioned in Roxbury church records as of January 24, 1671; on "26 7^{m} 1669," there appears an entry: "Thomas Lyons was excommunicated," but under date of "11.4.71," the records furnish the interesting information that "Thomas Lyons, upon his repentance, was absolved fro ye sentenc of excom," [41] and on February 20, 1673, Thomas and Sarah, children of Thomas Lyons, were baptised at the church in Roxbury. William Lyons was listed among "Massachusetts Freemen, 1634-1655." As in the cases of numerous others bearing names common among the Irish there is no mention anywhere of the nationality or racial origin of these people.

Several of the "Mac" families, besides those already referred to, were represented in New England in the seventeenth century, and while the names were not always spelled correctly by the recording officers, those here mentioned are unquestionably of Irish origin. Dennis MacBrian was transported to Barbados in the *Alexander* from London in October, 1633, and thence came to Massachusetts, but no trace of his whereabouts in the colony can be found. "John McGoune" was a landowner at Scituate in 1666,[42] and a "John Macgoune" witnessed a deed covering the sale of lands at Kittery on November 18, 1701. William McGraney, name also recorded "Mack Cranney," and Margaret Riley, daughter of the John and Margaret (O'Dea) Riley already mentioned, were married at Springfield on July 19, 1685.

Fairfield, Conn., records show that Bridget Baxter sold land to "John Makew" in that County, and the deed was recorded on March 28, 1661. This is the only reference to "John Makew" that has been located. But the statement will

40 Town Books, Vol. 7, p. 35.

41 *Ibid.*, Vol. 6.

42 William Berry Lapham, in *Maine Genealogist and Recorder.*

hardly be questioned that the proper form of his name, as well as that of "Timothy MaKue" who witnessed a deed covering a transfer of lands in York township, Maine, from Thomas Moore of Boston to Daniel Dill, dated March 17, 1693,[43] was MacHugh, or, as it is sometimes rendered, M^c^Cue. The marriage of "Tim^o^ Mackhew" and Ann Dry was recorded at Boston on May 15, 1699;[44] "Timothy, son of Timothy and Ann MacKue," was born there in 1700, and in the same year "Timothy Mackhue" was recorded as having his "taxes abated."[45]

"John MackDonell" came to Massachusetts in the *John and Sarah* from London in 1651. Probably he was the "John Magdoniell" whose marriage to Elizabeth Smith at Boston was recorded on May 17, 1658, and the births of their children, John, Elizabeth, Martha, Mercy and Mary, as well as of "Michael, son of John and Isabel Magdaniel," appear in the town records between 1659 and 1674.[46] "Dennis, son of Dennis and Alice Magdaniel," was born at Boston on November 25, 1671; as "Denis Mackdaniell" the father appears in the tax lists of the year 1691; and in the "Minutes of the Meetings of the Selectmen" of the year 1697 the Town Clerk made an entry that "Dennis MacDoniel dyed 20 Jan." Dennis was a Boston police officer and evidently lived there for more than a quarter of a century, and in 1714 Daniel MackDoniel, supposed to have been a son of Dennis, was one of the guardians of the municipal peace in the town of Boston.

"Widow MackMalley" was one of a number of "Poor widows in Salem" who received aid from the town in 1679; Thomas McMallen married Mary Gilson at that place on De-

43 York Deeds, Book 6, fol. 65.

44 Boston Town Books, Vol. 9.

45 *Ibid.*, Vol. 10.

46 *Ibid.*, Vol. 9.

cember 11, 1684, and as Thomas Mack Mallin he was mentioned as a "chair-maker or turner" at Salem in 1692. In Dorchester records, there is an entry: "Sarah Mackeone died September the 14, 1669."[47] "Daniel Makenny" was recorded as the grantee in a deed for lands at Taunton, Mass., from John Eddy on August 27, 1660;[48] "the estate of Daniel Mackenney of Taunton" was administered by the Court on October 27, 1685;[49] Alexander McKenny served under Captain James Oliver in King Philip's War in 1675 and John Mackenny, son of the John McKenna later referred to, owned lands at Yorktown, Maine, in 1691.[50] There was also a family of this name at Dedham, Mass., and among Dedham births are found such entries as: "John, son of William and Ruth Mecanie," on July 18, 1664, and "Daniell, son of William and Ruth MeacKenny," on February 15, 1676.[51] This name was recorded in various ways by the taxing officers. In 1659 "Willm McKeanie" was assessed for his taxes under "Countrey Rate" at Dedham, as "Willm Mackennie" in 1660, as "William MacKena" in 1672,[52] and as "William McKennys of Dedham" he was listed with service in King Philip's War in 1676.

On Dedham tax lists for the years 1660 to 1672 we find "James Mackarorie," "Jeams Macarory" and in various other forms; "James MaKarory" and Mary Everitt were married at Dedham in September, 1662, and the births of their children appear in local parish registers down to the year 1670.[53] The proper spelling, of course, was MacRory, the original

47 Dorchester Vital Records, in Boston Town Books, Vol. 12.

48 Plymouth Colony Records, in *Mayflower Descendant,* Vol. 14, p. 236.

49 *Ibid.,* Vol. 6, p. 176.

50 York Deeds.

51 Dedham, Mass., Vital Records.

52 Dedham, Mass., Town Records, Vol. 4, pp. 7, 25, 215, 225.

53 Parish Register, First Church in Dedham, in Dedham Town Records, Vol. 2.

form of the name of the Irish family of Rogers.[54] "John Mackmoran" was listed under "Country Rates" by the Boston Tax Commissioners in 1692;[55] the marriage of "Elisabeth Mackarta" and Thomas Bridgewater was recorded at Boston on April 7, 1696; John McShane was brought before the Quarterly Court at Salem "5 mo. 1653," on a charge of "uttering two oaths"; on September 25, 1660, he and Anthony Carroll were witnesses in a case tried in the Ipswich Court,[56] and "John MackShane" was again mentioned in the court records in November, 1678.[57] An Irishman named Fergus McDowell was a merchant at Stonington, Conn., and he received a power of attorney from Ezekiel Cleasby of Boston on December 26, 1692, filed at the Suffolk County Registry of Deeds.[58]

The name "Guire" turns up frequently in Fairfield County, Conn., records. "Eleanor Guire, daughter of Luke of Fairfield," was "born about 1691"; "Mary Guire, daughter of Luke," was "born about 1695," and "Hannah, daughter of Luke Guire," was baptised at Fairfield on April 19, 1697, and they married into Fairfield families named Turney, Stewart and Hall, respectively. Luke Guire (2) married Rebecca Odell, daughter of John and Mary Odell of Stratford; in 1699 Luke Guire, his brothers, Eben and John, and three sisters were mentioned in Fairfield County probate records, and on February 3, 1716, Samuel Hall conveyed to Luke Guire (2) lands in Fairfield formerly owned by Luke Guire (1).[59] These people are mentioned here because I am con-

[54] MacRory means "the son of Rory," the Irish baptismal name corresponding to the English Roger.

[55] Boston Town Books, Vol. 10, p. 133.

[56] *Records and Files of the Quarterly Court*, Vol. 2, p. 244.

[57] *Ibid.*, Vol. 7.

[58] Lib. 14, fol. 235.

[59] *History and Genealogy of the Families of Old Fairfield*, ed. by Donald Lines Jacobus, Vol. 1, parts 1 to 6.

vinced that the family name originally was McGuire. Many Irish families are known to have dropped the prefix "Mac" or "O" after coming to the colonies; in at least one instance, that of a Guire or Guier family in Gloucester, Mass., their immigrant ancestor was called "Maguier," and some of the descendants of one Patrick McGuire, who came from Ireland and settled at Falmouth, Maine, in the early part of the eighteenth century, are known as "Makquier" and "Quire."

Daniel McGinnis located at Woburn, Mass., where he purchased a plot of ground from his countryman, Michael Bacon, by deed dated June 29, 1674, recorded in Middlesex County. In the vital records of the year 1675 he was called "the first Irishman to settle in Woburn," [60] and he was also mentioned as "an Irishman" in a deed dated June 8, 1675, from John Tidd to Daniel McGinnis.[61] From the fact that he was called "an Irishman" it might be inferred that that designation was given to him because his countrymen were then so rare in Woburn. However that may be, local seventeenth century records show that in addition to Daniel McGinnis men named Timothy Burke, James and William Butler, John Creagan, Robert Doyle, Thomas Geary, William Healy, Thomas Kenny and John Molony resided at Woburn, and several of these men served in a troop of cavalry raised in that town for King Philip's War by Captain Thomas Prentice. In November, 1675, Captain Daniel Henchman recruited a company of twenty men for the war, and there were at least five Irishmen on the roll, Timothy Burke, William Healy and Dennis "Sihie," or Sheehy. Also, Daniel Malony of Boston and John Molony, or, as he was also recorded, "John Malloone of Wooborn- Towne." All were listed as "on garrison duty at Dunstable" down to August, 1676, and the last mentioned

[60] Vital Records, Woburn, Mass., Vol. 4, p. 184.

[61] Middlesex County Registry of Deeds.

received pay totaling £20. 6s. 4d. while in the military service.[62]

Daniel McGinnis served under Captain Thomas Wheeler in the "Three County Troop" in the defence of Brookfield in August, 1675, and down to June, 1676, "Daniel McKennys," as well as Richard Brien, John Casey, Hugh Collohane or Gollihu and James Wealsh, served under Captain Samuel Mosely. On December 19, 1675, these men took part in the "Great Swamp Fight," where the Narragansett Indians made a determined stand against the united forces of the Massachusetts Bay, Connecticut and Plymouth colonies.[63] McGinnis was corporal and at one time "Clerke" of Mosely's company. In September, 1676, "Daniel Meginny" was in Captain Daniel Henchman's company, then "in garrison at Medfield." [64]

The marriage of Daniel McGinnis and Rose Neill was recorded at Woburn on February 10, 1676; in the next year they removed to Billerica and they were the parents of Daniel, Edmund, Rose and Mary McGinnis, born at Billerica between 1677 and 1685.[65] The name was spelled in various ways. In December, 1677, it appeared in Middlesex County records as "Daniel Macginnys"; [66] and in June, 1684, Joseph Winn sued "Daniel Macginny" for money due on the sale of a horse.[67] By deed dated June 25, 1685, "Daniel Mackguines" bought from John Abbott for £40. sixty acres of land at Billerica, with the buildings thereon, and in October, 1685, "Daniell Mackginney" sued Michael Bacon "for defaming pltffs title to land bought of John Abbott and lying on the southeast of Shawskin River and part in Michael's

[62] Bodge's *King Philip's War*, pp. 75, 359, 376.

[63] *Ibid.*

[64] *Ibid.*

[65] Billerica, Mass., Vital Records. Also Woburn Vital Records, Vol. 1, p. 162.

[66] Middlesex County Records, Vol. 3, p. 206.

[67] *Ibid.*, Vol. 4, p. 115.

farm in Billerica." [68] The jury found for the plaintiff and in "an Acon for Appeale from the Judgement of the County Court," entitled "Michael Bacon plt. con^{ta} Daniel Maguinis deffendant," the Court ordered "Revision of the former Judgment and Costs of Court." [69] As "Dan Mackginnis" he appeared in the Billerica tax list of the year 1679, and the last entry of his name in the records was in 1687, at which time he was living at Rochester, Rhode Island, and was there recorded "Daniel Mackines, victualler." [70]

In 1674, "Dorman, ye Irishman," was included in a "List of the Names of p'sons ratable returned by Tho. Bingley, Constable," of Boston.[71] Apparently, it was only after he had acquired property that his full name was recorded; from 1675 to 1688 "Derman Maroone," "Dorman Morrean" or "Dorman Mareen" was on "Muddy River Valuation," and was assessed for taxes on "oxen, bulls and cowes, heyfors and steers, horses and mares" and "six acres of land." [72] A Brookline historian states that "Dorman Morean was one of the original grantees of Muddy River." [73] Under date of "20. 3. 1681," there was recorded in the Roxbury parish register the burial of "a young infant of Dorman Mareene, an Irishman living at Muddy River," [74] and under 1684 there are mentioned in the church records Elizabeth, Philip and William Mareen and Mary and Rebecca Murreene, all children of "Dorman Mareene." As "Dorman Morean" he took the oath of allegiance in 1679; [75] "Dorman Moraun" and Thomas Stedman were appointed "Tythingmen for Muddy River"

[68] Middlesex County Records, Vol. 4, p. 184.

[69] Records of the Court of Assistants, Vol. 1, p. 291.

[70] *Records of the Colony of Rhode Island*, Vol. 3, p. 234.

[71] "Tax Lists of Boston," in Town Books, Vol. 1.

[72] *Ibid.*, Vol. 1, pp. 56, 128, 145.

[73] *History of the Town of Brookline, Mass.*, by John Gould Curtis, p. 116, Boston, 1933.

[74] Roxbury Church Records, in Boston Town Books, Vol. 6, p. 184.

[75] *Ibid.*, Vol. 29, p. 168.

on March 12, 1694,[76] and the last entry concerning him was in 1695, when he appeared in a "List of the Inhabitants of Boston." There can be no doubt that all these entries referred to "Dorman, ye Irishman," and, as in the case of the Dermod O'Mahony before mentioned, sometimes recorded "Dorman Mahoone," it is probable that his proper baptismal name was Dermod. Apparently, he became a man of some little importance at Muddy River, since he was appointed by the town board as one of the tax collectors. His property passed to his son, William, who sold it to Joseph Goddard, and in 1705 when Muddy River was incorporated under its present name of Brookline, William Morean was made town constable. Several Mareans appear in the probate books of Middlesex County down to the end of the eighteenth century, and people named Morean and Mareene are in Roxbury vital records as late as the nineteenth century, all undoubtedly descended from "Dorman, ye Irishman," who paid his taxes at Boston two hundred and sixty-three years ago.

[76] *Ibid.*, Vol. 7, p. 217.

CHAPTER XIV

Irish settlers in York County, Maine—John McKenna, "a genuine Hibernian," and his many descendants—the O'Neils and O'Donnells—the Meades in Connecticut and Massachusetts—Andrew Meade from Cork, Ireland—the Massachusetts Mulligans and Murphys—the Moores from Cork, Dublin and Wexford.

A LARGE number of Irish emigrants came to York County, Maine, who settled chiefly along and adjacent to the Saco River and its tributaries, and in the neighborhood of Scarboro and Kittery. In York deeds and probate records are found the names of many of the pioneers of that territory, among them Irish lumbermen, fishermen, farmers, artisans and laborers, who lived there throughout the eighteenth century. One of the prominent families at Scarboro were the Gillpatricks, consisting of Thomas Gillpatrick and his four sons, who came to that place from Ireland in 1718, and it was also at Scarboro that Morris O'Brien, father of the famous O'Brien brothers of Machias, first located after his arrival in this country. For much of the genealogical history of the early families of this part of the State we are indebted to a local antiquarian, Rev. Gideon T. Ridlon, whose work, *Saco Valley Families and Settlements* is a monument to his patience and industry and has been long regarded as a most authoritative source of information. John McKenna is described as "the first Irishman who settled in Scarboro." He came originally to the Isles of Shoals, whence he removed to the mainland, and first appears at Scarboro in 1668, when he was recorded as the lessor of lands at that place to Joshua Scottow. In 1673 he purchased lands at Scarboro from Robert Jordan.[1]

The local historian informs us that "John McKenna came into the plantation of Little Ossipee with other families from the coast, and with his sons, all powerful men, sat down in the northern part of the town, where his descendants now live." Long after John McKenna passed away, the members of the family changed the name to McKenny, and it is usually under that form that they appear in the public records and in the muster rolls of the Revolutionary War. Among those from the town of Scarboro who bore arms for American independence and were engaged in the disastrous expedition to Castine, Maine, in 1779, were five McKennys, all grandsons of John McKenna, but no one bearing the name McKenna can now be found in that territory. Some of the McKennys claimed that their immigrant ancestor was a Scotsman, but Ridlon, who himself was descended from one of York County's pioneer settlers, warmly ridicules that idea and shows clearly that John McKenna was none other than an Irishman, as his name implies.

We are told "he was a genuine Hibernian and the prevailing physical and mental features exhibited in the old men of the name have strongly indicated Irish ancestry." "While we do not care a fig," declares Ridlon, "whether the McKennys are descended from a Scottish or Irish race, we would emphasize the fact that we have no sympathy for the class, and there are many of them, who are too proud to acknowledge their nationality or that of their ancestors. There have been as noble patriots and brave soldiers who were identified with the war by which our national independence was gained and that of the preservation of the Union during the Rebellion, in whose veins flowed pure Irish blood, as any who hailed from Scotia's heather-clad hills."

[1] *Saco Valley Families and Settlements*, by Rev. Gideon T. Ridlon, p. 913.

There appears to be nothing on record to indicate the exact time of John McKenna's emigration to this country, though it is said it was "about the year 1653." Drake, in his *History and Antiquities of Boston,* mentions a John McKenna who was "transported to New England in 1650." He calls him "a Scotchman," doubtless because he was taken with a number of "prisoners at the battle of Dunbar" in Scotland, and possibly also on the mistaken assumption, which is shared in by many American historians, that all names with a "Mac" or "Mc" prefix indicate Scottish origin. Aside from that, the name McKenna unquestionably is Irish, and that fact, coupled with the statements of such a careful investigator as Rev. Mr. Ridlon, fully justifies placing the Scarboro pioneer in the Irish category. In 1676 "John MaKenny," son of John McKenna, joined other inhabitants of Scarboro in a petition to the Massachusetts General Court, in relation to the distresses they suffered in King Philip's War,[3] and as John McKenny he was recorded as owner of lands at Yorktown, Maine, in 1691. In York County records is found the following entry relating to one of John McKenna's daughters-in-law: "Rebeckah MacKanney, wife of Robert MacKanney, presented by the Grand Jury to the Court January 3, 1696, for not frequenting the public worship of God upon the Lord's Day."

The name Donnell also appears in the early records of the Saco Valley, and for more than two centuries it has been a numerous one in that part of the State. The ancestor of all the families of the name in Maine is said to have been Henry Donnell, a fisherman and planter at Kittery before 1648.[4] In 1652 he was "admitted Freeman," and in the same year he and his son, Thomas, "signed submission to Massachusetts." On December 6, 1664, Henry Donnell appears as the mortgagor of houses and lands in security for a contract to deliver

[3] *New England Historic-Genealogical Register,* Vol. 43, p. 73.

[4] York, Maine, Deeds, Vol. 1.

a quantity of fish,[5] and as the owner of Jewell's Island, he conveyed to his son, Joseph, by deed dated February 29, 1671, "all his right and title to Jewell's Island with all boats, appurtenances and fishery rights in Casco Bay." [6] His son, Samuel, was a man of considerable importance in his day, a magistrate, Judge of the County Court and member of the Massachusetts Council in 1692. The "will of Samuel Donnel of York," dated March 7, 1718, in which he named as legatees his sons, Samuel, Nathaniel, William and James, and daughters, Alice, Elizabeth and Joanna, was recorded in the probate office [7] on May 15, 1718.

The records in no way indicate what the national origin of the Donnell family was, and the local historian says that he was unable to ascertain "whether they were descended from the McDonalds of Scotland or the O'Donnells of Ireland." As in the case of the descendants of Michael Donnell of Essex County, Mass., some members of the family in later times changed the name to Dunnell. However, William Berry Lapham, a distinguished authority on early Maine history, in referring to the Donnells of that State, says that originally they were O'Donnells.[8] The O'Neils likewise changed their name to Neil or Neal, and a Maine historian asserts the Neals of that State were "all of Irish extraction." At Harrison, Maine, "their names are among the first on the records of births," and we are told that one of them, "John Neal," was "noted for his Irish wit and many singular stories relating to his eccentricities are still told." [9]

There is an interesting tradition, which has received general acceptance in the families of some of the old settlers in Eastern

[5] *Ibid.*, Vol. 7.

[6] Pope's *Pioneers of Maine and New Hampshire*, p. 57.

[7] Lib. 2, fol. 152.

[8] "Mutations in Surnames," by William Berry Lapham, President Maine Historical Society, in *Maine Genealogist and Recorder*.

[9] *Early Settlers of Harrison, Me.*, by Rev. G. T. Ridlon, Skowhegan, Me., 1877.

Maine, that Orono, a celebrated chief of the Penobscot tribe of Indians, was one of the Donnell family! As related in the collections of the Massachusetts Historical Society, the tradition is to the effect that "his paternal name was Donnel," and that "he was one of the captive children taken in the winter of 1692, when that place (York) was ravaged by the Indians." From the same source we learn that "the Donnell family was one of the most distinguished in the Province, Samuel Donnell being in the same year (1692) one of the Council, and his brother a man of considerable note." [10] Another account says: "Orono was unquestionably of white origin. It is conjectured that he was a native of York, in the District of Maine; that his family name was Donnell; that, in 1692, when the place was, in a great measure, destroyed by the savage enemy, he was carried into captivity, and that his relatives, who escaped with their lives, not knowing what became of him, supposed him to have been killed." [11] Orono was born at York in 1688; so, therefore, if the tradition were correct, he would have been a grandson of Henry Donnell, the first of the name in Maine. He was one of the most remarkable men of his time among the Eastern Indians. He and all of his tribe were converts to Catholicity, and to this day their descendants have remained firm adherents of that faith. Throughout the Revolution, Orono was the most powerful influence among the Eastern Indians in resisting the attempts of the English agents from Canada to induce them to take the side of England, and to the end of the war he was the steadfast friend of the American cause. He died at Oldtown, Maine, on February 5, 1801, at the age of 113.

Gabriel Meade was witness to a deed dated February 10, 1652, between Thomas Holbrooke and John Gill, recorded

[10] Hon. William D. Williamson, in *Collections of the Massachusetts Historical Society*, 3d Ser., Vol. 0, p. 82.

[11] Alden's *Epitaphs*, Vol. 1, No. 69, New York, 1812.

in Suffolk County.[12] He was listed among "Massachusetts Freemen, 1634-1655," [13] and the "will of Gabriel Meade of Charlestown" was recorded in the probate books of Suffolk County.[14] I am informed that there is an entry in the printed records of the "Prerogative Court of Ireland," showing that "Robert Meade of Dublin," in his will dated August 26, 1677, mentioned his "brother, Gabriel Meade, now in New England," and it is probable that Gabriel Meade of Charlestown was the person here referred to. Thomas Meade and Mary Day were married at Salem on January 31, 1672; Nicholas Meade was mentioned as in Essex County, Mass.; [15] in 1681 a Nicholas Meade was appointed surveyor by the town of Bristol and in the following year he was in a lawsuit with Eliezer Dunham in the Plymouth County Court.[16]

Others of the name were among the early settlers at Horseneck, now Greenwich, Conn., and although some of the Connecticut Meads claim they are of English descent, the correctness of that statement is open to considerable doubt. The tradition is that the first of the name in Connecticut was "one of two brothers who emigrated from England," "the other emigrated to Virginia, where the family still exists." However, the Virginia Meade, Andrew, unquestionably was an Irishman, who came from London, England, to New York, whence he removed to Nansemond County, Virginia. His grandson, David Meade, compiled the *Records of the Meade Family*,[17] wherein he said: "Andrew Meade, my paternal grandfather, was an Irish Catholic born in County Kerry, Ireland, who left his native country and went to London, and from there to New York in the seventeenth century."

12 Registry of Deeds, Lib. 1, fol. 198.

13 List of Freemen in *New England Historic-Genealogical Register*, Vol. 3.

14 Lib. 16, fol. 163.

15 Records of the Essex County Court, Vol. 8, p. 384.

16 Plymouth Colony Records, Vols. 6 and 7.

17 In *William and Mary College Quarterly*, Vol. 13.

Another of his descendants, Patrick H. Baskervill of the University of Virginia, compiled a very complete history of the Meades[18] from the original family papers and Irish records. Therein he shows that Andrew was born in Ballintober, Barony of Kerry-Currihy in County Cork, a son of Sir John Meade and Catherine Sarsfield, daughter of Sir Dominick Sarsfield, Viscount of Kilmallock, County Limerick; that the ancestral seat of the family was the castle of Meadestown in Cork, where they were settled for centuries, and the records show that between 1379 and 1637, twelve of the Mayors of the City of Cork were members of this family.

There are many American families among whom, as in the case of the Connecticut Meads, there exists a belief that they are of English descent, because of the fact that their immigrant ancestors came here from England. But, all the authorities agree that the Meades are of Irish origin, and the name is almost as old as many of the better known Irish patronymics. They are mentioned in Burke's *Landed Gentry of the Kingdom of Ireland*, and in O'Hart's *Irish Pedigrees*. And the distinguished Gaelic scholar, Rev. Patrick Woulfe, the best authority on the subject of *Irish Names and Surnames*, in his work bearing that title,[19] shows that the name came from the Gaelic word, *midheac* (pronounced *mee-ach*), which, in the mutations of time, became *Miache, Miagh, Myah, Meagh* and finally Mead or Meade. *Midheac* means "the Meathman," *i.e.*, a native of or in some way connected with County Meath, Ireland. Rev. Mr. Woulfe describes them as "merchant families who settled at an early period in Cork and Limerick,"[20] that, "as the surname implies, they pre-

[18] *Andrew Meade of Ireland and Virginia,* by Patrick H. Baskervill, Richmond, Va., 1921.

[19] Dublin, Ire., 1923.

[20] George Meade, a prominent citizen of Philadelphia during the Revolution, ancestor of General George Meade of Gettysburg fame and of Admiral Meade of the United States Navy, was a son of Robert Meade of Limerick.

viously settled in Meath," and that "the anglicised form of the name to the end of the sixteenth century was always Meagh or Miagh."

Thomas Morrissie was taxed at Oyster River, N. H., between 1662 and 1675,[21] and "Thomas Morrisse and Mary of Antego" were married at Weymouth, Mass., on September 23, 1696. In 1674, "Denis Menan, Webb's serv^t^," was listed among "p'sons ratable" at Boston,[22] and on December 15th of the same year Dennis Monaane was "disallowed to be an inhabitant" by the Charlestown Selectmen.[23] An entry in the *Provincial Records of Maine* under date of April 7, 1685, shows that "Dennis Murrough claimed 50 acres at Falmouth by assignment of a deed of gift of Thomas Brackett"; "Dennis Morough and Jane, his wife," sold thirty acres of land to James Frees by deed dated December 7, 1686,[24] and "Denis Maroh" appears in Dorchester church records in 1696. Doubtless, all three entries related to the same identical person.

The marriage of "Nathaniel Masterson and Elilisabeth Coggswell" was recorded at Ipswich on July 31, 1657; Joanna Mullins and James Lawton were married at Boston on September 21, 1659; in 1674 letters of administration to the estate of William Mullen were granted by the probate court of Suffolk County; Philip Mullen took the oath of allegiance at Boston on November 11, 1678,[25] and James Mullen, a cooper on the ship *Herron* of Boston, was mentioned in the Court records in 1680.[26]

At Nantucket there were many Irish families in the early part of the eighteenth century, and their names appear in the parish registers under births, marriages and deaths. However,

21 Dover, N. H., Town Records.

22 Boston Town Books, Vol. 1, p. 7.

23 *Charlestown Genealogies and Estates*, by Thomas B. Wyman.

24 York Deeds, Book 6, fol. 23.

25 Boston Town Books, Vol. 29.

26 Records of the Court of Assistants, Vol. 1, p. 159.

the town records contain the name of only one Irishman in the period under review. That was Dennis Manning, the births of whose children, Betty, David and James, were recorded at Nantucket between 1679 and 1685, and there is also on record the marriage of William Stubbs and "Dinah, daughter of Dennis and Catherine Manning," at Nantucket on March 31, 1717. There was a Thomas Manning at Ipswich in 1657, in which year he was recorded as the grantor of a homestead and lands at that place to William Buckley.[27] He served in King Philip's War, and, "Thomas Manning, dying intestate, being slain in the war," the Essex County Court granted letters of administration to his brother, Daniel Manning.[28] Another Thomas Manning was at Ipswich in 1685, in which year the Selectmen voted "that Thomas Manning, gunsmith of Salem, may be an inhabitant and carry on his trade." Among "ye passengers that came in ye shipe *Hannah & Elizabeth,*"[29] which arrived at Boston on November 4, 1679, there were seven members of a family named Manning, described as "from St. Patrick's Parish, Darthmouth, England." With the exception of Dennis of Nantucket, I am unable to find any authority for saying that these Mannings were Irish, because there are English as well as Irish families of the name. The Irish Mannings originally were O'Maoineins, but in course of time the name was anglicised Mannin, Manion and Manning, and their coat of arms bears a triple three-leaf Shamrock.

The Mulligans were one of the pioneer families of New England who might be classed among the "elusive" Irish, since their record is practically unknown and they receive no mention in town or county histories. This name first appears on

[27] "Caldwell Records," p. 6, in *Ipswich in the Massachusetts Bay Colony,* by Thomas F. Waters, Ipswich Historical Society, 1905.

[28] Records of the Essex County Court, Vol. 6, p. 71.

[29] *New England Historic-Genealogical Register,* Vol. 28.

this side of the Atlantic in 1651, in which year, as we learn from a record known as "Book of Eastern Claims,"[30] "John Mulligan of Scarburrough" claimed "in right of his wife, Elizabeth," that he had sold "a tract of land beginning at ye mouth of ye River called Blew Point." There were four distinct families of the name in Massachusetts in the seventeenth century, those of Hugh, John and Thomas Mulligan of Boston and Robert Mulligan of Rowley. As "Hugh Mallagan," the former was assessed for taxes in Boston in 1681, but in later tax lists he appears as Hugh Mulligan.[31] And that he was a native of Ireland is indicated by an entry in the *Records of the Court of Assistants of the Colony of Massachusetts Bay*[32] of the year 1685, in a case before the Court, entitled "Hugh Mulligan, plain^{t} on Appeale from the Judgement of the County Court in Boston." The record of the case says: "the Jury brought in their verdict, they found a Confirmation of the County Courts sentenc and costs of Courts, *i.e.*, defraying ye charg of Tryall," and the Clerk of the Court made this notation on the margin of the docket: "Mulligan's sentenc to return to Ireland under poenalty of 20^{li}." From the fact that Hugh Mulligan was taxed at Boston several years later, it is assumed that the "sentenc" of the Court was not carried out and that he paid the "poenalty" of twenty pounds.

"John Mulligan, carpenter," was on the Boston tax lists between 1687 and 1691;[33] in 1695 he was listed as one of the "inhabitants of Boston,"[34] and in 1701 he received an "abatement of his taxes."[35] Savage[36] mentions "Robert Mulligan of Rowley, probably a brother of Hugh," and his chil-

30 Vol. 5, reproduced in *Maine Historical Genealogical Recorder*, Vol. 2.

31 "Tax Lists of Boston," in Town Books, Vol. 1, pp. 102 and 138.

32 Vol. 1, p. 280.

33 Boston Town Books, Vol. 1, pp. 110 and 152.

34 *Ibid.*, p. 165.

35 *Ibid.*, Vols. 1 and 10.

36 *Genealogical Dictionary of the First Settlers of New England*, Vol. 3, p. 253.

dren, "Robert, John and Mary Mulligan," but, like nearly all Irish names, in course of time the name suffered through misspellings. "Robert Mullican" appears in Newbury vital records in 1687; his daughter, "Rebecca Mullican," was married at Bradford, Mass., to Benjamin Gage on August 2, 1722, but on the death of his son, Robert, at Rowley in 1741 he was recorded Robert Mulligan, and down to the end of the eighteenth century many of the descendants of these early Mulligans turn up in Massachusetts records as "Mullekins" and "Mullergrens." Among Boston births and baptisms[37] we find:

"Robert, son of Hugh and Ellener Mullegin," August 9, 1681.

"John, son of John and Eliza Mullegan," December 27, 1691.

"Thomas, son of Thomas and Elizabeth Mullegan," April 27, 1693.

"James, son of John and Elizabeth Mulligan," December 4, 1694.

"Benjamin, son of John and Elizabeth Mulligin," April 1, 1699.

Although the Murphys were well represented in other colonies, it does not appear that many of them came to New England, and not more than twelve persons of the name can be located there in the seventeenth century, the earliest of whom was the Brian Murphy before referred to. "Thomas Murfey" signed by "his mark" as witness to a deed of conveyance dated December 8, 1662, covering the transfer of lands at Hingham, Mass., from Josiah Loring to John and Thomas Loring, recorded at the Suffolk County Registry of Deeds.[38] "James Murfee" was an indentured servant in the service of Jonathan Gage at Ipswich in 1669;[39] a James Murphy from Massachusetts served in King Philip's War and also a "James Murffey of New London County, Conn."[40]

37 Boston Town Books, Vol. 9, pp. 155, 196, 207, 215, 248.

38 Lib. 8, fol. 14.

39 Records of the Essex County Court, Vol. 4, pp. 159 and 318.

40 *Soldiers of King Philip's War*, by Rev. George M. Bodge, p. 444.

The last mentioned was one of a company of men who took part in an attack on an Indian fort during the "Great Swamp Fight" in Rhode Island on December 19, 1675, where the chronicler of the war says "they distinguished themselves by their gallant conduct." Others in the company were John Roach, Edward Larkin, James Welsh, Daniel Tracy and Edward, John and Thomas Fanning. James Murphy was listed as one of a number of "Volunteers who drew Cedar Swamp Lots" at Voluntown, Conn., for their services in the war.[41]

William Murphy was listed in 1669 among "Early Settlers of Essex and Old Norfolk," [42] and a William Murphy is mentioned as "Master of the ship *Friendship*," registered at Boston and trading with the West Indies in 1679.[43] In June, 1686, "Margaret Murffee of Scituate" was one of a number of "Persons licensed to sell spiritous liquors out of dores," [44] and "Ann Murfy" and George Young were married at Marblehead on June 16, 1696.[45] The files of the Essex County Court show that William Murphy and Thomas Murphy were residents of Salem in 1696, and in the same year "Thomas Murffee, boatswain on the Salem Galley," was recorded as receiving his share of some prize money.[46] Richard Murphy was at Marblehead in 1699, and in the *Boston News Letter* of November 20, 1704, he was referred to as "Master of the Arcana Galley of Marblehead," then about to sail on a voyage to Leghorn. If any more of the name were in New England in the seventeenth century, it is not disclosed in the public records.

One William Hibbins was at Boston at a very early date,

[41] *Ibid.*

[42] *New England Historic-Genealogical Register,* Vol. 7, p. 86.

[43] *Ibid.*, Vol. 8, p. 206. Also Boston Town Books.

[44] Plymouth Colony Records, Vol. 6, p. 187, and *American Antiquarian Society*, Vol. 1.

[45] Marblehead Vital Records.

[46] Essex Institute Historical Collections, Vol. 41, p. 186.

and while nothing can be found on record that would permit the statement that he was an Irishman, a conservative historical writer asserts that "William Hibbins came to the Colony from Ireland in the *Mary and John* about 1634." [47] He seems to have been a man of some importance, was selectman and surveyor of highways and held other town offices. He married Mrs. Anne Moore, who in 1656 fell a victim to the "witch-hunting" craze of the period and was hanged by order of the General Court. In her will [48] she bequeathed her property to her two sons, described as "John and Joseph Moore of Ballyhorick, County Cork, Ireland," both of whom later settled in Boston. At the Registry of Deeds for Suffolk County there were recorded two deeds dated December 28, 1657, in one of which "John Moore, late of Ballehonicke in the Countie of Corke in Ireland, Gentman, Eldest Sonne of the late Anne Hibbins, the relict of William Hibbins of Boston," acting as executor of the will of his mother, conveyed to John Winchester "a farme of upland or meadow comonly called or knowne by ye name of Ronton Farme in ye towne of Boston." In the second deed he conveyed to Isaack Stedman "all that farme of upland and meadow consisting of fower hundred and tenn Ack^{rs} comonly called or knowne by ye name of Stanford ffarme," etc., "scittuated at Muddy River in ye precincts of Boston," and the record shows that John Moore appeared in person before Governor John Endicott, acknowledging the transfer, and both deeds were recorded on January 4, 1658.[49]

In these deeds the grantor's brother was described as "Joseph Moore of Wexford in the Countie of Wexford in Ireland," and he gave John Moore a power of attorney as one of the legatees under the will of Anne Hibbins. Joseph

[47] *Echoes From Out the Past*, by Thomas Hamilton Murray, Boston, 1905.

[48] Suffolk County Probate Records, Lib. 6, fol. 283.

[49] Suffolk County Registry of Deeds, Lib. 3, fols. 82 to 85.

later emigrated to this country and both brothers were mentioned as residents of Charlestown, Mass.,[50] and the marriage of Joseph Moore and Hannah Gellune was recorded there in 1659. Several of this name were in the vicinity of Boston. Thomas Rawlins sold to Thomas Moore a house and lot at Boston on February 10, 1654;[51] by deed dated December 23, 1668, William Courser sold a dwelling house and land at Boston to Jeremiah and Samuel Moore;[52] "Alice Moore, widow of Jeremiah Moore," married Henry Langin of Boston;[53] another Jeremiah Moore was mentioned as owner of lands at Hingham, Mass., in a deed dated August 29, 1683;[54] Daniel and Richard Moore enlisted for King Philip's War under Captain Joshua Scottow and served in the "Black point garrison" in 1676;[55] John Moore, described as "formerly of Dublin, shipwright," was on the Charlestown tax list of the year 1680, and on January 15, 1683, his estate was administered by his widow, Mary Moore;[56] on April 5, 1686, Thomas and John Moore signed as witnesses to a mortgage between "Joseph Shaw of Boston, cooper, and Ruth, his wife," and "Elisabeth Condey, widow of William Condey of Boston, mariner."[57] The genealogical records show a long line of people of this name in Massachusetts, all through the eighteenth century.

50 *Charlestown Genealogies and Estates*, by Thomas B. Wyman.

51 Suffolk Deeds, Lib. 2, fol. 109.

52 *Ibid.*, Lib. 6, fol. 7.

53 *Ibid.*, fols. 7 and 8.

54 *Ibid.*, Lib. 13, fols. 21-2.

55 *New England Historic-Genealogical Register*, Vol. 43, p. 75.

56 *Charlestown Genealogies and Estates*, by Thomas B. Wyman.

57 Suffolk Deeds, Lib. 13, fol. 473.

CHAPTER XV

The sad fate of Ann Glover, hanged as a "Witch"—the Powers from Waterford—the Irish origin of the name Roe—Timothy Ryan of Marblehead—the Sullivans—James Stackpole from Limerick or Sligo—Dermond Shehee and Dennis Shihie.

THE sad fate of Anne Hibbins brings to mind the famous case of the Irish woman, Anne Glover, known as "Goody Glover," who in 1688 was hanged in Boston on the pretence that she was a "witch," but "for a certainty because she was a Catholic and would not renounce her faith." Drake, in his *Annals of Witchcraft in New England*, says "the magistrates, long annoyed by the presence of an obstinate Papist in Boston, ordered Goody Glover to be taken into custody," and the Puritan Minister, Cotton Mather, in a sermon preached in Old North Church, Boston, said of her that "she was a scandalous old Irishwoman, very poor, a Roman Catholic and obstinate in idolatry." A Boston merchant, one Robert Calef, who knew and sympathized with the unfortunate woman, thus wrote of her in *More Wonders of the Invisible World*, printed in London in 1700: "Goody Glover was a despised, crazy poor old woman, an Irish Catholic, who was tried for afflicting the Goodwin children. Her behaviour at her trial was like that of one distracted. They did her cruel. The proof against her was wholly deficient. The Jury brought her guilty. She was hung. She died a Catholic." Drake, in referring to Calef's comments, says "she was not a crazy person as we now understand the word; it was not meant that she was insane, but simply that she was weak and infirm." Anne Glover stated that "in the time of Cromwell" she and her husband "were sold to the Barbadoes," whence they came to this country some time before 1682, and she was employed in the family of one John Goodwin in Boston. The Glovers were "cruelly persecuted because of their refusal to attend the sermons of the Puritan Ministers," and on her trial, "she was only able to answer her tormentors in Irish"; but when Cotton Mather visited her in prison, he "asked her to say the Lord's Prayer, for the common belief was that this could not be done by a Catholic or a witch." "She recited the *Pater Noster* to me in Latin," he said, "and in Irish and in English, but she could not end it"; and on the day of her execution "there was a great concourse of people to see if the Papist would relent." But, "the old Irishwoman conquered Cotton Mather; she died a Catholic, and imitating her Divine Master, she died forgiving her enemies, all those from whom she had suffered grevious wrong." [1]

Besides the "Edward Nealand, Irishman," already mentioned as at Ipswich in 1654, vital records of towns in Barnstable, Plymouth and Essex Counties, Mass., for more than 250 years contain such names as Nealand, Newland, Nuland and Kneeland. These names are from the original O'Niallain. According to O'Hart,[2] the first in Ireland to assume that surname was Dermod O'Niallain in the tenth century, and in course of time the name was anglicised Nallin, Nealan, Nealand, Neyland, Newland and Niland. On April 16, 1640, John and William Newland of Sandwich received grants of land; [3] they were listed in 1643 among the "townsmen liable to bear arms," and Freeman, historian of Cape Cod, informs us that "the Newlands were of Irish extraction" and were

[1] From "A Forgotten Heroine," by Harold Dijon, in the *Ave Marie* of Notre Dame, Ind., and in *Journal of the American Irish Historical Society*, Vol. 5, pp. 17-22.

[2] *Irish Pedigrees*, Vol. 1, p. 604.

[3] Plymouth Colony Records, Vol. 1.

"prominent men."[4] Savage[5] also notices the Newlands but makes no mention of their origin. On September 7, 1641, William Newland was made a Freeman of the Colony;[6] on June 5, 1644, he was "lycensed to draw wine at Scituate";[7] on June 4, 1645, William Newland was "allowed to trayne the townsmen of Sandwich in armes," and on June 1, 1647, he was made Lieutenant of the Sandwich military company.[8] On May 19, 1648, he married Rose Holloway at Sandwich,[9] and the "will of William Newland of Sandwich," dated August 26, 1690, showing that he was possessed of considerable property, was probated in Barnstable County on May 6, 1695.[10]

An action for debt entitled "Symon Brodstreet *vs.* Jerymyah Newland" was tried in the Essex Court at Ipswich on July 26, 1654;[11] another Jeremiah Newland and "Daniell Muckenney" (McKenny), both of Taunton, were brought before the Plymouth County Court on June 7, 1659, "for being drunke." Each was fined five shillings and they were "admonished for giveing provaking speeches."[12] On July 12, 1695, the Probate Court of Bristol County, Mass., confirmed to "Katharine, widow of Jerimy Newland of Taunton," the ownership of a house and land at that place.[13] A "Jeremie Nueland" was also mentioned in Portsmouth, R. I., records of the year 1654.[14] The birth of "Anthony, son of Jeremiah

4 *History of Cape Cod—Annals of the Thirteen Towns of Barnstable County,* by Frederick Freeman, Vol. 2, pp. 61 and 69, Boston, 1869.

5 *Genealogical Dictionary of the First Settlers of New England,* Vol. 3, p. 274.

6 Plymouth Colony Records, Vol. 2, p. 23.

7 *Ibid.,* Vol. 2, p. 73.

8 *Ibid.,* Vol. 2, pp. 88 and 117.

9 Plymouth Colonial Records, in *Mayflower Descendant,* Vol. 15.

10 *Ibid.,* Vol. 3.

11 Court Records, Vol. 1, p. 363.

12 Plymouth Colony Records, Vol. 3, p. 168.

13 *First Book of Bristol County Probate Records.*

14 *The Early Records of the Town of Portsmouth,* Rhode Island Historical Society, Providence, 1901.

Newland," was recorded at Taunton on August 1, 1657; another Anthony Newland was "fined for a breach of the peace" at the Salem Court on February 10, 1658,[15] and Jeremiah and John Newland were mentioned in the records of the Plymouth probate court in 1662 and 1667.[16] Sandwich vital records show that "Elizabeth Nuland, wife of William Nuland," was buried there on September 4, 1658; "Elizabeth Nuland, wife of John Nuland," died on May 2, 1671, and Rose Nuland and John Buck were married at Sandwich on February 2, 1682. Many Kneelands are mentioned in the town records of Harrison, Maine, to which place Philip and Edward Kneeland, descended from Edward Nealand of Ipswich, removed in the eighteenth century.

The name Power or Powers, though not of Irish origin, has been a common one in Waterford, Ireland, for several centuries. The founder of the family, Sir Roger de la Poer, came to Ireland with Strongbow in the Norman invasion in the twelfth century,[17] and from him were descended many of the Powers families in New England. Several different accounts of these families have been published,[18] but they are not in agreement as to details. Farmer, in his *Genealogical Register,* refers to "John Power of Charlestown, 1643," as "probably the founder of the families of the name Powers in New England." Amos H. Powers, genealogist of the family, tries to establish for them an English ancestry. He begins his work by a reference to "Sir Roger de Poer" who received a grant of land in Waterford in 1172, but omits all reference to the fact that his descendants have been in Ireland ever since

[15] Plymouth Colony Records, Vol. 2, p. 149.

[16] *Mayflower Descendant,* Vol. 17, p. ?17.

[17] *Irish Pedigrees,* by John O'Hart, Vol. 1, p. 252.

[18] In Farmer's *Genealogical Register; The Powers Family,* by Amos H. Powers, Chicago, Ill., 1884. "Genealogical Register" in *History of Hardwick, Mass.,* by Lucius R. Paige, Boston, 1883, and *History of Woodstock, Vt.,* by Henry Swan Dana, Boston, 1889.

that time; states that "Walter Power, born in 1639, appears in Middlesex County (Mass.) records in 1654 as a boy fourteen years old"; that "he lived at Salem in 1654" and "with his wife, Trial Shepard, to whom he was married at Malden, Mass., on March 11, 1661,[19] he settled on a tract of land in or near Concord, now the town of Littleton, Mass."

On the other hand, Henry Swan Dana says the New England Powers descended from "Thomas and Walter Power, brothers, born in Waterford, Ireland, who came to this country somewhere near the year 1680. In Ireland the name of the family was Power, but these men, on coming to this country, added an *s* to their name, but for two generations after the Power brothers settled here, little or nothing is known of the history of the family." One William H. Powers compiled a genealogical chart of the family, in which he made no reference to their Norman or Irish descent, but claims for them a "Puritan ancestry."

In one way or another, all of these are in error. (1) The founder of the family in Ireland, as his name indicates, was a Norman and he was so called in Irish annals; (2) for nearly 500 years before his descendant, Walter Power, came to this country, the Powers were in Ireland, and history shows that their interests were identified solely with that country, and that is the determining factor which governs the racial category to which they belong; (3) if it be true that Walter Power "lived at Salem in 1654," the assumption is justified that he was one of the Irish "captives" who came in the *Goodfellow* from Kinsale, Ireland; (4) Dana erred in saying that Walter and Thomas Power were "brothers," for as a matter of fact they were father and son, Thomas having been born at Concord in 1667, the son of Walter and Trial Power; (5) he also erred in saying that they came about "the year

[19] The correct date was November 1, 1660. Malden, Mass., Vital Records, p. 281.

1680"; and lastly, the assertion that the New England Powers are of "Puritan ancestry," merely because the immigrant lived among the Puritans, is as ridiculous as if it were said they are of Dutch ancestry.

Whatever be the facts in respect of these matters, it is clear that the progenitor of the American branches of the family was an Irishman, and large numbers of his descendants appear in the eighteenth century records of Worcester County, Mass., towns.[20] Walter and Trial Powers were the parents of nine children; one of them, Daniel, born in 1669, was the father of ten children; Daniel's son, Peter Powers, born in 1707, served as a Captain in the French-English War, and was the father of thirteen children, and one of his sons, Rev. Peter Powers of Haverhill, N. H., a famous New England preacher in his day, also was the father of thirteen children. Thomas Powers settled at Greenwich and Jeremiah Powers at Hardwick, Mass., early in the eighteenth century, and were recorded among the "Proprietors of Hardwick" in the year 1733.[21] Both are said to have emigrated from Waterford, Ireland. Dr. Stephen Powers of Vermont, born at Hardwick in 1735, was a noted medical practitioner in his day; in every generation of the family there were physicians, and there are still physicians of the name in Massachusetts and Vermont who are descended from the Powers of Waterford, Ireland. We are also told that "the Powers of Brimfield, Mass., are descendants from Walter, the emigrant." They came to Brimfield from Hardwick in 1761 and were then "of the fourth generation removed from the emigrant." [22]

One Nicholas Power was an early settler at Providence, Rhode Island, and if a tradition handed down among his de-

[20] Vital records of Greenwich, Hardwick, Worcester, Grafton, Petersham, Winchendon and other Massachusetts towns.

[21] *Proprietors' Records, Town of Hardwick.*

[22] *Historical Celebration of the Town of Brimfield* (1876), by Rev. Charles M. Hyde, Springfield, Mass., 1879.

scendants is to be accepted, it is fairly certain that he also was a native of Ireland. This tradition is to the effect that "Nicholas Power left Drogheda, Ireland, during the siege of that town by the Cromwellians, for Surinam," whence he came to this country. However, there is considerable doubt about the correctness of that date, because of the reference to the siege of Drogheda, which occurred in the year 1649. He was first mentioned in Providence town records on May 27, 1643, and was listed with a number of inhabitants, each of whom received "a free Grante of Twenty five Akers of Land" on November 19, 1645.[23] By his will dated May 27, 1667, he left his estate to his wife, Jane, and son Nicholas. The latter married Hannah Rhodes at Providence on February 3, 1672; he served as a volunteer in King Philip's War and was killed in the "Great Swamp Fight"; Nicholas Power (3), Colonel of a regiment of Providence County Militia in 1731, married Anna Tillinghast on October 31, 1734; Nicholas Power (4) married Mary Hale, and Nicholas Power (5) married Rebecca Corey on April 20, 1766, all at Providence.

Christopher Piggott, a resident of Muddy River in 1655,[24] was sometimes mentioned as Christopher Picket; as for instance, in a deed dated May 19, 1662, by which he conveyed to Joshua Scottow a dwelling house and land at Muddy River,[25] and a "Christopher Picket" was a witness in a case tried at the Essex County Court in June, 1676. He probably was the Christopher Piggott who was mentioned in Boston town records in 1679, and "the ground of Elizabeth Pickett's or Piggott's" at Braintree was so referred to in a deed dated May 25, 1670, recorded in Suffolk County.[26]

[23] *The Early Records of the Town of Providence,* Vol. 1, pp. 30 to 33, and Vol. 2, pp. 1, 29, 31, Providence, R. I., 1893.

[24] *Genealogical Dictionary of the First Settlers of New England,* by James Savage, Vol. 3, p. 435.

[25] Suffolk County Deeds, Lib. 4, fol. 19.

[26] *Ibid.,* Lib. 7, fol. 155.

In the "Lane Family Papers," [27] written by Job Lane, an early settler at Malden, Mass., there is an entry dated June 15, 1666, to the effect that "John Quinne of the County of Corke in Ireland binds himself to Job Lane," and Savage mentions one "Arthur Quing or Quin" as at Boston in 1677. John Quin, with other "Inhabitants and Train Soldiers of ye Province of New Hampshire," signed an address to the Governor and Council of Massachusetts on February 20, 1689,[28] and on April 29, 1692, a John Quin was "chosen Cow Keeper for ye year ensuing" by the Boston Selectmen.[29] "William Quirk, a mariner," is mentioned as an inhabitant of Charlestown in 1636; he owned land in that town in 1638, which he sold in 1644, and then is said to have removed to Newport, R. I.[30] John Quirk was listed as corporal under Captain Samuel Gallop in a Plymouth military company, when on an expedition to Canada in 1690.

Some time prior to 1650 two young men, each named John Roe, cousins, came from Ireland, one of whom was indentured as a servant at Gloucester, Mass., the other settling at East Hampton, and later at Brookhaven, Long Island. In the genealogy of the last mentioned and his descendants,[31] it is stated that he was "born probably in Ireland in 1628," and the records show that down to the present time his descendants [32]

[27] In *New England Historic-Genealogical Register*, Vol. 2.

[28] Massachusetts Archives, Book 35, p. 229.

[29] Boston Town Books, Vol. 7, p. 212.

[30] *Charlestown Genealogies and Estates*, by Thomas B. Wyman.

[31] *American Ancestry*, compiled by John Munsell, Vol. 4, p. 184, Albany, N. Y., 1889.

[32] In tracing the descendants of the early Irish settlers in America, a reuniting of the Irish strains is noted frequently. Sarah Roe, descended from John Roe of Long Island, became the wife of William Connor of Orange County, N. Y., in 1799. He was a son of John Connor, born at Castle Pollard, County Westmeath, Ireland, in 1741, who served as a soldier of the Revolution. Hezekiah Connor, son of William and Sarah Connor, married "Caroline Corwin, fifth in descent from Matthias Corwin of Ipswich, Mass., 1633," who was the Matthias Currin or Curren already mentioned in these pages, and who, doubtless, was an Irishman,

have continued the form, Roe, as their family name. There was a David Roe at Flushing, Long Island, of whom it is said "he probably was a brother of John Roe of Brookhaven." He was "a carpenter and farmer" and is "supposed to have come to Flushing about 1666," and his name was on the rate list of the town in the year 1675.[33] Most of the descendants of the Gloucester Roe spelled their name Row or Rowe. In 1651 he bought land from one Thomas Drake in a district still known as the "Farms," then a wild territory several miles from Gloucester. He died there on March 9, 1662, leaving a wife, Bridget, and sons, John and Hugh; on April 2, 1662, the "inventory of the estate of John Roe of Gloucester, sworn to by his widow, Bridget Roe, and John Row, her son," was filed in the Essex County Court, and at Gloucester there was recorded the marriage of "William Colman, planter, and Bridget, widow of John Rowe," on November 14, 1662.

"Hugh Roe of Weymouth, currier," sold lands at that place to Stephen French on September 13, 1658;[34] he sold a dwelling house and land at Boston by deed dated June 13, 1679;[35] in 1675 he served in King Philip's War and for his services he received a grant of land at Kettle Cove, near Gloucester. In 1680 John Roe bought lands at Kettle Cove from Moses Dudy, which the latter had also received for military services. It may seem strange to those unacquainted with the methods by which certain Irish names originated, to say that the ancestor of the Roe or Rowe family in Ireland was Niall O'Neill of Tyrone, Prince of Ulster in the thirteenth century. There were various ways by which family names were formed in

though his descendants changed the name to Corwin. Dr. Leartes Connor of Detroit, one of the foremost American physicians of his time, was a son of Hezekiah and Caroline Connor.

33 *David Roe of Flushing, Long Island, and Some of his Descendants,* by Clarence A. Torrey, Tarrytown, N. Y., 1926.

34 Suffolk Deeds, Lib. 13, fol. 243.

35 *Ibid.,* Lib. 11, fol. 313.

Ireland. Some took their names from some peculiarity of an ancestor, the color of his hair or his eyes, his manner of speech, his occupation or place of abode, or from a nickname or other soubriquet by which he may have been known. Niall O'Neill was known as *Niall Ruadh*,[36] because he was red-haired, *ruadh* (pronounced *rua*) being the Irish word meaning red, synonymous with the Welch *rhydh* and the French *rouge*, also meaning red. In time the name was anglicised to Roe or Rowe.[37]

Also among the early families at Gloucester were Varneys or Verneys, who are believed to have been Irish or possibly Anglo-Irish. It is certain that families bearing those names were in Ireland, and O'Hart mentions Verneys as "Viscounts of Fermanagh" and "Barons of Belturbet in County Cavan." Bridget Varney sold lands at Gloucester to Bartholomew Foster in 1669; Thomas Verney is mentioned as a fisherman-man and landowner, and one of his sons, Francis Verney, settled in Ireland, and Gloucester town records show that he was "living in the City of Waterford, Ireland, in 1716." The town historian lists among "persons known to have settled in Gloucester before 1711" men named James Brady, three Butlers, John, Stephen and Valentine, Felix Doyle, David Downing, John Flynn, Joseph Greeley, Timothy Higgins, Daniel McAfee, James McCoy, William Moore and Richard Tandy, and these names appear in Gloucester vital records, though there is nothing to indicate that they were there in the seventeenth century.

A Thomas Roach resided at New London in 1651, and he there married Rebecca Redfin on December 12, 1661. On October 14, 1669, he was "admitted Freeman" by the General

[36] *Irish Pedigrees*, by John O'Hart, Vol. 1, pp. 718, 771.

[37] O'Hart lists Neal Roe O'Neale and Shane Roe O'Neale of County Tyrone. The head of one of the branches of the O'Connor family is called "The O'Connor Roe," and Hugh Roe O'Donnell, a famous figure in the history of Ireland, is popularly known there as "Red Hugh O'Donnell."

Court of the Colony, and as late as 1708 a Thomas Roach was a resident of the town. John Roach of Norwalk served in King Philip's War, and in Norwalk records he was referred to as "A soldier in the Direful Swamp Fight," and for his services the town gave him as a gratuity a tract of land "consisting of twelve acres, more or less, lying upon the west side of the Great Rock, so called." William Roche, described as "a whale fisherman," and Hannah Potter were married at Salem and they had four children born there between 1692 and 1699; as William Roache he was on Salem's tax list in the year 1700,[38] and Salem records mention without date "Francis Roache, shipmaster and chandler at Salem, a native of Ireland."[39] There is a "Roache's Point" on Winter Island opposite Salem, said to have been called after William or Francis Roache.

Timothy Ryan, a mariner, is mentioned as of Marblehead. On December 17, 1688, he married Jean Shelton, and in Marblehead vital records there are entries of the births of Elizabeth, Sarah, Deborah and Mary, "daughters of Timothy and Jean Ryan," between 1689 to 1698. No information as to Timothy Ryan seems to be obtainable; he is not mentioned in local history, and although numerous Ryans appear in Essex County records down to the end of the eighteenth century, it is not known if he left any descendants of the name. There was a Ryan family at Marblehead in 1723, and several families of the name appear in the vital records of the towns of Marblehead, Salem and Newburyport.

New Haven town records under date of June 25, 1650, show that "Daniell Selevant" was one of the sureties for a sailor named Michael Taynters, when brought up in Court on a charge of assault; but, that his proper name was Sullivan, is clearly indicated in Hartford records. He married Abigail,

[38] Tax Lists, in *Genealogical Quarterly Magazine*, Vol. 4.

[39] Town Records, in *Historical Collections of the Essex Institute*, Vol. 2.

daughter of James Cole of Hartford, who, in his will bequeathed his property to his "deare and well-beloved Sonne and Daughter, Danyell and Abigaill Sullivane." The will, as recorded, was undated, but the inventory of the testator's estate was taken in November, 1652, and is spread out in detail in the record.[40] The land books at the office of the Secretary of State show that on August 17, 1650, "Andrew Monroe of Appamatick, mariner, bargained, sold and delivered to Robert Lord and Daniel Sullivane," his equity in a sailing vessel, and on August 25, 1652, "Daniel Sullivane of Hartford made Mr. William Gibbons his lawfull attorney."[41] After the death of his wife, Sullivan married Elizabeth Lamberton of New Haven on October 17, 1654.[42] He was master of a Connecticut vessel trading with Southern ports and the West Indies, and in 1655 he died while on a voyage to Virginia. The "will of Daniel Sullivan" was recorded on June 4th of that year at Eastville, Northampton County, Va., and at the New Haven Court on March 4, 1656, "the last will and testament of Daniell Selevant, late of New Haven, deceased at Vergenia," was presented and "the Court accepted as good proofe the testimony of Obadiah Robbins, Magistrate, Northampton County."

The marriage of "Mackum Downing and Margaret Suleavan" was recorded at Lynn, Mass., in April, 1653,[43] and they were the parents of John, Margaret, Sarah, Mary, Priscilla, Catherine and Johanna Downing, all born at Lynn between 1654 and 1670.[44] Downing was a "forgeman" at the iron works in Lynn; he took the "oath of fidelity" there on February 26, 1677, and was then listed "MacCallum Mor Down-

[40] Hartford, Conn., Probate Records, Vol. 2, pp. 36-37.

[41] Land Books, Vol. 1, and Probate Records, Vol. 6.

[42] New Haven Vital Records.

[43] Lynn, Mass., Vital Records, Vol. 2, p. 123.

[44] *Ibid.*, Vol. 1.

ing," [45] and the records say that in 1677 "Macam Downing's wife" was a legatee under the will of "Teague Brann" of Lynn.[46] The death of "Ma Cullam Downing" was recorded in October, 1683.[47]

In 1664, "John Sullaven" and William Collins were listed among a number of "transient residents of New London, who were not grantees and householders," but who, on petitioning the Court, were permitted "to remain as inhabitants." [48] The will of John Dicksey of Swanzey, Mass., proved in the Plymouth County Court on June 4, 1674, mentioned "Daniel Sullavant" under "debts standing out." There is no further mention of "Daniel Sullavant," but it is probable that he was an indentured servant to John Dicksey, who was indebted to him for his wages. One William Sullivan was mentioned in Boston records of the year 1699.

The marriage of "Samuel Gregory and Mary Sillavan" was recorded at Fairfield, Conn., on December 28, 1699, and they were the parents of six children, all born at Stratfield (now Stratford), Conn.,[49] and in the source from which this information is obtained it is said that "Mary Sillivan is supposed to have been a daughter of Owen Sillivan who is mentioned as having a house at Stratfield in 1699." [50] There cannot be much doubt that Owen's proper name was Sullivan, and it is certain there was a Sullivan family in that vicinity less than fifty years later, since according to the genealogy of the Sanford family, "Patience, daughter of Daniel Sullivan," [51] born

[45] Essex County Court Records, Vol. 6.

[46] *Ibid.*, Vol. 6, p. 385.

[47] Lynn Vital Records, Vol. 2, p. 471.

[48] *History of New London, Conn.*, by Frances M. Caulkins, p. 145.

[49] *History and Genealogy of the Families of Old Fairfield*, ed. by Donald Lines Jacobus, Vol. 1, part 3, p. 240.

[50] *Ibid.*, part 5, p. 562.

[51] A Daniel Sullivan of Fairfield County enlisted in the Fourth Regiment of Connecticut Provincials, for service in the French-English War, on April 10, 1758.

December 10, 1746, at Easton, near Stratford, married David Sanford at that place on March 22, 1764.[52]

In one case this name was rendered "Suiflan" and "Shulavan." At a session of the Essex County Court on November 29, 1681, there was heard the "Petition of Joane Suiflan, a poore Irish servant woman," who charged Thomas Mawle of Salem with being "a cruell master," who "hath Many Tymes unreasonably beate me with an unlawful weapon to strike a Christian with, wch weapon is by the English called a maunatee or hors whip, and with this weapon my master Mawle had some tymes stroke me at least 30 or 40 blowes at a Tyme." Mawle brought a counter charge against her because of her refusal to attend religious meetings, and it is apparent that this influenced the jury, since the case was dismissed. There is a long account of the trial in the court records,[53] wherein the name of the complainant was written "Joane Suiflan" and "Joan Shulavan."

For centuries the name Stackpole has been numerous in Ireland, and according to Irish annals there were many Mayors, Aldermen and Recorders of the name in the City of Limerick between 1450 and 1650. They were descended from Sir Robert Stakpol, who came to Ireland in the Norman invasion in 1172. There have been many of the name in Maine and New Hampshire, whose ancestor, according to a long account of him in the genealogy of the family, was James Stackpole, who was "taken prisoner on the coast of Ireland when a boy only fourteen years old and brought to this country."[54] His descendants state "he probably came from Limerick, although a tradition says he came from Sligo,"[55] and it is possible the latter is correct, since he gave the name,

[52] *Sanford Genealogy*, Vol. 1, p. 156.

[53] Records and Files of the Quarterly Court, Vol. 8, pp. 222-6.

[54] *History and Genealogy of the Stackpole Family*, by Everett S. Stackpole, Lewiston, Me., 1920.

[55] *Ibid.*

Sligo, to a strip of land on Salmon Falls in Strafford County, N. H., where he first settled. In 1680 he was taxed at Cochecho, N. H., and for several years thereafter at Dover where he married Margaret Warren, and they were the parents of five sons and three daughters, all of whom are mentioned in the public records. From 1693 to 1699 he kept a tavern at South Berwick, Maine, and in 1710 he bought "the Samuel Hale estate in Rollingsford, N. H.," and lived there until his death in 1756, and for 150 years his descendants possessed this property. This place has been described as "opposite the mouth of the Great Works River, on the road to Sligo," and "Sligo Road" is still known by that name. In the will of "John Bready of Kittery," [56] dated August 30, 1681, he was referred to as "James Stagpoole," and the will of his son, "James Stagpole, Junr of Barwick, planter," dated November 11, 1706, recorded at the probate office of York County, Maine,[57] mentioned his father and his brothers, William, Philip and John Stackpole. Some members of the family settled at Waterville, Maine, and the town historian informs us that "James Stackpole (the immigrant) of Sligo, Ireland, came over in 1680, probably to Biddeford, Maine." [58] From the same source we learn that for several generations the Stackpoles were the most active and prominent people in that vicinity, and a grandson of the immigrant, Captain James Stackpole, commanded "the first military company raised there in defense of American liberty." [59]

Owen Swiney was one of the passengers on the *Goodfellow* which arrived at Marblehead from Kinsale, Ireland, in 1654, and as "Owen Swinn, a servant, age 16," he was a witness on a trial in the Ipswich court on July 28, 1658.[60] Thomas

[56] Mentioned in York County Registry of Deeds, Lib. 5, fol. 13.

[57] Lib. 4, fol. 130.

[58] Whittemore's *History of Waterville, Me.*

[59] *Ibid.*

[60] Records of the Essex County Court, Vol. 2, p. 112.

Skallin or Scallon was at Falmouth, Maine, in 1651, but in 1658 he bought land at Gloucester, Mass., and removed to that place, and his son, "Thomas Skallin," was mentioned in Gloucester records in the year 1676. One "Dennis Skalion" was mentioned in the Essex County Court records in 1664,[61] and "Brigitt" or "Bridgett" Skerrey was a witness in that court on June 17, 1679.[62] Thomas Sexton was mentioned in a deed dated October 16, 1661, from John Hart to Matthew Cushion and Thomas Joy, as owner of lands in Boston,[63] and by deed dated March 16, 1674, "Thomas Sexton of Boston, miller, and Mary, his wife," sold to George Healey and William Snell "a parcel of land scituate at the north end of Boston."[64] There can be no assurance, however, that he was an Irishman, because there were English as well as Irish families of the name at this period. "Dennis Springer of Ireland" probably was a resident of New London in 1687, and his marriage to "Mary Hudson of London in Old England" was recorded at New London in that year. "Peter Sheridon" was listed under "Country Rate" in Boston's tax list of the year 1692,[65] and as Peter Sheridan his name appears in a list of "Inhabitants of Boston" in 1695.[66]

A "Dermond Shehee" was at Portsmouth, N. H., in 1660,[67] and there can be very little doubt that the proper form of his name, and that of "Dennise Shihie" who came to Boston from the Island of Nevis on November 25, 1675, was Sheehy. Not long after his arrival, "Dennise Shihie" was enrolled as a soldier in Captain Samuel Mosley's company for King Philip's War, and was made "Company Clarke." He seems

61 *Ibid.*, Vol. 3.

62 *Ibid.*, Vol. 7, p. 238.

63 Suffolk County Deeds, Lib. 3, fols. 491 and 502-504.

64 *Ibid.*, Lib. 12, fol. 100.

65 Boston Town Books, Vol. 10.

66 *Ibid.*, Vol. 1, p. 168.

67 *Pioneers of Maine and New Hampshire*, by Rev. Charles Henry Pope, p. 186.

to have been an interesting character, serving under different Captains, and appears variously on the rolls as Sihy, Shyhy and Sihie, and one of the historians of the war states "the men's names are all in the handwriting of Dennis Sihy," which he describes as "a wonderful production in the way of misspelling names." [68]

[68] "Soldiers in King Philip's War," in *New England Historic-Genealogical Register,* Vol. 37, p. 181.

CHAPTER XVI

The Healys in Massachusetts—"Willyam Heally, ye Iersman," at Cambridge, 1664—Sarah Healy, early Boston schoolmistress —William Collins taught school at Hartford, 1640—"Master O'Shane, an Irish scholar," taught the children of "the best families" of the town of Boston, 1678—"Kathleen, daughter of a Lord of Galway," kidnapped in Ireland.

WE are told that "Philip Towle, the patriarch of the Towle families now numerous in New England and elsewhere, came to Hampton, N. H., as early as 1657"; that "he was of Irish extraction and the locality in Hampton where he settled was, on that account, early called Ireland, a name it still retains." [1] From this it is inferred that the family name originally was Toole. In actions at law in the Essex County Court he appears as "Philip Toule"; as, for instance, a case entitled "John Wheelrite *vs.* Philip Toule," tried on August 13, 1663, and "James Pendleton *vs.* Philip Toule," tried in October, 1666, and in 1675 he was mentioned as "Philip Toule of Hampton." [2] The marriage of "Mary Tooll" and Nehemiah Hunt was recorded at Concord on June 1, 1663, and they had two sons, Nehemiah and John, born at Concord.[3]

One Michael Tandy was mentioned as in Essex County, and at a session of the court in April, 1673, administration was granted to Joseph Lancaster "upon the estate of Michaell

[1] Towle Genealogy in *History of the Town of Hampton, N. H.*, by Joseph Dow, Vol. 2, Salem, Mass., 1893.

[2] Essex County Court Records, Vol. 3, pp. 98, 147 and 364, and Vol. 6, p. 139.

[3] Concord, Mass., Vital Records.

Tandy, deceased," and he was ordered "to bring in an inventory to the next Hampton Court." [4] John Tulley was a resident of Boston in 1685; [5] "Richard Thomas of Dublin in Ireland, 18 years old," was listed with a number of "servants" who came to New England in the *Virginia Merchant* in March, 1699,[6] but that is the only mention of his name. Margaret Taylor, an Irishwoman, and Alexander Bulman were married at Watertown on December 22, 1690, and when registering the marriage in the "Record Book of the Pastors," the celebrant, Rev. John Bailey, referred to her as "one of my Ireland friends and once my serv^{t}." [7] According to the "Diary of Samuel Sewall," [8] the minister himself came to Watertown "from Dublin, Ireland," although John Dunton wrote in his *Journal* that he came "from Limerick, Ireland." [9]

In the eighteenth century, Welsh or Walsh [10] was a common name in New England. Thomas Welsh was "admitted to the church" at Charlestown on February 12, 1650; in 1658 he was mentioned in the town records as "Tythingman," and in the rolls of the troops raised for King Philip's War are found Thomas, Philip and John Welsh and James Wealsh. Peter Welsh signed as witness to a deed dated September 18, 1666, recorded in Suffolk County; [11] Elizabeth Walsh, also listed Hannah Walsh, was one of "ye Passengers that came in ye shipe, *Hannah and Elizabeth*," which arrived

4 Essex County Court Records, Vol. 5, p. 166.

5 Boston Town Books, Vol. 10, p. 88.

6 List in *New England Historic-Genealogical Register*, Vol. 64, p. 259.

7 Watertown, Mass., Town Records, Vol. 4, p. 100.

8 In *Massachusetts Historical Society Collections*, 5th Ser., Vol. 5, p. 452.

9 *Ibid.*, 2nd Ser., Vol. 2.

10 The idea prevails in this country that Welsh and Walsh are separate names, because of their different spellings, but that opinion is erroneous. In Ireland Walsh is never pronounced with the sound of *waw*, but always as if spelled Welsh.

11 Suffolk County Deeds, Lib. 5, fol. 85.

at Boston on November 4, 1679;[12] Mary and Sarah Welsh, daughters of Thomas Welsh, Jr., and his wife, Hannah, were born at Charlestown in 1688 and 1692, respectively, and in later years seven other children of Thomas and Hannah Welsh were baptised at the First Church in Charlestown. John Miles and Mary Whelan were married at Salem "18th 11 mo. '61," and she "died in ye year '63."[13]

Healy is another very common name in Massachusetts records. A Thomas Healey was at Cambridge as early as 1635 and Robert Healy was mentioned in a deed dated December 28, 1643, as owner of lands at Watertown.[14] William Healy was recorded several times at the Suffolk County Registry of Deeds. On March 24, 1649, John Roberts conveyed a house and lot to William Healy;[15] in October, 1650, William Healy was the grantor in a deed to Thomas Dudley, covering a plot of ground and barn;[16] Robert Starkweather sold a house and lot to William Healy on March 31, 1652;[17] and William Healy conveyed land to John Weld by deed dated June 16, 1659,[18] the property in all four deeds being described as in Roxbury. This William Healy was a resident of Cambridge in 1664, in whose town records he was written down "Willyam Heally, ye Iersman," and on August 17th of that year he signed a petition to the General Court with other residents of the town. He was the "prison keeper" at Cambridge from 1672 to 1682, when he was "removed from office." He married five times, and in 1680 his wife, Sarah (Brown) Healy, to whom he was married at Charlestown on

[12] Essex County Court Records, Vol. 7, p. 303, and *New England Historic-Genealogical Register*, Vol. 28.

[13] *Essex Institute Historical Collections*, Vol. 2, p. 297.

[14] Registry of Deeds, Suffolk County, Mass., Lib. 1.

[15] *Ibid.*

[16] *Ibid.*

[17] *Ibid.*

[18] *Ibid.*, Lib. 3.

November 29, 1677, was schoolmistress in the famous university town, Cambridge, Mass., and the record says she had "nine scholars."

Exclusive of the numerous persons of the name mentioned in records of the early part of the eighteenth century, we find Nicholas Healy of Pemaquid, Maine, who took the "oath of fidelity" in 1674, and Paul Healy who in 1675 settled at New Hampton, N. H.[19] The family evidently removed to Rehoboth, Mass., since in the parish registers at that place there were recorded Paul, Henry, Samuel, Thomas, William and Phebe, children of Paul Healy, all baptised on the same day, January 2, 1703,[20] and the death of "Paull Healey" appears in the vital records as of March 12, 1718. "Nathaniel Healy of Newton or Cambridge" served in King Philip's War 1675-6,[21] and on July 14, 1681, he married Rebecca Hagar and brought up a large family at Watertown, Mass.[22] George Healy was one of twelve "Tythingmen" at Boston, appointed by the General Court in October, 1677; [23] "Dennis Healey or Haley" married Joanna Ballard at Watertown on March 22, 1681,[24] and "Joanna, daughter of Dennis and Joanna Healey," was born at Sudbury on August 23, 1682. But, when their daughter, Tabitha, was born on November 2, 1684, the parents were recorded "Dennis and Joanna Headley," and the birth of Joanna (2) on September 25, 1689, was thus entered in the register: "Joanna, daughter of Dennis and Joanna Heyland." [25]

William Healy signed a "peticon of several inhabitants of

[19] *Provincial Papers of New Hampshire.*

[20] Rehoboth, Mass., Vital Records.

[21] Bodge's *King Philip's War*, p. 171.

[22] Watertown, Mass., Vital Records.

[23] *History and Antiquities of the City of Boston,* by Samuel G. Drake, Vol. 2, p. 438.

[24] Watertown, Mass., Vital Records.

[25] Sudbury, Mass., Vital Records.

Hingham," Mass., to the General Court on May 30, 1679.[26] Samuel Healy of Salisbury married Hannah Smith at that place on May 22, 1685, and a Samuel Healy was at Hampton, N. H., in 1693.[27] Mary and Sarah, daughters of William and Sarah Healy, were born at Bradford, Mass., on October 10, 1691, and February 18, 1693, respectively.[28] Terence Healey was at Boston in 1694, but in 1698 he was listed as "Terrence Henley";[29] John Healy was enrolled as a soldier in Major Simon Willard's Middlesex County Company on October 5, 1675, and he probably was the John Healy who resided at Newton, Mass., in 1698.

Some of the Healys were recorded "Haley" and "Hayley," a common method of pronouncing the name in some parts of Ireland. In 1654 there is mention of "Mary Hayley, servant to Hugh Williams of Boston," and in all likelihood she was one of the Irish "captives" transported in the *Goodfellow* in that year. Richard Haley "acknowledged judgment to Mr. Moses Maverick" at the Essex County Court in 1670;[30] John Haley married Ruth Gaylord at Hadley, Mass., in 1681 and died there in 1688.[31]

The Andrew Haley before mentioned is called "the first settler from Ireland on Isles of Shoals." With the three Kelly brothers elsewhere referred to, he settled on "Smutty Nose Island" in the year 1653, and he and his descendants long occupied this island, which is now called Haley's Island. We are told "he was extensively engaged in the fisheries at the Isles of Shoals, where he settled at an early colonial day and for him Haley's Island was named. He seems to have been a

[26] *The Records of the Colony of Massachusetts Bay in New England*, Vol. 5, p. 232.

[27] *Provincial Papers of New Hampshire.*

[28] Bradford, Mass., Vital Records.

[29] Town Books, Vol. 10, p. 88.

[30] Essex County Court Records, Vol. 4, p. 310.

[31] Savage's *Genealogical Dictionary*, Vol. 2, p. 332.

man of wealth and social standing and was known as 'King of the Shoals.' A seawall was built by him to connect two islands and improve his harbor," [32] described as "the only secure harbor on these islands." [33] In 1662, he bought lands at York, Maine, which passed to his son, Andrew, and in 1694 and 1697 the latter was recorded as the patentee of certain lands in York County, and the will of Andrew Haley (2), dated April 8, 1725, indicates him to have been a man of considerable wealth for the time. He left a long line of descendants; the name, Haley, is found in profusion in New England down to the present day, and a local chronicler states that "descendants of the original Andrew Haley have lived on Haley's Island for 250 years."

Thomas Haley, brother of Andrew (1), settled at Saco, Maine, in 1653,[34] and on July 5th of that year he acknowledged himself "subject to the government of Massachusetts." In 1654 he received a license for a tavern and ferry on the Saco River, and in 1673 the York Court fixed the tariff for his ferry at "two pence for every one he setteth over the river," and the Haley family operated this ferry for many years. In York records of the year 1692 he was referred to as "Thomas Healy," but he signed his name Haley to a deed dated May 21, 1683, whereby he conveyed his entire property to his son, Thomas, and named him "the only legal heyre to my estate." [35] In 1684 and 1687 the latter was recorded as the purchaser of lands in the vicinity and in the deeds he was called "Thomas Haley, the younger, of Saco, planter." [36]

[32] *Saco Valley Families and Settlements*, by Rev. Gideon T. Ridlon, p. 706, and *Genealogical and Family History of the State of Maine*, by Dr. George T. Little.

[33] *Collections, Massachusetts Historical Society*, Year 1800.

[34] Town Records, in *History of Saco and Biddeford*, by George Folsom, p. 86, Saco, Me., 1830.

[35] York Deeds, Lib. 3, fol. 124.

[36] *Ibid.*, Lib. 9, fols. 64-65.

He served as sergeant of the Saco military company during the Indian War in 1689, saw service in many of the frontier alarms and in August, 1695, according to the "Diary of Rev. John Pike," "Serj Tho Haley was kill^d by Ind^ns a little out of Saco fort."

In 1695, Sarah, widow of Thomas Haley (2), removed with her family to Boston, where she married Richard Carr of Amesbury on February 26, 1701, and when her daughter, Sarah, married Samuel Carr at Salisbury on August 24, 1709, her name was recorded Sarah Healey. Thomas Haley, grandson of the immigrant, born at Saco in 1692, was a house builder at Exeter, N. H., and lived there to the great age of 105 years. In Connecticut annals of the year 1682 there are some references to "Captain Ohely," sometimes mentioned as "Haley." He was master of a coasting vessel and at one time was characterized as "a pirate," but I have never been able to obtain any information as to him, though it is probable, from his name, that he was an Irishman. New England town records of the eighteenth century show that some of the Healys and Haleys followed the teaching profession and generally were an important factor in the educational progress of their respective communities.

Among teachers of New England youth in the eighteenth century there were many natives of Ireland and sons of Irish immigrants,[37] but in the seventeenth century traces are found of only two Irishmen engaged in that calling, William Collins and "Master" O'Shane. In his *Ecclesiastical History of New England*,[38] Rev. Joseph B. Felt states: "This summer (1641) a number of families not permitted to enjoy their religion at

[37] See the author's researches on this subject, entitled "Early Irish Schoolmasters in New England," in *Catholic Historical Review*, Vol. 3, and "Irish Schoolmasters in the American Colonies," in *Journal of the American Irish Historical Society*, Vol. 25.

[38] Vol. 1, pp. 456-7.

Christopher[39] without persecution, left, and came to New Haven. They dispersed in different directions and some returned to Ireland. They were accompanied to this country by their minister, Mr. William Collins, who began to teach school at Hartford." Collins was also mentioned in the *Journal of John Winthrop* as "a young scholar, full of zeal," but as to how long he taught is unknown. He married Bridget, daughter of the celebrated Ann Hutchinson, and then removed to Boston, where he was arraigned before the General Court because of his refusal to accept certain religious doctrines. On December 10, 1641, the Court fined him £100 and ordered him to leave Boston and "not return at his utmost peril." He and his wife returned to Connecticut, but in September, 1643, they met a tragic fate, having been killed by Indians in the vicinity of New Rochelle, N. Y. Although no definite statement is made in New England annals as to Collins's nationality, yet, since it is said that some of the refugees from the West Indies, with whom he came to this country, "returned to Ireland," the natural assumption is that he was an Irishman.

O'Shane is not mentioned in the public records or by any of the historical societies, but some information as to him has been obtained from a very scarce little book entitled "Leaves from Margaret Smith's Journal of the Province of Massachusetts Bay, 1678-9," published in London in the eighteenth century. Margaret Smith was an English girl, niece of Edward Rawson, Secretary of the Colony of Massachusetts Bay, and during her residence in this country she recorded in her *Journal* many interesting things which came under her observation. Writing about her school days in Boston under date of "March ye 15" (1679), she referred to "one Master O'Shane, an Irish scholar, of whom my Cousins here (the daughters of Edward Rawson) did learn the Latin

[39] The Island of St. Christopher, West Indies.

tongue . . . Rebecca tells me he is a learned Man, as I can well believe," but "lost the favour of many of the first Families here who did formerly employ him." Whence he came or the period of his service as a teacher cannot be ascertained, and though it is probable he did not conduct a school but was a private tutor, it is apparent that he was a competent teacher. All we know is, from a source that can hardly be questioned, that as far back as 258 years ago the children of "many of the first families" of the town of Boston learned their letters from "an Irish scholar," but he has received no place in Massachusetts history!

Master O'Shane evidently was a versatile individual, and like many of the Irish schoolmasters of the olden days, he seems to have "courted the Muse." Margaret Smith related in her *Journal* how her tutor, "exceeding merry, entertained us rarely with his stories and songs. There was one Ballad which he saith is of his own making, concerning the selling of the daughter of a great Irish Lord as a Slave in his land, which greatly pleased me, and on my asking for a copy of it, he brought it to me this morning in a faire hand. I copy it in my Journal, as I know that Oliver, who is curious in such things, will like it." Then followed the "Ballad," which is of twenty-nine stanzas, bearing the simple caption, "Kathleen." The subject of the poet's effusion was described as the daughter of "a Lord of Galway," who was "stolen from the castle," "sold to a sea Captain in Limerick," who was supposed to have again sold her into captivity. On her father offering "her hand in marriage" to whoever would rescue the maiden, "a handsome youth" undertook the search, and the ballad goes on to relate how the daring youth "sailed east and west and north and south until he came to Boston town," but after his arrival there, he believed he had come to "the end of the rainbow"! However, after many vicissitudes, and when about to give up the search in despair, he located

"Kathleen" somewhere in Massachusetts, employed as a menial in the home of an English planter. On offering her "master" his "purse of gold," the maiden was released and the couple returned to Ireland, and as the ballad informs us, they afterwards married and "resided in their castle looking down the pleasant Galway shore."

CHAPTER XVII

General comment on the foregoing—Irishmen in other colonies occupied high places in public life—the Virginia McCarthys cousins of George Washington—the early Irish settlers in America mainly Catholics—how they suffered for their faith—why their descendants are non-Catholic.

THE facts herein related, collected from sources that cannot be called into question, vindicate beyond cavil the frequently derided contention that the Irish came to New England in large numbers in the seventeenth century. And it is proper to assume that much more evidence of the same character is available, if one had the time and opportunity to make a more extensive examination of the records. It is regretted that the full story of the first Irish in New England has not been obtained, since it is clear that a vastly greater number of Irish people than are here listed lived in New England, which statement is amply supported by the English State Papers of the time. It is evident, however, that most of the "Exiles from Erin" never rose above the status in which they began life in this country; many of them stood on the lower rungs of the "social ladder," according to the standards of the day; they lived in obscurity and died poor and practically unknown. But, on the other hand, as has been clearly demonstrated, there were Irish in New England in that early day who were numbered among the property owners, farmers and business men; their names are on the tax rolls; they stood side by side with their English neighbors in battling with the primeval conditions of the time; they enrolled in defense of the settlements when men were needed to repel the assaults of the Indians, and in the communities where they lived they unquestionably played some part in the everyday life of their times. Few of their descendants, however, are now recognized among the class designated the "old New England stock."

Perhaps it should be said here also that in seventeenth century records of New York, New Jersey, Pennsylvania, Maryland, Virginia and the Carolinas, there are so many Irish people mentioned, that a mere list of their names would be a revelation to those who think that the Irish did not begin to come to this country until the forepart of the nineteenth century, as has been stated so frequently by historical writers. In that early period of American history there were Irishmen who occupied places of much importance in these colonies. Florence O'Sullivan from Kerry was Surveyor-General of South Carolina in 1676, and his name is perpetuated in Sullivan's Island in Charleston harbor. George Talbot from Roscommon held a similar post in Maryland in 1680; and Thomas Holmes, a native of Dublin, was the surveyor who first laid out the lands on the west bank of the Delaware, now part of the City of Philadelphia. An Irishman, James Dalton, was the first Land Register of South Carolina (1670); in the same year his countryman, Michael Moran, was a member of its Commons, and this same Michael Moran is said to have been "the father of the first white child born in South Carolina." Richard Kyrle, an Irishman, was Governor of the Province of South Carolina in 1684; sixteen years later James Moore, son of the famous Irish Chieftain, Rory O'Moore, was chosen its Governor. Moore came to this country from Ireland in 1655, settled in Charleston and there married a daughter of Sir John Yeamans, and his son, James Moore, also became Governor of South Carolina. Thomas Dongan from Kildare, the distinguished Governor of the Province of New York, 1683-1688, induced many of his countrymen to emigrate to this country, who settled on Long Island and along the Hudson River in Dutchess and Columbia Counties.

We find Irishmen among the colonial merchants and traders. Cornelius Dougherty, an Indian trader from Virginia, was the first white man known to have penetrated the territory now embraced in the State of Kentucky (1690). "John Anderson, the Irishman from Dublin," or, as the Dutch expressed it, "Jan Andriessen, de Iersman van Dublingh," traded with the Indians on the Hudson River between 1649 and 1657, and Thomas Lewis, usually referred to in the Dutch records as "Thomas, the Irishman," also traded with the Indians on the Hudson River in 1662. Thomas Lynch and Anthony Duane, both from Galway, Ireland, appear in New York records of the late years of the seventeenth century as prominently as any of the Dutch or English merchants of their time. Among merchants and landowners in New York, 1674-1677, we find William Walsh and Hugh O'Neil; and Dr. William Hayes from Barry's Court, Ireland, is mentioned by O'Callaghan as the physician who attended to the ills of the Dutch and English residents of New Amsterdam in the year 1647. "William Hogan, van Bor in Ierlandt in de Kings County," *i.e.*, William Hogan, who was born in Birr, in Kings (now Offaly) County, Ireland, was a merchant in Albany in 1680. The Newlins from Mountmellick, Ireland, who came in the *Welcome* with William Penn in 1682, were active business men in Philadelphia. Dennis Rochford from Wexford, who also came in the *Welcome*, was a man of much prominence in Philadelphia, and in 1683 he was a member of the "First Provincial Council" of the Province of Pennsylvania. Few of these receive any mention in the historical works that are read by the general public; their racial identity became submerged with the English, and consequently, they are almost unknown to the American people.

Captain William O'Brian, who emigrated to this country after the defeat of the Irish army at Limerick in 1690, was an extensive trader and lumber merchant in North Carolina, and he was the ancestor of a distinguished American, William Jennings Bryan of Nebraska, three times nominated for the Presidency of the United States. Charles O'Carroll from Tipperary, Attorney-General of Maryland in 1688, was one of the largest landowners in the colony and was the grandfather of the illustrious Charles Carroll of Carrollton. The Kings of Kingston Hall, a famous colonial family in Maryland, were Irish, and Lord Baltimore gave recognition to the fact that the Irish were an important element in the colony, when he designated the territory now embraced in Cecil County, as the "County of New Ireland," by proclamation dated St. Marie's, Md., April 4, 1684. "New Ireland" comprised three subdivisions, known as New Munster, patented by Edmund O'Dwyer from Tipperary, New Leinster, patented by Bryan O'Malley from Wicklow, and New Connaught, patented by George Talbot from Roscommon. Indeed, the records at the Land Commissioner's office in Annapolis show that a very large number of the grantees of lands in the "County of New Ireland" in the last quarter of the seventeenth century, were Irish immigrants, and their names clearly indicate that they were of the ancient Race.

Captain Hubert Farrell of James City County, Virginia, is mentioned in connection with the defence of Jamestown during the "Bacon Rebellion" in 1676, and it was he who commanded the colonial troops at the famous battle of King's Creek in that year. Andrew Meade from Cork, Ireland, settled in Nansemond County, Va., in 1690, and became an extensive trader, landowner and member of the Legislature. He was the grandfather of Colonel Richard Kidder Meade, Aide-de-Camp to General Washington. Daniel Sullivan of Suffolk, Va., was a man of much prominence in that part of the Colony, a Burgess for Nansemond County, County Clerk and Clerk of the Court. Among his descendants were Lucas Sullivant, mentioned in the history of the Ohio Valley as one of its most noted pioneers, and William Sullivant, a famous American bryologist.

Daniel McCarthy came from Cork, Ireland, to Westmoreland County, Va., in 1692; in time he owned lands in five Virginia Counties; from 1710 to 1715 he was Speaker of the House of Burgesses, and through the marriage of his son, Dennis, and Sarah Ball on September 19, 1724, his grandchildren were second cousins of the immortal Washington.[1] The records of their land grants may be found in the Patent Books at the Land Commissioner's office in the State Capitol at Richmond, Va. Numerous other emigrants from Ireland and their sons are recorded among the seventeenth century landowners in Virginia. That Irishmen of good standing and education came to the colony at this early period, is seen from the fact that in some instances they held as high a social position as any of their neighbors of English descent. Yet the country which gave them birth receives little or no credit in history!

It would be impracticable to furnish exact figures showing how many Irish came to the colonies in the seventeenth century, though it can be said with certainty that they numbered several thousands. Today, there are numerous Americans holding the same views as our present critic, but who, if the facts had been related in history, might be disposed to give due credit to the Irish as part of the "original stock." In some instances, successive generations of the descendants of these people can be traced through the public records, although at the present time comparatively few of the old names can

[1] Sarah Ball was a first cousin of Mary Ball, wife of Augustine Washington, and mother of George Washington. See *The McCarthys in Early American History,* by Michael J. O'Brien, New York, 1921.

be found in the localities where the Irish originally settled. In time, some of the Irish families died out and in other cases there were no male children born in some generations, which to some extent explains why so many of the old names have disappeared. These things, of course, also occurred in New England, and eventually all had the effect of lessening the number of Irish names in later American records.

In support of the theory that no Irish came to New England in the seventeenth century, it is stated "there were then no Roman Catholics in the Colony." That is true only in so far as it means that none practiced the Catholic faith; for despite all opinion to the contrary, the majority of the Irish who came to the colonies at this period were Catholics, or had been in their own country. On their arrival here, however, they encountered as bitter hostility to their religion as ever existed among the ruling element in Ireland; there were neither priests nor churches of their own faith to commune with, and in many places, if one dared avow himself a Catholic, the consequences would be serious. In Massachusetts the town was the nominal unit of government; but in every case, by virtue of an ordinance enacted by the General Court, the minister of the local church dominated all affairs of the community, and all rules and regulations formulated by the town officials were first submitted to the minister, who approved or disapproved of them at his pleasure. Attendance at religious "meetings" by every man, woman and child was made compulsory; refusal was punishable by fine or by whipping, as a consequence of which the records furnish a long list of victims of religious intolerance.

Under such conditions, a Catholic had no earthly chance to succeed in life unless he renounced his religion; and although it is evident that many of the Irish in time were forced to do so, instances are not wanting indicating that some refused to comply with the regulations. An extreme case was that of the martyred Irishwoman, Anne Glover. In 1665, David Frou of Northampton, Mass., was ordered "to sit in the stocks during the Court's pleasure for contemning the constable's authority commanding him into the meeting house," and in 1667 Teague Jones was "returned by the Selectmen of the Town of Yarmouth for not coming to meeting." And at the Salem Court in 1681, when Joane Sullivan brought a charge of cruelty against her master, the clerk of the court thus recorded the testimony of one of the witnesses: "I asked the Irish maide about going to the public meeting and she replied that it was a develish place, for thay did not goe to mast, and what suld shee doe there, for shee was resolved to stay out her time with her master and misteris and then goe whome to her owne contry againe wher shee mit goe to mast." Joane Sullivan was lashed with a whip when she refused to attend "the public meeting," but she evidently lived in the hope that some day she would find her way back to "her own country," where she could receive the consolations of her religion and "goe to mast," that is to say, that she would have the privilege of attending the holy sacrifice of the Mass. It is probable that her ambition was never realized, and with the entry here quoted from the records of the Court, Joane Sullivan disappeared from history.

We have observed from the references to "Cornelius, the Irishman," an indentured servant at Northampton between 1658 and 1663, that his surname was omitted from the records when the town gave him a grant of land, on the expiration of the period of his service. Evidently, his fellow townsmen refused to acknowledge that he was on an equality with them, because he was an Irishman and probably a Catholic. And it was only when he had risen to what they regarded as a "respectable" status, that his full name began to appear in the local records, and the community consented to grant Cornelius Merry those civic rights that were enjoyed by others. The relationship between master and servant was not then like that which obtains today between employer and employe. The social conditions of the time permitted the master to regard his servant as a mere chattel or other property that he could dispose of at will. Oftentimes, the servant had a better social background than his master, and instances are noted where the servant had education, and even culture, beyond the compass of the master. But the servant was so tied down by his indentures, that he was not permitted to use his intelligence; he was not allowed to have a will of his own and was entirely at the mercy of the whims and caprices of his master.

The Irish and Scotch servants seem to have been particularly unfortunate, because the Puritans looked upon them as of an "inferior" race. One means of reminding them of the lowly place they occupied in life was by withholding recognition of their full names, and continually reminding them of their racial origin. In many cases, the servant was known only as Mr. So-and-So's "Irishman," or "Scotchman," as the case might be, and thus we find that in 1658 when Joseph Parsons received a grant of land from the town of Northampton, it was recorded by the Town Clerk that it was "for the estate hee hath in his Irish man" (unnamed). On April 12, 1677, Samuel Gardner of Salem had a warrant issued for the apprehension of his runaway servant, and the latter was described as "Mr. Samuel Gardner's Irish man." Also, in a deed dated January 7, 1679, by which Bozoun Allen conveyed to Nathaniel Green a dwelling house and ground in Boston, it was recited that the premises were "in the present tenure and occupation of one Teige, an Irishman." [2]

True, some of the English in Massachusetts were generous

[2] Suffolk County Deeds, Lib. 11, fol. 105.

and considerate to their servants, and recognized that their position in life was not in all cases compatible with their family origin. On the other hand, impartial students of the public records must admit there are indications that in other instances the English settlers were, as a matter of fact, of lowly origin and were destitute of honor or dignity or kindness toward their fellowmen of other races. In their opinion, to be English was to be superior to all other human beings on "God's footstool." Their lilliputian minds would not permit them to acknowledge that their Irish servants could possibly be their equals, or should aspire to a higher level in the social scale, and as the record is scrutinized, it is with difficulty that one suppresses his indignation at the treatment meted out to those whose fate it was to live among them! They refused to give any recognition to the Irish, except in such a way as to bemean them, and they called them by the contemptible phrase, "the Irishry," sometimes coupled with references to the "Papish church." How many Irish hearts were crushed by their cruelty, the world will never know, and one can only wonder how much Cromwell and his myrmidons had to answer before God for consigning them to a life of slavery! Doubtless, many of Cornelius Merry's countrymen were known only by their baptismal names during their period of service. And throughout this book will be noted references to another "Cornelius, the Irishman," "a certain Irishman named Cornelius" at Barnstable (1664),[3] "David, the Irishman," at Yarmouth (1655),[4] "Dennis, the Irishman," at Piscataqua (1657),[5] "Michaell, the Irishman," at Ipswich (1657),[6] "Dorman, ye Irishman," at Boston

[3] Barnstable County Probate Records.

[4] *Ibid.*

[5] *Pioneers of Maine and New Hampshire*, by Rev. Charles Henry Pope, p. 163, Boston, 1908.

[6] Essex County Court Records, Vol. 2, p. 41.

(1674),[7] "William, the Irishman," at Topsfield (1666),[8] and a man recorded only as "Alexander, the Irishman," was in business as a "brickmaker" at Rehoboth, Mass., in 1663.[9]

Some comment by Rupp, a Pennsylvania historian, although applying to a later period, is of considerable interest in connection with the history of the early Irish Catholics in America. During the first quarter of the eighteenth century, there were large emigrations from Ireland to Pennsylvania, and Rupp refers to a custom among the Irish families in assembling in prayer around their firesides at night. Undoubtedly, this was the beautiful custom of "reciting the Rosary," which has prevailed in Ireland for centuries. In their homes they had pictures of Christ and the Virgin, besides other religious objects, and their prayer books were printed in Gaelic and English. Springing from a traditionally religious people, they adhered to the old faith as far as practicable; they attended services at any place set aside for the worship of God, and on Sundays these Irish Catholics went to the Lutheran Church, the only church in their locality, where they "told their beads" with as much fervor and devotion as if they were attending services in a Catholic Church! Their children were baptised by the Lutheran Minister, and in time, after the "old folks" had passed on, as a result of their constant association and intermarriages with Protestant families, the children lost the faith of their fathers, for in nearly all cases their living descendants profess some of the many forms of the Protestant faith. The Protestant Germans in Pennsylvania were friendly to their Irish Catholic neighbors, but how inexpressibly sad was the lot of the Irish in New England who were compelled to live with the intolerant English Puritans!

7 Boston Town Books, Vol. 1.

8 Essex County Court Records, Vol. 2, p. 243, and Topsfield Town Records.

9 *History of Rehoboth, Mass.*, by Leonard Bliss, p. 59.

CHAPTER XVIII

The New England Irish and their descendants in the War of the Revolution—many officers of the army and navy of Irish birth or descent—numerous old Gaelic names in the muster rolls—the "Scotch-Irish" myth—how history is falsified.

AS already pointed out, since the average reader of history does not examine records, he has no personal knowledge of what they contain; so he assumes that the truth was related impartially by the historians and that nothing which would put a different complexion on the facts was withheld or covered up. Therefore, since the records so clearly demonstrate that the population of New England did not consist of Englishmen alone, but that numerous Irishmen also came there, and they and their sons bore their part in the hard tasks which confronted the pioneers, it will be readily seen that the historians mentioned, in whom readers of history place such unfounded faith, wandered far from the path of truth. In face of the foregoing facts, no one can deny that the Irish were entitled to a "fair show" in history. They were not accorded that simple right, however; they were refused a place in American history, with the result that generation after generation of Americans have steadfastly believed that the credit for laying the foundations of the country is wholly due to Englishmen and their descendants. This method of writing resulted in what may be called the publication of "history by suppression." It was deliberately followed by a number of historians in dealing with the Revolution, in which the Irish were also denied any part, notwithstanding the conspicuous services rendered by men of our race and blood in that great conflict. In later days, such "histories" achieved the result which apparently was desired by their authors, and at times they have proven to be most effective propaganda against Irish influence in the United States. So, it is no wonder that Americans of Irish descent sometimes express themselves bitterly against historians like Lodge and Palfrey and their many imitators.

This review of the subject would be incomplete without some reference to the so-called "Scotch-Irish." The critic's reference to the "Scots-Irish" indicates his failure to do his own thinking and his willingness to accept the preposterous position taken by certain writers of history, who insist upon placing the people of Ireland in two separate classes, calling them "Irish" and "Scotch-Irish." The "Scotch-Irish" theorists have been so well "scotched" in recent years, that we do not often now hear from them. But, I suppose we must expect still to find an occasional person unconvinced of the absurdity of this theory, because it has been harped upon to such an extent by historical writers and after-dinner speakers that it has become, in the minds of some, an axiomatic truth. It is a strange fact that the Irish are the only people in the world whom the historians have divided into two distinct nationalities, because of different religious beliefs. That illogical inference never seems to occur to some writers of history, and they go on repeating it, *ad infinitum, ad libitum*. According to their "reasoning," or that of the "authorities" on whom they rely, a native of Ireland of the Protestant religion is, as a matter of course, a "Scotch-Irishman," and he is an "Irishman" only when he professes the Catholic faith! Yet, they admit that every native of France is a Frenchman, no matter what his religion may be or if he has none at all, and even though his ancestors in far back time may have come to France from some other country!

All authorities upon the subject of the relations between

Scotland and Ireland agree that for several centuries before the "Plantation of Ulster" (1611), there were constant migrations back and forth between the two countries, which at one point are only eleven miles apart. This fact is fully supported by records quoted by historians and antiquarians of unquestioned standing. In the fifth century, so many Irish went to Scotland that three Irish Chieftains were sent over, one of whose descendants became King of Scotland. It was thus that Argyle, which means "Eastern Irish," received its name. In the thirteenth and fourteenth centuries, Scottish settlers infiltrated into north-eastern Ireland. But, during the past two centuries the Irish again went to Scotland in large numbers, and settled there permanently. Historians do not use the term, *Irish-Scotch,* to describe the nationality of the descendants of the Irish who settled in Scotland; so, why use *Scotch-Irish* to describe the descendants of the relatively small number of Scots who went to Ireland in the Plantation of Ulster?

The Irish Census taken under the direction of Sir William Petty in the year 1659 enables us to form a fair idea of the proportionate numbers, by national origins, of the emigrants from Ireland to this country in the seventeenth and eighteenth centuries. Petty came to Ireland with Cromwell's army in 1652, and was the author of the famous "Down Survey of Ireland" and many scientific works. He was the direct ancestor of the Marquis of Landsdowne, and the original manuscript of the Census is among the collections of the present Lord Landsdowne, at Landsdowne House, Berkeley Square, London. It was not a complete Census, however, because the Counties of Tyrone, Cavan, Galway, Mayo and Wicklow and thirteen baronies in Cork and Meath were missing. Of the total number of inhabitants enumerated, 500,091, the Province of Munster had 153,282 inhabitants, Connaught 87,352, Leinster 155,534, and Ulster 103,923. An interesting feature of the returns is the relative proportions of Irish, English and Scotch, which were shown as follows:

In Munster, 100 Irish to 10 English
In Connaught, 100 Irish to 10 English
In Leinster, 55 Irish to 10 English and Scotch
In Ulster, 15 Irish to 5 English and Scotch.

If the figures for the missing districts had been included, it stands to reason that the ratio of the Irish to the English and Scotch would be far greater than is here shown. But, even when the above figures are considered, in the light of Prendergast's statements, in his "Cromwellian Settlement of Ireland," it can readily be seen that the great majority of those who came from Ireland to America in the seventeenth century must have been of the old Irish Race.

The natural inference to be drawn from our critic's reference to the "Scots-Irish" is, that no "genuine Irishmen" were in this country about the time of the Revolution, and therefore could have had no part in the conflict which resulted in our independence. This subject is discussed at great length in my book, "A Hidden Phase of American History," the result of twenty years' research among American, English and Irish records, and those interested in the details are referred to that book for further data. New England historians would have the world believe that certain officers of the Continental Army and Navy in New England, bearing names which in some instances can be traced back through the history of Ireland for more than fifteen centuries, were not Irish; that the men who flocked from the farms and the workshops to enroll under the banner of freedom, and marched to Concord, Lexington and Bunker Hill, were mainly English with a slight admixture of "Scotch-Irish"; and by inference, that the only "Irish" who fought in the Revolution were on the side of the enemy! But, let us review the record. Among officers of the Continental Army, the Navy and Militia, and including those who served as captains of the privateers which played such havoc to English shipping and captured many valuable prizes during the Revolution, there are recorded in New England:

General—John Sullivan.

Colonels—John Greaton, Moses Kelly, Pierse Long, Hercules Mooney, Daniel Moore, John McClary, Alexander McCloskey, Matthew Thornton.

Lieutenant-Colonels—John Barrett, Samuel Connors, George Dorrance, John McDuffie.

Majors—James Collins, John Goffe, Joseph Kelly, Andrew McClary, Daniel Reynolds, Michael Ryan.

Captains—

Michael Barry
Joseph Barrett
Oliver Barron
Timothy Barron
William Barron
James Bourke
John Burke
William Burke
Clifford Byrne
Simon Bryne
Henry Butler
Joseph Butler
Charles Callaghan
John Callahan
William Callaghan
Henry Cargill
William Carnahan
John Casey
Peter Coburn
Daniel Collins
William Collins
Dennis Condry
Thomas Connolly
Benjamin Connors
Florence Crowley
James Dalton
Michael Dalton
Anthony Divver
John Donaldson
James Donnell
Timothy Donnell
Morris Doran
Samuel Dunn
Thomas Dunn
John Farris
Daniel Flood
Simon Forrester
James Gilmore
Roger Gilmore
Daniel Hand
Patrick Hare
Nathaniel Healy

Captains—

Jeremiah Heggarty
Hugh Hill
Lawrence Hogan
John Kehoe
Daniel Kenrick
Daniel Larey
Bernard Magee
James Magee
William Maley
James Mallone
William Malone
——— Malony
Michael Melally
Thomas Moriarty
Francis Mulligan
John Murphy (A)
John Murphy (B)
Zachariah Murphy
John McCall
John McCarthy (C)
John McCarthy (B)
Richard McCarthy
Michael McClary
Samuel McConnell
Daniel McDuffie
William McDuffie
John McGra
Thomas McLaughlin
Daniel Nevins
James Norris
Jeremiah O'Brien
John O'Brien
Joseph O'Brien
——— O'Hara
Edward Phelan
John Power
Thomas Powers
A. Riley
John Riley
John Reilly
Francis Roach
William Roche
Daniel Shay
Daniel Sullivan
Eben Sullivan
James Sullivan
James Tracy
John Tracy
Michael Tracy
Nathaniel Tracy
Nicholas Tracy
Patrick Tracy

Lieutenants—

John Aiken
John Barron
Daniel Bradley
Charles Butler
Thomas Butler
Richard Carney
Jonathan Carroll
Gideon Casey
Patrick Cogan
Daniel Collins
John Dealey
Darby Driscoll
John Driskill
Charles Dougherty
Michael Dougherty
Michael Dunning

Lieutenants—

William Ennis
Charles Fanning
Joseph Fay
Thomas Fitzgerald
L. Fling
Andrew Garrett
James Garvin
William Gilmore
James Griffin
Cornelius Higgins
William Higgins
Robert Kalley
David Kelly
Robert Kelly
Samuel Kelly
John Kennedy
William Lawless
James Leary
John Larey
Matthew Lyon
John Maloon
William Manning
Hugh Molloy
Benjamin Mooney
Daniel Murphy
James McCauley
John McCauley
William McClannen
David McClure
James McClure
Andrew McGaffey
Neil McGaffey
William McKenny
Daniel McMurphy
Robert McMurphy
William Nevins
Thomas O'Brian
William O'Brien
John Phelan
Patrick Phelan
John Powers
Thomas Powers
James Reilly
Cornelius Russell
Matthew Ryan
William Ryan
James Taggart
John Taggart
Joseph Walsh
John Welsh
Peter Welsh
Richard Welsh

Surgeon—John Quinn.

Commissary—James Sullivan.

Quartermasters—Richard Coughlan, John Flynn, Timothy Gleason, John Handy, John Patton, William Taggart.

Adjutants and Ensigns—John Butler, Oliver Barrett, Thomas Logan, Cornelius Lynch, Michael Madden, Timothy McCarthy, William McCarthy, James McClure, Henry McCrellis, John McMurren, John O'Neal.

(A) Rhode Island, (B) Massachusetts, (C) Connecticut.

Pioneer Irish in New England

Among the rank and file of the New England troops in the Revolution, there were numerous soldiers bearing Irish names; and while the records generally lack information as to their nativity, there can be no doubt that many of these men were American-born descendants of Irish immigrants. A careful examination of the muster rolls and enlistment papers, in the cases of sixty selected surnames, shows the following are listed in the Connecticut, Massachusetts, Maine, Rhode Island and New Hampshire rolls:

33 Barrys
80 Burkes
62 Byrnes, Burns
22 Callahans
67 Carrolls
33 Caseys
16 Cavanaughs
15 Condons
51 Connellys
70 Connors
10 Crowleys
61 Dalys
12 Dempseys
29 Dohertys
28 Donnellys
10 Donovans
36 Doyles
16 Driscolls
10 Duffys
18 Dugans
25 Dwyers
27 Farrells
63 Fitzgeralds
39 Flynns
17 Healys
12 Hennessys
22 Hogans
13 Keatings
12 Keefes
213 Kellys
18 Kennys
27 Learys
15 Lynch's
29 Maddens
30 Magees
23 Mahonys
23 Malones
38 Maloneys
26 Molloys
13 Mooneys
116 Murphys
11 McBrides
14 McCaffreys
62 McCarthys
12 McCormacks
23 McGuires
27 McLaughlins
10 McMahons
13 McManus's
12 Mullens, McMullens
13 McNamaras
13 Nolans
102 O'Briens
12 O'Neills

10 Prendergasts	102 Ryans
18 Quinns	19 Sheas
66 Reillys	60 Sullivans

And of men bearing such names as

Brady	McCann
Clancy	McConnell
Delany	McDonnell
Donohue	McGinnis
Doran	McGowan
Dowling	McKenny
Fitzpatrick	McNally
Flanagan	McSweeney
Gorman	O'Hara
Haggerty	Roche
Hickey	Rourke
Kearny	Sheehan
Lafferty	Sheridan
Lawlor	Sweeney
Moran	Walsh

there were nearly 200, making a total of 2,300 New England soldiers and sailors bearing these ninety names. Many other Irish names appear in the muster rolls, and all told, approximately 3,000 men bearing Irish names enrolled with the New England forces in the Revolution, exclusive of many natives of Ireland bearing non-Irish names, such as some of those before described. Some historians, wishing to make sure that their readers would not get the idea that such men were "Irish," go to great lengths to explain that their forebears were "Scots" and had nothing in common with the Irish. No greater injustice has been done the Irish in America and their descendants than robbing them of the credit to which they were entitled, for what men of their race and blood contributed to the success of the Revolution, and conferring that credit on a people, who, on the whole, had little sympathy with the cause of the revolting colonists.

APPENDIX

PERSONS MENTIONED IN NEW ENGLAND RECORDS OF THE SEVENTEENTH CENTURY

Name	*Where Recorded*	*Year*
Cormac Annis	Newbury, Mass.	1666
Peter Barron	Marblehead, Mass.	1675
Teague Barron	Boston, Mass.	1674
Timothy Barron	Watertown, Mass.	1689
Clement Barry	Boston, Mass.	1633
James Barry	Boston, Mass.	1688
James Barry	Pemaquid, Maine	1674
John Barry	Boston, Mass.	1682
John Barry	Ipswich, Mass.	1670
John Barry	New London, Conn.	1659
Matthew Barry	Wethersfield, Conn.	1689
Peter Barry	Boston, Mass.	1685
Teague Barry	Boston, Mass.	1687
William Barry	Rye, N. H.	1683
Margaret Bird	Boston, Mass.	1656
John Blaney	Charlestown, Mass.	1675
William Bodkin	Boston, Mass.	1680
Michael Bowden	Topsfield, Mass.	1668
Peter Bowden	Salem, Mass.	1686
Patrick Boyce	Brunswick, Maine	1683
Brian Bradene	Boston, Mass.	1688
John Brady	Kittery, Maine	1681
Margaret Brene	Boston, Mass.	1681
Mary Breen	Boxford, Mass.	1699
Alexander Bryan	Milford, Conn.	1639
Darby Bryan	Boston, Mass.	1677
Dennis Brian	Oyster River, N. H.	1685
Richard Brien	Dedham, Mass.	1675

Name	*Where Recorded*	*Year*
Richard Bryan	Milford, Conn.	1639
Teague Brian	Lynn, Mass.	1675
Nicholas Brogan	Boston, Mass.	1635
Richard Bulger	Boston, Mass.	1632
Bryan Bourke	Boston, Mass.	1635
Daniel Burke	Boston, Mass.	1635
Edward Burke	Boston, Mass.	1656
Rickard Burke	Salem, Mass.	1687
John Burke	Boston, Mass.	1676
Joseph Burke	Boston, Mass.	1699
Richard Burke	Northampton, Mass.	1685
Rickard Burke	Sudbury, Mass.	1670
Roger Burke	Cambridge, Mass.	1664
Thomas Burke	Middletown, Conn.	1670
Thomas Burke	Rowley, Mass.	1681
Thomas Burke	Salem, Mass.	1681
Timothy Burke	Woburn, Mass.	1675
Walter Burke	Boston, Mass.	1687
James Butler	Lancaster, Mass.	1663
John Butler	Saybrook, Conn.	1653
Nicholas Butler	Boston, Mass.	1674
Peter Butler	Boston, Mass.	1699
Stephen Butler	Boston, Mass.	1679
Thomas Butler	Kittery, Maine	1695
Philip Cadogan	Isles of Shoals, N. H.	1653
Richard Cadogan	Isles of Shoals, N. H.	1650
Ann Callahan	Charlestown, Mass.	1658
James Carney	Boston, Mass.	1687
John Carney	Boston, Mass.	1681
Anthony Carroll	Topsfield, Mass.	1658
Christopher Carroll	Boston, Mass.	1634
Edward Carroll	Salem, Mass.	1699
John Carroll	Boston, Mass.	1685
John Carroll	Topsfield, Mass.	1666
Joseph Carroll	Salem, Mass.	1699

Name	*Where Recorded*	*Year*
Joseph Carroll	Hartford, Conn.	1687
Thomas Carroll	Salem, Mass.	1688
Philip Cartey	Exeter, N. H.	1668
Teague Cartey	Essex County, Mass.	1674
John Casey	Boston, Mass.	1675
Jonathan Casey	Roxbury, Mass.	1678
Mary Casey	Salem, Mass.	1694
Samuel Casey	Essex County, Mass.	1670
Thomas Casey	Newport, R. I.	1658
John Cassidy	Boston, Mass.	1635
Teage Clark	Wells, Maine	1681
John Clary	Northfield, Mass.	1682
John Cleary	Boston, Mass.	1676
Matthew Clesson	Northampton, Mass.	1668
Bridget Clifford	Suffield, Conn.	1635
John Clifford	Hampton, N. H.	1667
Humphrey Cogan	Boston, Mass.	1648
John Cogan	Boston, Mass.	1633
Hugh Collahan	Dedham, Mass.	1675
Hugh Collane	Boston, Mass.	1675
Matthew Colane	Isles of Shoals, N. H.	1650
Cornelius Collins	Boston, Mass.	1687
Christopher Collins	Boston, Mass.	1645
Daniel Collins	Boston, Mass.	1695
Daniel Collins	Enfield, Conn.	1690
Edward Collins	Boston, Mass.	1645
Edward Collins	Boston, Mass.	1687
Henry Collins	Lynn, Mass.	1635
Joane Collins	Gloucester, Mass.	1661
John Collins	Guilford, Conn.	1691
John Collins	Boston, Mass.	1697
Joseph Collins	Eastham, Mass.	1672
Matthew Collins	Boston, Mass.	1678
Peter Collins	New London, Conn.	1655
Roger Collins	Essex County, Mass.	1669

Name	*Where Recorded*	*Year*
Thomas Collins	Boston, Mass.	1674
Timothy Collins	Salem, Mass.	1678
William Collins	New Haven, Conn.	1640
Jeremiah Connaway	Charlestown, Mass.	1678
Patrick Conoway	Salem, Mass.	1653
Philip Connel	Malden, Mass.	1688
Sarah Connell	Portsmouth, N. H.	1655
Thomas Connell	Boston, Mass.	1638
Timothy Connell	Boston, Mass.	1680
William Connell	Boston, Mass.	1680
Abraham Connelly	Kittery, Maine	1640
Daniel Connelly	Boston, Mass.	1635
Patrick Conly	Boston, Mass.	1635
Cornelius Connor	Salisbury, Mass.	1659
James Conniers	Boston, Mass.	1696
Jeremiah Conner	Exeter, N. H.	1681
John Connor	Salisbury, Mass.	1660
John Connor	Middletown, Conn.	1686
Joseph Connor	Salisbury, Mass.	1691
Joseph Conners	Boston, Mass.	1635
Patrick Connyer	Boston, Mass.	1635
Richard Conners	Boston, Mass.	1699
Samuel Connor	Salisbury, Mass.	1661
William Conner	Plymouth, Mass.	1621
David Conway	Boston, Mass.	1642
Margaret Conway	Boston, Mass.	1635
Morris Conway	Boston, Mass.	1679
John Cosgrove	Boston, Mass.	1658
John Cotter	Essex County, Mass.	1680
Philip Cotter	Dover, N. H.	1689
Richard Cotter	Charlestown, Mass.	1653
Robert Cotter	Charlestown, Mass.	1653
William Cotter	New Haven, Conn.	1657
John Couney	Boston, Mass.	1678
Benjamin Crehore	Milton, Mass.	1689

Pioneer Irish in New England

Name	*Where Recorded*	*Year*
Cornelius Crehore	Essex County, Mass.	1670
Teague Crehore	Dorchester, Mass.	1650
Timothy Crehore	Milton, Mass.	1666
David Cremin	Dorchester, Mass.	1699
Cornelius Croggin	Barnstable, Mass.	1664
Bryan Crowley	Boston, Mass.	1635
David Crowley	Boston, Mass.	1690
Gilbert Crowley	Boston, Mass.	1699
Robert Crowley	Boston, Mass.	1635
Thomas Crowley	Exeter, N. H.	1639
Thomas Crowley	York, Maine	1668
James Cullen	Boston, Mass.	1676
Thomas Cullen	Salem, Mass.	1675
David Cummins	Boston, Mass.	1678
Patrick Cunningham	Hartford, Conn.	1685
Timothy Cunningham	Boston, Mass.	1695
Matthias Currin	Ipswich, Mass.	1634
William Dadey	Charlestown, Mass.	1679
Michael Dalton	Boston, Mass.	1678
Nicholas Dalton	Boston, Mass.	1678
Philemon Dalton	Dedham, Mass.	1636
Timothy Dalton	Essex County, Mass.	1677
John Daly	Braintree, Mass.	1669
John Dayly	Mendon, Mass.	1679
John Dailey	Providence, R. I.	1689
Nicholas Daly	Woodbury, Conn.	1663
Samuel Daly	Braintree, Mass.	1669
Thomas Daly	Salem, Mass.	1682
Darby Daniell	Oyster River, N. H.	1662
Patrick Daniell	Boston, Mass.	1655
Teague Daniell	Essex County, Mass.	1678
Dennis Darley	Braintree, Mass.	1662
Edmund Deare	Ipswich, Mass.	1660
Michael Delaney	New Haven, Conn.	1667
William Dempsey	Boston, Mass.	1679

Name	*Where Recorded*	*Year*
Andrew Devin	Dedham, Mass.	1652
John Devin	Essex County, Mass.	1661
Joseph Devitt	Providence, R. I.	1685
Bridget Dexter	Boston, Mass.	1641
John Dexter	Malden, Mass.	1677
Richard Dexter	Boston, Mass.	1641
John Dillon	Monhegin, Maine	1673
William Dillon	Essex County, Mass.	1659
Mary Dinan	Lynn, Mass.	1685
Christopher Dolan	Essex County, Mass.	1678
Mary Dolens or Dowling	Boston, Mass.	1653
Hannah Dongan	Oyster River, N. H.	1695
Jude Donley	Boston, Mass.	1638
Henry Donnell	Kittery, Maine	1648
Joseph Donnell	Kittery, Maine	1671
Michael Donnell	Topsfield, Mass.	1657
Samuel Donnell	York County, Maine	1692
Thomas Donnell	Topsfield, Mass.	1673
John Donnogen	Essex County, Mass.	1677
John Dowgin	Boston, Mass.	1678
John Downey	Ipswich, Mass.	1665
William Downey	Boston, Mass.	1691
Dennis Downing	Kittery, Maine	1697
William Downing	Ipswich, Mass.	1654
Robert Doyle	Woburn, Mass.	1680
William Doyle	Westerly, R. I.	1698
Florence Driscoll	Windsor, Conn.	1674
Lawrence Driscow	Boston, Mass.	1691
Mary Driscoll	Dorchester, Mass.	1679
Teague Drisco	Exeter, N. H.	1664
Philip Dudy	Exeter, N. H.	1698
John Duffy	Exeter, N. H.	1645
Richard Duffy	Ipswich, Mass.	1633
Barbara Dugan	Newport, R. I.	1696
Daniel Duggan	Portsmouth, N. H.	1685

Name	*Where Recorded*	*Year*
Samuel Duggan	Portsmouth, N. H.	1683
Edward Dulen	Boston, Mass.	1651
Hugh Dunn	Dover, N. H.	1664
John Dunn	New Haven, Conn.	1657
Nicholas Dunn	Cochecho, N. H.	1689
Richard Dunn	Newport, R. I.	1682
William Dunne	New Plymouth, Mass.	1641
"Crobar" Dunnevan	Essex County, Mass.	1678
Henry Dwier	Hartford, Conn.	1696
Edward Dwyer	Exeter, N. H.	1696
James Dwyer	Exeter, N. H.	1695
John Egan	Boston, Mass.	1674
Thomas Fallon	Yarmouth, Mass.	1681
Andrew Fanning	Stonington, Conn.	1679
Edmund Fanning	Groton, Conn.	1652
Thomas Fanning	Watertown, Mass.	1656
William Fanning	Newbury, Mass.	1668
Michael Farley	Ipswich, Mass.	1675
Timothy Farley	Billerica, Mass.	1675
Benjamin Farrell	Boston, Mass.	1675
James Farrell	Boston, Mass.	1685
John Farrell	Dedham, Mass.	1654
Thomas Farrell	Cohannett, Mass.	1689
Darby Field	Exeter, N. H.	1638
Thomas Finnan	Ipswich, Mass.	1635
David Fitzgerald	Boston, Mass.	1682
Elephel Fitzgerald	New Bedford, Mass.	1687
Gerald Fitzgerald	Hartford, Conn.	1664
James Fitzgerald	Saybrook, Conn.	1678
——— Fitzgerald	New London, Conn.	1664
Edward Fitzmorris	Boston, Mass.	1676
Patrick Flannery	Scituate, Mass.	1677
Thomas Flynn	Sudbury, Mass.	1639
Thomas Foley	Boston, Mass.	1652
John Fynn	Boston, Mass.	1635

Name	*Where Recorded*	*Year*
Owen Garrett	Boston, Mass.	1635
John Garvin	Salem, Mass.	1661
Arthur Geary	Roxbury, Mass.	1638
Dennis Geary	Lynn, Mass.	1635
Nicholas Garey	Roxbury, Mass.	1659
Thomas Geary	Stoneham, Mass.	1675
William Garey	Roxbury, Mass.	1651
William Geary	Boston, Mass.	1679
Alexander Gilligan	Marblehead, Mass.	1670
Ferdinando Gilligan	Boston, Mass.	1683
Andrew Greeley	Salisbury, Mass.	1654
John Greeley	Newbury, Mass.	1675
Andrew Haley	York County, Me.	1662
Andrew Haley, Jr.	York County, Me.	1697
James Haley	York County, Me.	1653
John Haley	Hadley, Mass.	1681
Thomas Haley	Saco, Maine	1653
William Haley	Salem, Mass.	1669
John Hannigan	Boston, Mass.	1681
Edward Harnett	Salem, Mass.	1639
Peter Harney	Salem, Mass.	1676
Mary Hayes	Boston, Mass.	1658
Patrick Hayes	Reading, Mass.	1685
Bridget Hayes	Boston, Mass.	1658
Christopher Hayes	Charlestown, Mass.	1669
Edmond Hayes	Kittery, Maine	1665
Edward Hayes	York County, Maine	1675
John Haies	Boston, Mass.	1635
John Hayes	Dover, N. H.	1686
John Hayes	Boston, Mass.	1686
Nicholas Hayes	Windsor, Conn.	1646
Robert Hayes	Ipswich, Mass.	1635
Sylvester Hayes	Charlestown, Mass.	1668
Thomas Hayes	Boston, Mass.	1658
William Haies	Boston, Mass.	1635

Name	*Where Recorded*	*Year*
Dennis Healey	Watertown, Mass.	1681
George Healey	Boston, Mass.	1677
John Healy	Newton, Mass.	1698
Matthew Healy	Boston, Mass.	1699
Nathaniel Healy	Cambridge, Mass.	1675
Nicholas Healy	Pemaquid, Maine	1674
Paul Healy	New Hampton, N. H.	1675
Samuel Healy	New Hampton, N. H.	1683
Terence Healy	Boston, Mass.	1694
Thomas Healy	Cambridge, Mass.	1635
William Healy	Boston, Mass.	1649
William Healy	Hampton, N. H.	1682
Thomas Hearn	Boston, Mass.	1678
William Hearn	Boston, Mass.	1676
John Heffernan	Portsmouth, N. H.	1680
John Heffernan	Wickford, R. I.	1674
Robert Heffernan	Wickford, R. I.	1674
Samuel Heffernan	Wickford, R. I.	1674
William Heffernan	Scituate, Mass.	1661
Luke Heneberry	Newton, Mass.	1638
Thomas Hickey	Bristol County, Mass.	1697
Cornelius Higgins	Providence, R. I.	1682
Dennis Higgins	Farmington, Conn.	1700
James Higgins	Exeter, N. H.	1680
John Higgins	Suffield, Conn.	1635
Owen Higgins	Newport, R. I.	1699
Richard Higgins	Newport, R. I.	1697
Richard Higgins	Eastham, Mass.	1644
Robert Higgins	Boston, Mass.	1660
Thomas Higgins	Boston, Mass.	1699
Daniel Hogan	Boston, Mass.	1685
"Pater" Hogan	Hartford, Conn.	1659
Darbie Hurlie	Boston, Mass.	1633
Matthew Hurley	Boston, Mass.	1676
Sarah Hurley	Cambridge, Mass.	1690

Name	*Where Recorded*	*Year*
Thomas Hyland	Scituate, Mass.	1638
Teague Jones	Yarmouth, Mass.	1645
Mary Jordan	New London, Conn.	1674
Stephen Jordan	Newbury, Mass.	1670
Christopher Joyce	Kittery, Me.	1682
James Joyce	Newcastle, Me.	1693
Jeremiah Joyce	Yarmouth, Mass.	1699
John Joyce	Lynn, Mass.	1637
Samuel Joyce	Yarmouth, Mass.	1699
Thomas Joyce	Yarmouth, Mass.	1699
William Joyce	Boston, Mass.	1648
Mary Keeffe	Boston, Mass.	1693
Christopher Kehoe	Dorchester, Mass.	1695
Andrew Kelly	York County, Me.	1699
Charles Kelly	York County, Me.	1698
Christopher Kelly	Dorchester, Mass.	1694
Daniel Kelly	Exeter, N. H.	1664
David Kelly	Boston, Mass.	1666
George Kelly	Danvers, Mass.	1658
James Kelly	New London, Conn.	1652
John Kelly	Exeter, N. H.	1648
John Kelly	Hartford, Conn.	1655
John Kelly	Newbury, Mass.	1635
John Kelly	Isles of Shoals, N. H.	1653
Joseph Kelly	Newbury, Mass.	1695
Michael Kelly	Conanicut Island, R. I.	1667
Peter Kelly	Danvers, Mass.	1671
Richard Kelly	Newbury, Mass.	1691
Robert Kelly	York County, Maine	1690
Roger Kelly	Isles of Shoals, N. H.	1653
Thomas Kelly	Marblehead, Mass.	1696
William Kelly	Boston, Mass.	1637
William Kelly	Isles of Shoals, N. H.	1653
Andrew Kenny	Malden, Mass.	1690
Daniel Kenny	Salem, Mass.	1680

Name	*Where Recorded*	*Year*
Henry Kenny	Salem, Mass.	1653
James Kenny	Danvers, Mass.	1682
John Kenny	Salem, Mass.	1657
John Kenny	Boston, Mass.	1672
John Kenny	Danvers, Mass.	1682
Richard Kenny	New Hampshire	1680
Thomas Kenny	Gloucester, Mass.	1664
Edward Kiely	New Haven, Conn.	1666
Edward King	Windsor, Conn.	1656
Henry Langin	Charlestown, Mass.	1660
Edward Larkin	Voluntown, Conn.	1676
Edward Larkin	Charlestown, Mass.	1638
Edward Larkin	Newport, R. I.	1655
Henry Larkin	Braintree, Mass.	1670
Hugh Larkin	Essex County, Mass.	1659
John Larkin	Charlestown, Mass.	1664
John Larkin	Newport, R. I.	1655
Peter Larkin	Lancaster, Mass.	1700
Richard Larkin	Boston, Mass.	1635
Roger Larkin	Charlestown, Mass.	1699
Thomas Larkin	Charlestown, Mass.	1674
Timothy Larkin	Salem, Mass.	1676
Gerrard Lawler	Boston, Mass.	1649
Cornelius Leary	Salisbury, Mass.	1664
Cornelius Leary, Jr.	Exeter, N. H.	1699
Daniel Leary	Exeter, N. H.	1699
John Leary	Saybrook, Conn.	1659
John Leare	Essex County, Mass.	1669
Katharine Lary	Lynn, Mass.	1657
Sarah Larey	Charlestown, Mass.	1639
Thomas Leary	Exeter, N. H.	1699
Gabriel Lynch	Hartford, Conn.	1656
George Linche	Essex County, Mass.	1666
Mary Lynch	Boston, Mass.	1693
Nicholas Lynch	Boston, Mass.	1683

Name	*Where Recorded*	*Year*
John Lyons	Roxbury, Mass.	1671
Joseph Lyons	Roxbury, Mass.	1654
Thomas Lyons	Roxbury, Mass.	1669
William Lyons	Roxbury, Mass.	1654
Rory Mackey	Boston, Mass.	1651
Darby Maguire	Boston, Mass.	1676
Daniel Mahone	Boston, Mass.	1646
Edward Mahone	Wethersfield, Conn.	1693
Darby Mahoone	Boston, Mass.	1655
Darby Makloney	Charlestown, Mass.	1655
Hendrick Malone	Dover, N. H.	1660
Luke Malone	Dover, N. H.	1670
Daniel Malony	Boston, Mass.	1676
John Moloney	Woburn, Mass.	1676
Darby Manning	Essex County, Mass.	1678
Dennis Manning	Nantucket, Mass.	1679
Denis Maroh	Dorchester, Mass.	1696
Nathaniel Masterson	Ipswich, Mass.	1657
Gabriel Meade	Boston, Mass.	1634
Nicholas Meade	Charlestown, Mass.	1681
Richard Meade	Boston, Mass.	1678
William Meade	Boston, Mass.	1683
Denis Menan	Boston, Mass.	1674
Cornelius Merry	Northampton, Mass.	1658
Cornelius Merry, Jr.	Hartford, Conn.	1698
Teague Merrihew	Yarmouth, Mass.	1676
Garrett Mickery	Sudbury, Mass.	1660
Dennis Monaane	Charlestown, Mass.	1674
John Moore	Boston, Mass.	1657
Joseph Moore	Charlestown, Mass.	1659
Matthew Moore	Newbury, Mass.	1662
Thomas Moore	Charlestown, Mass.	1680
Dermod Morean	Roxbury, Mass.	1674
Patrick Moran	New Haven, Conn.	1664
Patrick Moran	Essex County, Mass.	1673

Name	*Where Recorded*	*Year*
Darby Morris	Marlboro, Mass.	1675
Hannah Morrissie	Dover, N. H.	1675
Thomas Morrissie	Oyster River, N. H.	1662
Denis Mortagh	York County, Maine	1686
Edmund Mortimore	Boston, Mass.	1675
James Mullen	Boston, Mass.	1680
Philip Mullen	Boston, Mass.	1678
Thomas Mullen	New London, Conn.	1658
William Mullen	Boston, Mass.	1674
Hugh Mulligan	Boston, Mass.	1681
John Mulligan	Scarboro, Maine	1651
John Mulligan	Boston, Mass.	1681
Robert Mulligan	Rowley, Mass.	1668
Thomas Mulligan	Boston, Mass.	1693
Joanna Mullins	Boston, Mass.	1659
William Mullins	Braintree, Mass.	1672
William Mullins	Duxbury, Mass.	1643
Elizabeth Murrin	Boston, Mass.	1635
Ann Murfy	Marblehead, Mass.	1696
Brian Murphy	Boston, Mass.	1661
Edward Murphy	Boston, Mass.	1635
James Murffey	New London, Conn.	1675
James Murphy	Ipswich, Mass.	1669
Margaret Murphy	Scituate, Mass.	1686
Richard Murphy	Marblehead, Mass.	1699
Thomas Murfey	Hingham, Mass.	1662
Thomas Murfie	Boston, Mass.	1634
Thomas Murphy	Salem, Mass.	1676
William Murphy	Salem, Mass.	1696
William Murphy	Essex County, Mass.	1669
Dennis Murrough	Falmouth, Me.	1685
Dennis McBrian	Boston, Mass.	1635
Andrew McCarthy	Salem, Mass.	1687
Charles McCarthy	East Greenwich, R. I.	1677
Daniel McCarthy	Boston, Mass.	1686

Name	*Where Recorded*	*Year*
Florence MacCarty	Boston, Mass.	1680
James McCarthy	Salem, Mass.	1687
Jeremiah McCarthy	Salem, Mass.	1687
John McCartey	Salem, Mass.	1674
Owen McCarthy	New London, Conn.	1670
Peter McCarthy	Salem, Mass.	1687
Thaddeus MacCarty	Boston, Mass.	1664
Thomas McCarthy	Boston, Mass.	1695
Thomas McCarty	Boston, Mass.	1689
Timothy McCarthy	Newport, R. I.	1700
William McCarty	Salem, Mass.	1661
Dennis McCormack	York County, Maine	1657
Hugh MacCoy	Wethersfield, Conn.	1683
William Mack Cranney	Springfield, Mass.	1685
Dennis McDoniel	Boston, Mass.	1671
Michael MacDaniel	Boston, Mass.	1666
John Magdoniell	Boston, Mass.	1658
Matthew Mackenetine	Newbury, Mass.	1699
Patrick Mackfassy	Charlestown, Mass.	1670
James MacGill	Suffield, Conn.	1685
John MacGill	Suffield, Conn.	1685
Thomas MacGill	Suffield, Conn.	1685
Daniel McGinnis	Woburn, Mass.	1674
William McGinnis	Dedham, Mass.	1676
John McGoune	Scituate, Mass.	1666
John MacKannah	Hingham, Mass.	1679
John McKenna	Scarboro, Maine	1668
Daniel McKenny	Boston, Mass.	1660
Daniel Makenny	Taunton, Mass.	1660
John McKenny	York County, Me.	1691
William McKenny	York County, Me.	1691
William McKenny	Hingham, Mass.	1679
Sarah McKeone	Dorchester, Mass.	1669
John Makew	Fairfield, Conn.	1661
Timothy MacKue	York County, Maine	1693

Pioneer Irish in New England

Name	*Where Recorded*	*Year*
Robert McLaughlin	Wenham, Mass.	1664
William McLoughlin	Boston, Mass.	1688
John McMahon	Windsor, Conn.	1690
John Mackmoran	Boston, Mass.	1679
James McRory	Dedham, Mass.	1660
John McShane	Essex County, Mass.	1653
Teague Nacton	Boston, Mass.	1635
Edward Nealand	Ipswich, Mass.	1664
Jeremiah Newland	Taunton, Mass.	1657
John Newland	Sandwich, Mass.	1643
William Newland	Sandwich, Mass.	1643
Margaret Norris	Boston, Mass.	1661
Desmond O'Bryan	Boston, Mass.	1635
William O'Brien	Salem, Mass.	1669
Teague O'Connell	Boston, Mass.	1662
Teague O'Crimi	Massachusetts	1643
Grace O'Dea	Wethersfield, Conn.	1643
Margaret O'Dea	Springfield, Mass.	1660
Bryan O'Dougherty	Salem, Mass.	1683
Darby O'Flynn	Boston, Mass.	1700
Charles O'Grady	York County, Maine	1687
Patrick O'Hogan	Boston, Mass.	1674
Benjamin O'Kelly	Yarmouth, Mass.	1692
David O'Kelly	Yarmouth, Mass.	1655
David O'Kelia, Jr.	Yarmouth, Mass.	1692
Henry O'Kelly	Dorchester, Mass.	1696
Jeremiah O'Kelly	Yarmouth, Mass.	1692
John O'Kelly	Yarmouth, Mass.	1690
Jonathan O'Kelley	Yarmouth, Mass.	1699
Josiah O'Kelly	Dorchester, Mass.	1688
Peter O'Kelly	Dorchester, Mass.	1668
Teague O'Leary	Boston, Mass.	1634
Dermod O'Mahony	Salem, Mass.	1642
Tege O'Mahonie	Salem, Mass.	1642
Daniel O'Neale	Boston, Mass.	1651

Name	*Where Recorded*	*Year*
Edmund O'Neil	East Hartford, Conn.	1682
John O'Neil	Wethersfield, Conn.	1682
"Master" O'Shane	Boston, Mass.	1678
Daniel O'Shaw / Daniel O'Shea	Great Island, N. H.	1693
James O'Shaw	New Castle, N. H.	1699
John O'Shaw	New Castle, N. H.	1697
Christopher Piggott	Brookline, Mass.	1655
Arthur Power	Boston, Mass.	1693
John Power	Charlestown, Mass.	1643
Nicholas Power	Providence, R. I.	1643
Peter Powers	Charlestown, Mass.	1643
Thomas Power	Concord, Mass.	1680
Thomas Powers	Boston, Mass.	1680
Walter Power	Salem, Mass.	1654
Edward Plunkett	Boston, Mass.	1635
Thomas Plunkett	Boston, Mass.	1635
Thomas Prendergast	Boston, Mass.	1635
John Quinn	Malden, Mass.	1666
John Quinn	New Hampshire	1689
John Quin	Boston, Mass.	1692
John Quirk	Plymouth, Mass.	1690
William Quirk	Charlestown, Mass.	1638
Garret Riley	Boston, Mass.	1634
Henry Reilly	Rowley, Mass.	1649
Jeremiah Ryley	Ipswich, Mass.	1678
John Reilly	Wethersfield, Conn.	1643
John Ryley	Hartford, Conn.	1674
John Reyley	Charlestown, Mass.	1671
John Riley	Springfield, Mass.	1660
James Riley	Wethersfield, Conn.	1677
Miles Riley	Boston, Mass.	1634
Patrick Riley	Hockanum, Conn.	1648
Richard Riley	Middletown, Conn.	1648
Sarah Reiley	Rowley, Mass.	1646

Name	*Where Recorded*	*Year*
Thomas Riley	Boston, Mass.	1635
William Reyley	Cambridge, Mass.	1664
John Reylean	Boston, Mass.	1661
Darby Rylean	Boston, Mass.	1633
Peter Reynolds	Little Compton, R. I.	1696
Teage Rial	Dover, N. H.	1661
John Ring	Ipswich, Mass.	1654
Francis Roche	Salem, Mass.	1692
John Roche	Norwalk, Conn.	1676
Thomas Roche	New London, Conn.	1669
William Roache	Salem, Mass.	1692
Timothy Ryan	Marblehead, Mass.	1688
Richard Sexton	Windsor, Conn.	1662
Thomas Sexton	Boston, Mass.	1679
Dennis Sheahone	Norfolk County Mass.	1667
Dermond Shehee	Portsmouth, N. H.	1660
Dennis Shihie	Boston, Mass.	1675
Peter Sheridan	Boston, Mass.	1692
Dennis Skalion	Essex County, Mass.	1664
John Smith	Dedham, Mass.	1640
James Stackpole	Dover, N. H.	1680
Daniel Sullivan	New Haven, Conn.	1650
Daniel Sullivant	Swanzey, Mass.	1674
Jael Sullivan	Braintree, Mass.	1660
Joan Sullivan	Salem, Mass.	1681
John Sullavan	New London, Conn.	1663
Margaret Suleavan	Lynn, Mass.	1653
William Sullivan	Boston, Mass.	1699
Owen Swiney	Ipswich, Mass.	1658
Richard Talley	Boston, Mass.	1679
Margaret Taylor	Watertown, Mass.	1690
Michael Tandy	Essex County, Mass.	1673
Mary Tooll	Concord, Mass.	1663
Philip Toule or Toole	Hampton, N. H.	1657
John Tulley	Boston, Mass.	1685

Name	*Where Recorded*	*Year*
Elizabeth Walsh	Boston, Mass.	1679
Edward Welch	Ipswich, Mass.	1654
James Wealsh	Boston, Mass.	1676
Joseph Welsh	Boston, Mass.	1676
Philip Welsh	Ipswich, Mass.	1654
Peter Welch	Charlestown, Mass.	1650
Thomas Welsh	Charlestown, Mass.	1650
Robert Ward	Charlestown, Mass.	1692
Mary Whelan	Salem, Mass.	1661
Cornelius White	Boston, Mass.	1678
Teague Williams	Boston, Mass.	1633

SOME NEW ENGLAND IRISH OF THE FIRST QUARTER OF THE EIGHTEENTH CENTURY

In New England records of the years 1700 to 1725, names of distinctive Celtic flavor occur so frequently and in such variety, as to make it perfectly clear that the Irish part of the population at that time was very much larger than is generally supposed. I am convinced that many of those hereunder listed were in the Colony as early as the last quarter of the seventeenth century. For although their names did not get into the records of that period, there are certain indications, such as the dates of their wills, the ages of their children, and in some cases the length of time they had been in possession of property, which amply justify that conclusion. Some examples of these are here listed, the year shown in each case being the earliest when the name appears in the public records. The names are spelled as they were written in the records, and only those marked with an asterisk (*) are mentioned as natives of Ireland.

That the Irish continued to come to New England during the first quarter of the eighteenth century is shown clearly by the Custom House lists of ships arriving at New England ports from Ireland, many with passengers. According to the Boston *News Letter*, 62 ships arrived there between 1714 and 1725, and 22 cleared out for Ireland, some of which subsequently returned. Of the arrivals at Boston, 35.5% of the shipping was from Cork, Dublin and Waterford, 12.9% from Belfast, Londonderry and Coleraine, and 51.6% "from Ireland," without naming the ports of departure. The *Elizabeth and Kathrin* arrived "from Ireland" in the week of May 31-June 6, 1714, and the government ordered her master "to place his sick passengers ashoar on Spectacle Island," [1] in Boston harbor. The "*York Merchant* from Cork, Ireland," arrived in September, 1714, with "Irish servants," and "the *Globe* from Dublin" arrived in the week of August 12-19, 1717, "with sundry servants to serve for 4 to 9 years." The "*Mary Anne* from Dublin" arrived in the week of June 18-25, 1717, and in the Province Laws of that month there is a record of an order to the effect that "the passengers just arrived from Ireland be sent to Spectacle Island." [2] A report in the *News Letter* of September 9-16, 1717, said "the ship *Friends Goodwill* from Dublin" arrived at Boston "with 250 passengers."

The "ship *Dolphin* from Dublin" arrived in the week of September 1-8, 1718, "with Servants, Boys, Tradesmen, Husbandmen and Maids, to be disposed of by Mr. John Walker, at his warehouse at the lower end of Woodmansy Wharff, in Merchants Row." A despatch from Marblehead, Mass., in the *News Letter,* dated May 16, 1718, said "Captain Gibbs has arrived here from Dublin with Irish and Scotch servants"; that paper announced on June 17, 1718, the arrival at Piscataqua, Maine, of "Captain Caldwell from Ireland with 178 passengers," and "Captain Yoa, six weeks' passage from Waterford," arrived at Piscataqua in the week of May 11-18, 1719. Other similar news items appeared in this paper down to 1725.

Name	*Where Recorded*	*Year*
Timothy Barron	Lancaster, Mass.	1725
Benjamin Barry	Wenham, Mass.	1709
James Barry *	Boston, Mass.	1707
John Barry	Wenham, Mass.	1721
Joseph Barry	Boston, Mass.	1719
Thomas Barry	Boston, Mass.	1707

[1] Province Laws of 1714, Chap. 45.

[2] *Ibid.,* 1717, Chap. 52.

Name	*Where Recorded*	*Year*
William Barry *	Newcastle, Maine	1718
James Blane *	Boston, Mass.	1718
Daniel Blaney	Lynn, Mass.	1724
Francis Boilan	Newport, R. I.	1724
Patrick Brinan *	Newport, R. I.	1723
Patrick Brown	Boston, Mass.	1725
John Burke	Hartford, Conn.	1709
John Burke	Hatfield, Mass.	1714
Richard Burke	Brookfield, Mass.	1720
Thomas Burke	Rowley, Mass.	1719
Peter Butler	Boston, Mass.	1706
Philip Butler	Middleboro, Mass.	1722
Philip Caine	Marblehead, Mass.	1710
Patrick Campbell *	Boston, Mass.	1711
James Carey	Newport, R. I.	1716
John Carey	Newport, R. I.	1711
Matthew Carey	Boston, Mass.	1703
Michael Carney *	York County, Me.	1723
Daniel Carroll	Killingly, Conn.	1711
Edward Carroll	Salem, Mass.	1701
John Carroll	Salem, Mass.	1723
Joseph Carroll	Salem, Mass.	1700
Michael Carroll	Middletown, Conn.	1725
Adam Casey	Westerly, R. I.	1705
John Casey	Newport, R. I.	1719
Mary Casey	Salem, Mass.	1714
Charles Cassidy	York County, Me.	1723
John Clary	Brookfield, Mass.	1701
Joseph Clary	Watertown, Mass.	1702
Humphrey Cochran *	Newport, R. I.	1714
John Cochran *	Brunswick, Me.	1723
William Cochran	Brunswick, Me.	1723
John Cody	Beverly, Mass.	1723
Darby Collety *	York County, Me.	1722
Daniel Collins	Boston, Mass.	1704

Name	*Where Recorded*	*Year*
John Collins	Amesbury, Mass.	1700
John Collins	Portsmouth, N. H.	1708
Matthew Collins	Amesbury, Mass.	1702
Robert Collins	Amesbury, Mass.	1700
Jeremiah Condey *	Boston, Mass.	1707
John Condon	Boston, Mass.	1725
Richard Condon *	Woburn, Mass.	1716
John Connally	Salem, Mass.	1722
John Connely	Boston, Mass.	1714
Daniel Connery *	Stoneham, Mass.	1725
Benjamin Conry	Stratford, Conn.	1705
Daniel Connor	Boston, Mass.	1714
John Connor	Salisbury, Mass.	1704
John Corbett	Lebanon, Conn.	1725
Darby Cotter *	New Haven, Conn.	1725
Robert Cunningham *	Spencer, Mass.	1707
John Curry *	York County, Me.	1722
John Curtin	Lynn, Mass.	1711
John Dalton	Haverhill, Mass.	1710
John Dalton *	Salem, Mass.	1722
Mary Dalton	Salisbury, Mass.	1716
John Daly *	Easton, Mass.	1708
John Daly	Boston, Mass.	1725
John Daley	Colchester, Conn.	1708
Joseph Daley	Colchester, Conn.	1725
Samuel Dailey	Stratford, Conn.	1708
John Dealin	Kittery, Me.	1715
Christopher Dempsey *	Salem, Mass.	1724
Margaret Dempsey	Danvers, Mass.	1725
Owen Denny *	Brunswick, Me.	1725
John Dillon	New London, Conn.	1725
Elizabeth Dolan	Manchester, Mass.	1723
William Donahy *	Framingham, Mass.	1720
John Donnavin	Scarboro, Me.	1724
Daniel Donovan *	Portsmouth, N. H.	1725

Name	*Where Recorded*	*Year*
Daniel Downing	Gloucester, Mass.	1722
Bartholomew Doyle *	Boston, Mass.	1723
Elizabeth Doyle	Boston, Mass.	1716
John Drisco(l)	Salisbury, Mass.	1710
Joseph Drisco(l)	Salisbury, Mass.	1712
Cornelius Driscoll	Dover, N. H.	1715
Daniel Driskell *	Boston, Mass.	1714
Mary Driskel	New London, Conn.	1725
John Duggan	Marblehead, Mass.	1725
William Duly	York County, Me.	1722
William Dunaghoe *	Hopkinton, Mass.	1723
Charles Dunn	Newport, R. I.	1725
John Dunn	Boston, Mass.	1720
William Dunn	Boston, Mass.	1723
Andrew Dunning *	Brunswick, Me.	1717
David Dunning *	Brunswick, Me.	1723
Robert Dwyer *	Newburyport, Mass.	1707
Thomas Dwier	Newburyport, Mass.	1706
Patrick Egan *	Boston, Mass.	1706
John Ennis *	Boston, Mass.	1716
George Fagan	Boston, Mass.	1712
John Fagan	Boston, Mass.	1710
Katherine Fallon	Newport, R. I.,	1723
Patrick Fargison *	Boston, Mass.	1712
Patrick Farren	Ipswich, Mass.	1722
Sarah Fennell	Portsmouth, N. H.	1715
James Fitzgerald	Boston, Mass.	1713
John Fitzgerald	Boston, Mass.	1708
Maurice Fitzgerald	York County, Me.	1723
Patrick Fitzgerald	Boston, Mass.	1709
Richard Fitzgerald *	Scituate, Mass.	1725
Richard Fitzgerald	Portsmouth, N. H.	1715
Thomas Fitzgerald	Boston, Mass.	1717
Elizabeth Fitzpatrick	Boston, Mass.	1722
William Fitzsimmons	York County, Me.	1722

Name	*Where Recorded*	*Year*
Patrick Flanagan	Boston, Mass.	1723
George Flinn	Newburyport, Mass.	1707
John Flynn	Gloucester, Mass.	1719
John Flynn	Boston, Mass.	1725
Mary Flynn	Boston, Mass.	1722
Patrick Flynn *	Malden, Mass.	1713
John Foley	York County, Me.	1722
Benjamin Geary	Charlestown, Mass.	1720
John Geary	Stoneham, Mass.	1725
John Geary	Kittery, Me.	1720
Thomas Geary	Stoneham, Mass.	1725
Jeremiah Gillpatrick *	Scarboro, Me.	1718
Joseph Gillpatrick *	Scarboro, Me.	1718
Thomas Gillpatrick *	Scarboro, Me.	1718
Bryan Gilmore	Boston, Mass.	1701
Charles Gilmore	York County, Me.	1722
John Gilmore *	Weymouth, Mass.	1700
David Giveen *	Brunswick, Me.	1717
John Giveen	Brunswick, Me.	1723
William Giveen	Brunswick, Me.	1723
Thomas Gleason	Oxford, Mass.	1714
Martha Glyn	Beverly, Mass.	1708
Ann Glynn	Marblehead, Mass.	1725
Patrick Googins *	Old Orchard, Me.	1722
John Grady	Salem, Mass.	1714
James Grealy	Boston, Mass.	1712
Joseph Greeley	Gloucester, Mass.	1715
Philip Greeley	Kingston, N. H.	1712
Thomas Greeley	Portsmouth, N. H.	1723
Patrick Greegory *	York County, Maine	1722
William Currin	Boston, Mass.	1714
Benjamin Haley	Boston, Mass.	1710
John Haley	Portsmouth, N. H.	1721
Joseph Haley	Marblehead, Mass.	1725
William Haley	Boston, Mass.	1710

Pioneer Irish in New England

Name	*Where Recorded*	*Year*
Abigail Harney	Salem, Mass.	1705
Patrick Hay	Charlestown, Mass.	1713
John Hayes	Boston, Mass.	1705
Luke Hayes *	Farmington, Conn.	1705
Peter Hayes	Dover, N. H.	1725
Sarah Healy	Salisbury, Mass.	1709
William Healy	Hampton, N. H.	1716
William Healy *	Boston, Mass.	1717
William Healy	Hopkinton, Mass.	1724
Robert Hewes *	Boston, Mass.	1714
Patrick Hickey	Marblehead, Mass.	1725
Thomas Higgins	Boston, Mass.	1724
James Hines *	Boston, Mass.	1716
Daniel Hogan	Boston, Mass.	1714
Daniel Hogin	Braintree, Mass.	1715
Matthew Hogin	Charlestown, Mass.	1724
Arthur Hunter *	Marblehead, Mass.	1712
James Joyce	Newcastle, Me.	1718
Thomas Joyce	Marshfield, Mass.	1701
Samuel Keating	Boston, Mass.	1716
Charles Kelly	Hartford, Conn.	1722
Charles Kelly	Kittery, Me.	1712
Darby Kelly *	Kingston, N. H.	1725
Faylam Kelly *	Boston, Mass.	1725
George Kelly	Newport, R. I.	1719
George Kelly	Boston, Mass.	1708
Henry Kelly	Boston, Mass.	1706
Hugh Kelly	Salem, Mass.	1725
James Kelly *	Boston, Mass.	1716
John Kelly	Bradford, Mass.	1715
Joseph Kelly	Norwich, Conn.	1715
Joseph Kelly	New London, Conn.	1716
Richard Kelly	Newbury, Mass.	1711
Steven Kelly	Kingston, N. H.	1725
Thomas Kelly	Marblehead, Mass.	1700

Name	*Where Recorded*	*Year*
Timothy Kelly	New London, Conn.	1719
William Kelly	Hartford, Conn.	1722
William Kelly	Middleboro, Mass.	1722
Michael Kennard *	Portsmouth, N. H.	1711
Hugh Kennedy	Boston, Mass.	1720
Robert Kennedy	New London, Conn.	1719
William Kennedy *	Middleboro, Mass.	1722
Daniel Kenny	Salem, Mass.	1704
Daniel Kenny	Sutton, Mass.	1725
Henry Kenny	Salem, Mass.	1704
John Kenny	New London, Conn.	1703
Joseph Kenny	Concord, N. H.	1700
Samuel Kenny	Boston, Mass.	1721
Thomas Kenny	Salem, Mass.	1701
John Kinnacan *	Gloucester, Mass.	1711
Hannah Larey	Portsmouth, N. H.	1725
John Larkin	Boston, Mass.	1716
Philip Larkin *	Lancaster, Mass.	1725
Thomas Larkin	Boston, Mass.	1700
John Lawler *	Boston, Mass.	1708
Thomas Lawler	York County, Me.	1722
John Logan *	Woodbury, Conn.	1716
John Logan	Boston, Mass.	1717
Susanna Loobey	Boston, Mass.	1716
James Lunnagen *	Marblehead, Mass.	1716
John Lunagen	Marblehead, Mass.	1716
Ann Linch	Salem, Mass.	1720
Eugene Lynch *	Beverly, Mass.	1714
William Lynch	Boston, Mass.	1725
Ruth Lyons	New Haven, Conn.	1724
Daniel McAfee	Gloucester, Mass.	1717
Daniel Maccane *	Dedham, Mass.	1710
John Maccanis *	Boston, Mass.	1719
Alexander McBride	Concord, Mass.	1725
John McBride *	Brunswick, Me.	1723

Name	*Where Recorded*	*Year*
John McBride	Concord, Mass.	1725
Christian Maccarty	Boston, Mass.	1714
Esther Maccarty	Gloucester, Mass.	1720
James McKarte	Kittery, Me.	1723
John Maccarty	Boston, Mass.	1724
Joseph MacCarthy	Roxbury, Mass.	1713
Margaret McCarty	Boston, Mass.	1708
Mary MacCarty	Boston, Mass.	1708
Michael MacCartey *	Ipswich, Mass.	1724
Prudence McCarthy	Salem, Mass.	1715
Robert McCarthy	Salem, Mass.	1716
Thomas Maccarty	Boston, Mass.	1719
William MacCarty	Boston, Mass.	1714
James McCausland *	York County, Me.	1722
John McConoughy *	Londonderry, N. H.	1719
Daniel McCoone	Newport, R. I.,	1705
Alexander McCoy	Watertown, Mass.	1722
William MacCoy	Grafton, Mass.	1724
Daniel MackDaniel	Boston, Mass.	1723
John MacDaniel	York County, Me.	1722
Eleanor McDonnell	Portsmouth, N. H.	1722
James McDowell *	Stonington, Conn.	1723
Daniel Mackdonald	Sudbury, Mass.	1724
Daniel MacDuffee *	Bradford, Vt.	1720
Andrew MacFadden *	Boston, Mass.	1722
John Macfadden	York County, Me.	1722
Edward Macgonnel	New London, Conn.	1720
Elizabeth Mackgowan	Ashford, Conn.	1719
Daniel Macinerney	Boston, Mass.	1722
Dennis McInerney *	Charlestown, Mass.	1723
Dennis McKahan *	Boston, Mass.	1718
Dennis McMahon	Boston, Mass.	1718
William MacMakin *	Boston, Mass.	1717
James McMallon	Salem, Mass.	1717
Dennis Mackmarty	Newport, R. I.	1719
John Mackmaster *	Boston, Mass.	1722

Name	*Where Recorded*	*Year*
Timothy McMullen	Lynn, Mass.	1717
John McMurphy *	Londonderry, N. H.	1719
Samuel McNamara	Portsmouth, N. H.	1722
Thomas Madden	Boston, Mass.	1725
James Magee	Boston, Mass.	1712
Timothy Magraugh *	Boston, Mass.	1724
Michael Maher *	Brunswick, Me.	1723
Richard Maher	Boston, Mass.	1720
Thomas Mahone	Boston, Mass.	1725
Cain Mahony *	Beverly, Mass.	1710
Thomas Mahony	York County, Me.	1722
Mary Mahony	Marblehead, Mass.	1724
James Mahoone	Salem, Mass.	1725
Daniel Malley *	Marblehead, Mass.	1720
Walter Malone	Lancaster, Mass.	1725
Timothy Manen *	Reading, Mass.	1712
John Meade	Portsmouth, N. H.	1708
William Melady	Charlestown, Mass.	1714
Henry Mitchell *	Brunswick, Me.	1723
Hugh Mitchell *	Brunswick, Me.	1723
Roger Mitchell	Kittery, Me.	1720
Charles Molloy	Boston, Mass.	1725
William Mooney	Marblehead, Mass.	1725
James McKean *	Amherst, Mass.	1718
William McKean	Amherst, Mass.	1718
Neal Mackuagh *	Dover, N. H.	1720
David MacKhue	Boston, Mass.	1702
William McKenery	Boston, Mass.	1718
William McKinley	Boston, Mass.	1718
John Maclanon	Boston, Mass.	1721
Daniel McLoughlin	Hartford, Conn.	1709
Michael Maclowd *	Boston, Mass.	1712
Thomas Maclowd	Boston, Mass.	1712
Daniel McMain *	Rutland, Mass.	1720
James Moore *	Waterville, Me.	1723
Thomas Moore *	Scituate, Mass.	1724

Name	*Where Recorded*	*Year*
Charles Mullen	Boston, Mass.	1711
Allen Mullins *	New London, Conn.	1725
Edward Mullins *	New London, Conn.	1725
John Mullins	Boston, Mass.	1711
Thomas Mullens	Boston, Mass.	1700
Thomas Mullins	Boston, Mass.	1722
George Murphy	Kennebunkport, Me.	1722
Hugh Murphy	Hingham, Mass.	1722
John Murphy	Kennebunkport, Me.	1724
John Murphy *	Middleboro, Mass.	1722
John Murphy	Hingham, Mass.	1722
Simon Murfe *	New London, Conn.	1710
William Murphy	Danvers, Mass.	1716
James Nolan *	Boston, Mass.	1711
William Knolen (Nolan)	Portsmouth, N. H.	1713
Charles O'Hara *	Boston, Mass.	1716
Henry O'Neil	New Haven, Conn.	1713
Ann O'Ryan	Boston, Mass.	1704
Jeremiah Philbrick	Boston, Mass.	1712
Daniel Power	Lancaster, Mass.	1725
Morise Powers	Boston, Mass.	1719
Thomas Powers	Woburn, Mass.	1702
Thomas Powers	Charlestown, Mass.	1714
Nicholas Roach	Charlestown, Mass.	1715
Edmund Rourk	Boston, Mass.	1725
Mary Ryan	Marblehead, Mass.	1718
Daniel Ryley	Wethersfield, Conn.	1712
Daniel Shannon	Portsmouth, N. H.	1714
Joseph Strahan	Marblehead, Mass.	1718
Humphrey Sullivan *	Dover, N. H.	1714
William Sullivan	Boston, Mass.	1711
Moses Sweeney *	Killingly, Conn.	1720
Richard Tandey	Gloucester, Mass.	1724
Bryan Toole *	Boston, Mass.	1722
Thomas Walker *	Boston, Mass.	1718

INDEX OF NAMES
Pioneer Irish in New England

Index of Names

Index of Names

Index of Names

Index of Names

Index of Names

Index of Names

Index of Names

Index of Names

Index of Names

www.ingramcontent.com/pod-product-compliance
Lightning Source LLC
Chambersburg PA
CBHW071639270326
41928CB00010B/1982
* 9 7 8 1 5 5 6 1 3 1 0 6 6 *